D0916287

Lola's Luck

Lola's Luck

MY LIFE AMONG THE
CALIFORNIA GYPSIES

CAROL MILLER

GEMMA

BOSTON

Iosco-Arenac District Library
East Tawas, Michigan

First published by GemmaMedia in 2009.

GemmaMedia
230 Commerical Street
Boston, MA 02109 USA
617 938 9833
www.gemmamedia.com

© 2009 by Carol Miller

All rights reserved. No part of this publication may be reproduced in any manner whatsoever without written permission from the publisher, except in the case of brief quotations embodied in critical articles or reviews.

Printed in the United States of America

13   12   11   10   09   1   2   3   4   5

ISBN: 978-1-934848-00-5

Library of Congress Control Number: 2008932715

ACKNOWLEDGMENTS

*T*his book has been an enduring part of my life since 1975, the year Lola died, when I began scribbling notes about her because I missed her and in an effort to better understand the miracle of our unlikely relationship. This final edition owes much to the editors, Louis Chunovic and my neighbor Barbara Lehman, the former for his cutting and compacting, the latter for her work on my carefree use of colons and both for their interest and support.

Many good friends have read and offered their opinions of my book in its various guises, among them the anthropologists Rena Gropper and Maggi Nicholson, the photographer/linguist Diane Tong, Mill Valley's Frank Rosenberg, my dear Bev Manber Anderson, the expatriate Don Bovee, filmmaker Diana Gerba, my aerobics classmate Jan Cox and the talented Victoria Scott who has helped the writing process along in so many ways, as well as others whose names, over the decades, I seem to have forgotten, an omission for which I ask to be forgiven. My sisters, Nancy Latourelle and Joan Davis, and my children, Colin and Leslie, knew Lola; they have shared my fieldwork and my passions. My heartfelt gratitude to my teacher, Anne Lamott, for her enthusiastic response to my work, to former agent Robin Straus, to Gayle Delaney for her help with my dreams and to my granddaughter Elicia Ho, a New Yorker of charm and infinite grace who, in a vain attempt to promote my memoir into a movie, once engaged the media consultant and marketeer, Soffie Kage.

A special thanks is due Zella who, in my hippie phase, shared the names and addresses of her California artist friends, friends with whom, driving down the coast, looking for Psychic signs and Machvanki, I sometimes enjoyed a hot meal and an overnight.

I never got a grant to study Gypsies and will be eternally beholden to those Machvaia who, whenever I ran out of funds, took me in. Ritual/belief was my focus and, in the effort to attend as many gatherings and parties as possible, I usually worked part-time. Katy and I were often live-together companions, and I consider myself especially lucky to have been sponsored by her husband King and, later, husband Chally. My blessings on all those Machvaia who tolerated my foreign presence at the sacred events normally forbidden Outsiders and who, in the generous spirit of good times, shared the bounty of their company, food, drink, crowded motel rooms, inspired music and dancing, the latest gossip and the immediate nature of their feelings. I speed good luck and good health to you all.

Mostly, I am indebted to my beloved Lola, for her love, example and guidance.

In the following, the names of the Machvaia who are living have been changed—with the exception of those who have requested their real names be used.

The Roma names familiar to Americans and speakers of English are spelled accordingly: Katy, Miller, Boyd, Lyla, for example.

The Roma names that reflect the people's mixed East-European origin, like Duda (Doo-dah), Zhurka (Zhoor-kah), Duiyo (Doo-ee-yo), Stevo (Stay-vo) and the words from Sanscrit, like *baX*, luck, are spelled according to the following sound tips:

R̲, as Roma, Romani, a post-velar sounded/aspirated roll at the back of the throat.

X̲ = as in Scottish pronunciation of lo<u>ch</u>.

r̲ is like the French light flap.

e̲ or é̲ = say   i̲ = see,   a̲ = saw,   o̲ = sew,   g̲ = go,   u̲ = goo

*K*ATY, A GYPSY OF SOME SIGNIFICANCE, lived an easy fifteen-minute drive from the University District, in the biggest Gypsy storefront in the city, with the whitest, fullest ruffled curtains. But the inside of the building was even more imposing. I was a divorced graduate student, an aspiring anthropologist from the University (there because one of the professors in my department said he knew someone who knew a local Gypsy family), and I remember looking around that first visit and feeling propelled at warp speed away from all that I knew.

Home to me was a well-lit flat with the no-bother statement of Scandinavian furniture. My only luxury stood on a carved rosewood folding stand, an oversized and open *Oxford English Dictionary* with tissue paper pages.

In contrast, Katy's storefront was a dark, two-storied Oriental box designed to gobble up my courage. Only the walls at the front and back had windows, doors and access to outside air and natural light. Chandeliers, pinpoints far above our heads, projected pale pools of light toward the vastness, dangerously unstable and propelled to sway by the drafts that issued through cracks in the molding. Wide stripes of red and green Art Deco lilies writhed and stretched across the carpeting that Katy told me crisply, chin in the air, had been cleverly salvaged from a theater lobby "for nothing."

Where to rest my eyes? Every wall was curtained, draped and papered, pattern to paisley pattern. I supposed the bravura effect might be an egregious attempt to re-introduce the coziness of

1

childhood's tent and the fertility of nature's luxuriant form and color. Within the twilight space, I counted bedrolls, one bed, two sofas, several overstuffed chairs, a dining set, televisions, a variety of sound systems, two phones but no phone book. The more precious items, gleaming Saint statues and aging maroon-red Easter eggs, were stored in a carved Italian cabinet.

Pointing to an egg that was accidentally chipped, Katy showed me that the yolk had miraculously changed to glass. "How does that happen?" I wondered, expecting sulfur fumes, and earnestly hoping she wouldn't ask me to hold it.

"That's because it's from Easter," she explained, explaining nothing, as she carefully put the egg back on the shelf. I can still see the imperious height of the black ceilings, the awesome openness of the room—room enough to perform ten handsprings, front to back.

I tried to enlist her support by explaining I needed a larger sample to study, that one family wouldn't do and that a community was what I had in mind. Could she help me meet more Gypsies?

Katy said there were three kinds in the city, two of them *Kalderasha*, but she came from the best, the highest class, being a *Machvanka*. Apparently, from Katy's view, I had reached my objective; a Machvanka should be quite enough. Whatever I might have said wouldn't have mattered. She knew outsiders were suspect and couldn't be trusted.

I had already tried several local Gypsy storefronts, pretending to be a prospective client. When I timidly asked, "Do you tell fortunes?" the women claimed that they didn't give readings. The ones that obviously did (the sign read "Palm Readings") said they were "too busy." While suggesting I come another day, the expressions on their faces made it clear that when I did, they intended not to be in.

I was puzzled as to why Katy, unlike the others, didn't order me out or tell me to come back "another day." In fact, she never locked her door. In those days, an open door proved that the Gypsies inside had nothing to hide or to be ashamed of—at least that's what it meant to other Gypsies. There were, however, other possibilities. She was a woman who made her living "reading" people and their motives, and perhaps I intrigued her. She certainly intrigued me, and I have always been a sucker for a mystery.

I found the slender Katy aloof and hard to figure. I had read that Gypsy royalty is a fiction invented for outsiders. I learned first-hand that the fiction conveys a deeper truth: the serious regard with which all Roma would like to be treated.

In truth, I was a bit overwhelmed by the shock of her straw-berry-orange-colored hair and the way she claimed she achieved that color with successive stubborn treatments of household bleach. Katy, the redheaded Gypsy Red Queen—all stride, disdain and angles—chain-smoked and made incessant phone calls. I was a bit dismayed by the arrogance of her style, nimbly twisting to hold an ear to the phone while she perched on her zebra-print barstool and painted strong nails with another leisurely coat. I was seriously impressed by the way she made her living, telling for-tunes. I wondered how she managed to support that big family, five children and a variable number of adults, with whatever income she got from the dismally hard-up clients who arrived at her store-front. But I was drawn to Katy in ways that I didn't, at the time, con-sciously comprehend. Although she was an unknowing informant, I considered Katy an expert at survival, and the most gallantly resourceful woman I had ever met.

The preceding years of my own life had seemed unending, an exercise in futility and postponement. Before my divorce and for too many years, I had hid in my husband's shadow, the diminish-ing tail to the kite of his success. His corporate promotions, invari-ably received like the word of Adam Smith, the capitalist god, allowed no discussion or negotiation. Every year or two, sturdy uni-formed men from a national trucking company would appear, pack all our belongings into numbered cardboard boxes and smooth-move us to another city. Each new rung up the corporate ladder cost my children and me our small and our more significant triumphs, our ongoing aspirations, familiar neighborhoods and schools and the support of our cherished friends. We weren't always good sports about these transitions. Whatever we ruefully left behind usually seemed more precious to us than what we were likely to be gaining—the bigger house, another car, a boat.

Now, I had to worry that my recent divorce had jeopardized my children's prospects for the future. I was scared that I wouldn't be able to manage, that my children would suffer unduly from the loss of private schools and find our newly frugal lifestyle oppressive. As it turned out, my fears were not entirely unfounded. My daughter soon moved back with her father who, to her dismay, switched from pushover parent into a firm disciplinarian. After that, for years, I saw her only on weekends and during vacations.

THAT FIRST YEAR of my fieldwork was a lesson in accommodation. Hoping to please, hoping to glean whatever scraps of information might become available, I had good reason to obey Gypsy edicts of respect. That's how I came to spend hours sitting on Katy's sofa, tugging at an old skirt that never seemed quite long enough or full enough to completely cover the disgrace of my knees. I became particularly annoyed at my legs. Accustomed to the cover of jeans, they had begun to feel goose—pimply, vulnerable and odd.

I was repeatedly and painfully impressed with the global nature of my ignorance; even Katy's youngest child knew worlds more than I did and he seemed to flaunt the fact. Carefully, whenever he thought I wasn't paying close attention, Baby Jelly John dared to pelt me with a few high-pitched taunts over the arm of the sofa. His sister was more inventive, hoping to scare me with stories about gigantic ancestors who ate people's heads, stories about "old, really old and mean" great aunts who were witches, or of the encounters her relatives had had with malevolent ghosts.

The teenagers, Sophie and Lana, had been systematically trained by their mother and their silent, austere hospitality dismayed me. I was invariably seated and served by myself, isolated as an icon of sorts in the middle of the ten-foot sofa. The service was always quick, courteous and impeccable, the coffee kept at the

4

scald, the paper napkin continually replaced. Meanwhile, the younger children peeked at me in black hate beneath the sweep of long black lashes, and, in Romani—this I could only guess—cursed and threatened me with unending misfortune.

The summer passed with too few pages of field notes. But, in the meantime, I learned something new about myself: the more I was ignored or harassed, the more determined I became. I found myself empowered by rejection. Feeling that I was a likable person, I wanted passionately to prove it. I wanted them to like me and I wouldn't accept their cool refusal as final.

At the same time, each touch-and-go encounter held the awful possibility of proving to be the last. Without warning, Katy might move, leave no forwarding address, change her telephone number or name, play hide-and-seek, escape. The Gypsies kept me on the edge of my seat, spellbound and wanting more. For decades thereafter I had nightmares that a caravan carrying everyone I knew was disappearing over the brow of a distant hill and that I was about to lose them forever.

SEVERAL EVENINGS A WEEK I headed for Katy's storefront. From the sidewalk, the only sign of life was a discrete gleam of light over the partition. I would park at the curb, leave my notebooks in the car and wrestle open the badly fitted door. Smiling inanely, I'd pass by the "reading room," trying for a show of confidence I never truly felt. My desperate desire to gain some measure of acceptance did pay off, however. Fate had apparently sent me to that storefront and no other, for that's where I met Katy's mother.

"Come here, dear," a voice boomed out of the shadows. I saw a pair of well-muscled legs thrust into platform-soled shoes with vinyl bows, chartreuse straps and heels high and sharp enough for stabbing. A dumpling woman with bright eyes and a sparkly hair bow nodded a cheery hello and patted the space on the bed beside her.

"Come here, honey. You got a car?" she asked. "My Cadillac is in the garage and I need a ride home. A Volkswagen? Those are nice. Do you know where I live? Never mind. We can follow the bus."

Then she was on those improbable feet and on her way, the children shouting "Hooray!" and applauding and bowing us out the door. The tide of enthusiasm carried us onto the freeway.

Until that moment, I hadn't the least idea that Katy's mother lived nearby. Indeed, the woman who called herself Ruth didn't look or act in the least like Katy.

Although I felt a bit chagrined when I couldn't find her Number 7 bus, that didn't keep Ruth's spirits down. After several wrong turns and dead ends, all of which she obviously enjoyed—"Look, look at that!"—we turned off Aurora Boulevard and pulled up at a modest gray triplex.

Whereas Katy's place was large, Ruth's was small and certainly more conventional—her furniture style was Duncan Phyfe, the same as my mother's—Ruth's apartment nevertheless contained a few items of a special conversational interest. The dining-room chair seats, for example, were covered in leopard-spotted faux-fur print. The entire kitchen, including the stove and refrigerator, had been purposefully hand-enameled in a bright pink.

When I asked about the pink, Ruth explained the obvious, with hauteur, "I like that color better." She bustled about, offering me a variety of refreshments—maybe everything she had to eat in the house—and returned the favor of the ride by offering to give me a reading. She secured my appreciation when her voice dropped to a caramel baritone as she confided, "I usually charge fifty dollars."

My fortune began with the advice to make a wish. Apparently, my response—I wanted, I said, to write a true and wonderful book about Gypsies—was not what she had expected. She turned instead to the circumstances surrounding my divorce, a topic that proved to be even more unsettling. I think she thought she was asking questions, but her questions sounded more like demands. Quickly, without losing momentum, "Your husband left you? Your husband had no money? He didn't take care of you? He didn't take care of the children? He beat you? He was chasing girls?"

Finally, all my answers to the contrary sparked the light of lucid inspiration and she announced in triumph, "You didn't love him." An oversimplification of a complex situation, but I didn't bother to deny it. I assumed, from her expression, that she found such a reason exotic. The man I had divorced was by her standards "rich" and admittedly kind enough not to beat either me or my children.

She claimed to know everything there is to know about children and, when I called mine to tell them where I was, the phone virtually jumped from my hand into hers. She talked to my daughter and son by turns, advising them to lock the door and not to let anyone in, "You understand?"

She promised to cook them "a little dinner." My watch said midnight, but that's what she did, made what she called *paprikash*, a spicy chicken stew. After she and I ate our helpings, she ladled the remainder into a restaurant-size pot and handed it to me at the door. Healthy children, she assured me, can eat anytime and sleep whenever they like.

Bundled in my raincoat, holding the stew and the gift of a partially eaten box of chocolates, my feet felt fastened to the stoop. I paused while she, wearing nothing over ample, bare arms and shoulders, shivered in the drizzle. To release me, she beamed a wagon-load of cheer and dance-stepped back into the lit doorway.

She apparently didn't care that I was an outsider, a stranger, the enemy. She didn't mind what the other Gypsies might think. Nodding good-bye with genial affirmation, she announced, "We're two women alone and we need each other."

I was an option, an available option, and the dear lady had a quick eye for the main chance.

SHE HAD INTRODUCED HERSELF to me as Ruth, "Sister Ruth, expert advisor on love, business, marriage." Ruth's Seattle family addressed her as *Dei* (pronounced "day") and referred to her as *Phuria* or *Phuri Dei*, the Old Mother—Lady, a glamorous term conveying spiritual power, a productive life and the glory of numerous kinsmen.

I usually referred to her simply as The Old Lady. So, on occasion, did her family. Gypsies tend to acquire a number of names according to need, circumstance and personal preference. Sometimes I heard her people refer to her as Lola. It took me a while to realize who they meant.

For several years, she remained Ruth, or The Old Lady, to me and my family. Not until I began traveling to California and met hundreds of her near and distant relatives would I make the switch to calling her Lola.

She hated hearing herself called The Old Lady. Although her people, the Machvaia Roma, are quick to acknowledge old age as reward and blessing, the capstone to a well-spent life, Ruth was also well aware of the derogatory connotations of old age in America. She was probably in her late sixties, but whatever age she was, she certainly possessed a youthful *joie de vivre*.

"Men still like me," she acknowledged frankly, and her flamboyant manner of dressing made me suspect she felt more siren than serene. One time, overhearing my reference to her as The Old Lady, she became pettish, reminding me that the date and place of her birth were uncertain. "We don't know how old," she cautioned, twisting on her toes in a girlish pirouette.

I had never met anyone like Lola. In my memory she looms fierce and feminine, an irrepressible beguiling Circe. Lola's buoyant enthusiasm and prevailing sense of fun and pleasure offset any lack of finesse she might possess. Within the year of our first meeting, she won my heart, becoming the pivot and inspiration for my studies.

She was a Machvanka of Serbian Gypsy background, a bright, short, plumpish parrot, propelled to energy and movement by an abiding taste for the good things of life. She knew how to seize the moment and, just a few hours after we met, Lola announced with abrupt decision that we were bound to be best friends. It was hard not to believe her. But her statement amazed me: What did she mean? How could anyone make friends so quickly?

It began by phone. My siblings all lived in Seattle and, without hesitation, she called my sisters, my brother, as well as my children, to give them the daily news and keep them informed about what was happening in her family. Appointing herself gossip coordinator, Lola added us to the already appreciable telephone list scribbled on the wall behind her phone in two-inch wobbly and cryptic numbers. She called me from the grocery, the department store, the jeweler's, dressmaker's, her son's house, Katy's storefront, street corners. She would often call me to come over to her apartment "right now." "I just fixed the best meal in town," she would say. "What you doing? *Studying?*"

She did not approve. In her silence I recognized dismay and disapproval at an enterprise resembling inertia, and one lacking the immediate joy of jokes and conversation, human sympathy, financial reward or anything else she cherished.

When she called, my teenaged children often answered. I'd come home to find a list of messages: "Milo's got a *sla* (Saint-day)." "Keka has a baby." "Come quick, I'm at the sale at Sears."

On the phone her drill-sergeant voice—untempered by the warmth of her expressive face, her curving hands, the rapid swings of her restless samba sandals—could be intimidating. At first my children were uncertain how to respond to queries of "What you doing?"

Raised to honor privacy, they found her unfailing intimacy and the flood of personal questions about their lives and their friends disconcerting. They repeated the details of what she said when she called, what they said, and looked to me for direction, trying to get it right. But they likely knew, as children often do and probably better than me, how I really felt about the situation: my admiring dismay, my vexed adoration.

Sometimes when I came in, my daughter would stomp about, tossing her hair—long, brown and ironed curtain straight—in frustration. "She kept me on the phone for an hour!" she complained, and I knew how she felt. Even I couldn't seem to terminate our conversations. "Now I really must go, Lola," I'd say, sounded damaging and cold when the voice on the other end was so full of concern and so devoted to contact.

9

THE FIRST SIGNIFICANT Gypsy lesson to be learned was that a cold and unfeeling heart is unforgivable. California, not Washington, is the Machvaia people's community headquarters, and Lola lived alone in North Seattle, far from her aging peers. The Roma in Seattle are of the Vlax-Roma variety—two-thirds of the American Romani population are Vlax-Roma—Gypsies who had been enslaved in Romania for hundreds of years and had developed ample reason for resentment. To the Roma, an old woman living alone implied that no one cared, which was a shame to her family, a slur to the credit of family reputation, a wounding blow to the corporate strength of community life. It was a notion arousing fear and dismay. For whatever happened to any one of their number might happen to them all.

Even still, I can hear this sentiment in the extended phrasing of the Machvaia table songs, addressing the mournful separation from a child, a mother, a husband—songs that were born in the days of traveling. "Alone," the men sing, "*Korkorvo!*" clasping one another for support, poignantly dragging out the final syllable.

For Lola, being alone was a recent development. Her early years had been spent in an overloaded wagon, traveling across America with her mother, father and siblings. As a young woman, she had been an invaluable member of her husband's expanding family unit, his four brothers, their wives, children, aging parents; they slept in tents and traveled, at first by horse and wagon, and later in a caravan of several cars. Then, she was the mother and central feature of a family of ten growing children living in a single storefront. Now, as the fates would have it, after so much company, laughter, body warmth, conversation, mutual challenge and sharing, she lived alone. She never complained, however. Having been through "all the trouble and misery in the world," as she defiantly put it, what was left to be afraid of?

At any rate, she claimed to live alone by choice. Bahto, her decorously polite former husband, an ailing old man, bow-tied and fragile, and whose name she never mentioned—she respectfully referred to him as "he"—lived two miles away with Miller, their youngest son, and his family. Daughter Katy's downtown storefront was a bit farther. Before moving to Los Angeles, Boyd, another son, was about the same distance away. Three children, thirteen grandchildren, one godchild, several cousins, all in the same city. To me, she hardly seemed alone.

When asked why she no longer lived with any of her nearby children, she explained, "I tried it with all my children all over America. That didn't work. They argued. They said things to each other I shouldn't hear. I left. I can't stand arguing." What she meant, of course, was that their households showed a lack of solicitude for her mental comfort, advancing age and the respect she felt was owed to an elder.

She never stayed home for long and went everywhere by city bus. Sometimes the routes changed and she got on the wrong bus, and would call to ask in that insistent musical voice if I knew where she was. No, she wasn't lost, she had been there before, she'd tell me. She was between a gas station and a Safeway. But I struggled to respond to her calls for help. How could I tell which gas station and which Safeway?

She would insist that I drop what I was doing and head off in whatever direction my intuition might suggest, utilizing the mind-to-mind connection she presumed was universally given, searching the entire north end of Seattle for her, if necessary. But when I tried, I failed, having not yet developed the psychic radar necessary to give me her whereabouts. Later, when I asked how the lost lady who couldn't read the street signs managed to get home, she would irritably refuse to say.

I knew I wasn't her only transportation option; she had others, her customers, her sons plus one enterprising daughter-in-law, Duda, who could drive. Still I hated to refuse her and she knew it. She may have preferred me to Miller—by tradition, the youngest son has the chief responsibility for the care of the parents—because I was more compliant. This was certainly the case at ceremonial events. There, "good-time Miller" liked to leave last, and Lola liked to leave whenever she liked.

I WAS GRATEFUL, of course, to find the frustrating evenings on Katy's sofa no longer a necessity for fieldwork. But Lola was demanding, at times even abrasive.

We were oddly matched; her flamboyant appearance attracted more notice that I had ever known or was ever likely to command. Dressed for town, she danced along, perfectly balanced on pretty legs and graceful clear plastic Springolator sandals that conveyed the effect that she was walking on bare toes. She liked vividly printed, soft materials and the unfettered style of plunging necks and flowing lines.

To get enough air, to ensure the chance to breathe and move, as she explained it, she routinely cut down the necklines and armholes in her dresses. Like many older Gypsies who grew up traveling, her body thermostat had been "cold-adjusted" and she never needed a coat or seemed bothered by the cold.

She always left the house well put together. But her accelerating motion and the tipsiness of her pinned-on ringlet soon prevailed. The tucks and dips hand-basted in her bodice added to the slapdash effect. I was so preoccupied with Lola that I didn't consider how my teenage daughter felt about appearing in public with Carnival-in-Rio Lola. Leslie was at that self-conscious age when her image had to be worriedly addressed in every store window we passed. Even today she admits the pain of being seen with such an eccentric was considerable.

LOLA WAS ACCUSTOMED to challenge. When the linen clerk at I. Magnin (at that time a high-end department store) stared huffily at her outfit, then acted as if she hadn't heard us, I wanted to complain to the manager. But Lola had a better idea. She insisted on viewing, at slow seated leisure, two dozen tablecloths, unfolded, smoothed and experimentally set with fine china. "No, that's a little flashy. Now let's see how the table looks with this pattern over here."

Lola talked with everyone. And if they averted their eyes to establish a need for privacy, or tried to profess a polite lack of curiosity at the unconventional statement of her dress, she was bound, as she said, to "bring them out."

Her chutzpah was incredible. She had discovered something I had never before realized, that many people are geared to do exactly as directed. Once, when we had stopped for a red light, Lola rolled down the window on her side and signaled an adjacent truck driver to follow us home. Sputtering in protest, the trucker arrived at her door just behind us and was persuaded to pick up a sofa from Katy's, four miles away, and deliver it to Lola. Then, while telling his fortune as payment, Lola extracted his promise to return the following weekend to fix the roof "so I won't have rain where it doesn't belong." Later, realizing how a younger woman can be a lure in attracting clients, I suspected I might have been an unwitting agent to the trucker's compliance.

The smallest thing, like not being able to sign her name, could provide Lola with the opportunity to perform. One day, when we were shopping, she made a number of purchases at the five-and-dime and tried to pay with her Social Security check. Instead of signing her name, she made an X, and while the cashier went for the manager's authorization, the line of women behind us began to shift and grumble. Lola, hands on hips, assumed a dramatic pose. Her voice rose huskily to reassure her Woolworth audience: "It's all right. Don't worry. I'm a responsible woman. I make my own living. I raised ten children here in America, the United States of America. I did it by myself. And without any reading and writing."

She was never too proud to ask for help; it was, I suspect, by virtue of the good will of passing strangers that she had gotten by from day to day and raised all those children. Her insurance against hard times was a continuing network of favors owed and favors given. She was curious about how I had managed to survive with my noblesse oblige policies, my awkwardness at confessing human need, my cavalier attitude toward money.

"You must be lucky," she decided. When my chronic lack of ready cash challenged this opinion, she suggested I get a job making airplanes at Boeing.

LOLA KNEW EVERYTHING about feelings; the currency of feelings was her specialty. She cried at the sad parts in the movies, sighing audibly, and then during the recounting—she loved the showmanship of telling stories—she cried again. She cried at the sight of little children walking to school in the rain: "Why do they do that, the mothers? They let those babies out by themselves in this terrible weather."

I took her to see the musical *Fiddler on the Roof.* Our seats were cheaply bought and high in the balcony, and she kept standing up to see more of the stage. When the good-hearted Tevya agreed to give his lovesick daughter in marriage to a poor tailor, Lola, enthralled, hollered and clapped. "That's like us! We do that! The older people tell the children who to marry." Then, realizing everyone was looking, she sat down, unabashed, and lowered her voice only slightly. "But we get paid for the girl! You know that!" Yes, feelings were something Lola never hesitated to share.

Her explanations, on the other hand, could cause alarm and confusion. When Lola arranged for the remarriage of a middle-aged daughter, she received a tidy cash sum from the asking family. I drove her to her local bank. There, she rented a box for the privilege of occasionally unlocking it and holding the money. Elated at this turn in her luck and what she regarded as a benevolent sign for the future, Lola joked and chatted with everyone, customers and employees alike. Approaching a loan officer, she handed him a business card that read, *Mrs. Johnson, Famous Expert on Love and Business.* On impulse, she merrily confided her recent good fortune of selling a daughter: "This is the third time for her and twice they gave full price." Explaining further, she admitted she was exceedingly lucky to have seven daughters and that she liked girls better than boys because "they help with the money and they're the best company."

Then, she paused, aware that her credibility was somehow eroding as she spoke. Not being one to waste the possibilities of the moment, comic or otherwise, she backed us out the door, compounding their shock by pointing to me, "I might sell that one, too." I roared with laughter, as she knew I would. She had discovered how easily a laugh could dispatch my embarrassment. With Lola, I laughed a lot. The truth is, I loved her. I loved that pesky old woman.

THAT FIRST SUMMER, to Lola's unending delight, I drove her wherever she liked. But classes started again in the fall and she didn't know how to take my sudden unavailability. She called more often, "constantly" according to my son, who was usually home after school hanging out with his friends and answering the phone. I tried to allay Lola's fears. "No, I'm not mad at you. Of course we're still friends. But this is what I do. I go to school, you tell fortunes."

I was beginning to understand some words of Romani and heard it said that Lola was *barvali,* which means big, powerful and lucky. She was also described as beautiful, rich, "up there."

But the Old Lady was not rich. If she had been rich, she might have stayed in a house she liked and bought it, rather than moving. If she had the funds, she might have done what she said she would do as soon as she got some money: take her daughters and me to Paris for the weekend. "I hear it's good times," she'd say.

She got the idea when we heard that two of her aging sisters-in-law were planning a trip to France—they never went because, according to the gossip, their doctors refused to let them out of the country. But Lola was hurt and disbelieving that they hadn't included her in their traveling plans and sniffed, "I would have taken them."

I knew Lola wasn't rich. There were times at the end of the month when I realized she must be short, when I opened the refrigerator door and found nothing inside except the half-and-half she liked in her coffee. But she never let on; a complaint might have hexed her luck. So I pretended not to notice.

Eventually, from others in the family, I learned that for a number of years, before and after the Second World War, Lola had lived very well in Sacramento, in an area now called Old Town. After they got their first daughter-in-law, the family ran two storefronts: the smaller had a picture-taking booth on display in the window; the larger, where Lola lived, had a shoe-shine stand on one side and a domed sound-and-light nickelodeon on the other.

There was always a party on "J" Street in those wartime years. Servicemen soon to ship out lined up on the sidewalk all the way to the corner. During the intervals between readings—"You'll come back safe. The cards say you won't die."—Lola's daughters practiced the jitterbug, a dance that was popular at the time. A drink or two might put Lola into such a festive mood that she sang her favorite song, "There'll Be Bluebirds over the White Cliffs of Dover."

"We didn't have much at that time," one of her in-laws remembers, "but Lola always had three or four girls bringing in money. I'll never forget Bandji. She was short and kind of skittish and she kept her money in her bra. We'd say 'Look, look at little Bandji and that big chest full of money.'"

Reputation is historical, like a letter of credit; and fame, once established, carries star qualities that endure and spangle the passing years, transcending the generations. When she was younger, Lola had been a Machvanka "Lucky Star," and reputation-wise, she still was.

It was enough that she had once been favorably situated in company with her many growing daughters, all pretty, industrious and clever, telling fortunes and making money—girls other families wanted and she was proud to have.

FOR THE MACHVAIA WOMEN, any appearance at a glamorous Seattle party began with the purchase of discount fabrics. The favorite place to go was Pacific Iron and Metal, a store in the upstairs of a vast and drafty wood-planked warehouse. Shopping for yardage was a carnival of choice, islands of color in brocades, silks, threaded sheers, lamé prints, ribboned laces. It also meant getting away from child and husband, getting away from the demand of customers and business, getting a short vacation. For these welcomed outings, Lola extended the invitations.

Fortunately, considering the size of my sub-compact car, usually no more than three women at a time ever deigned to accept. Sometimes Katy came with one of her daughters, or perhaps Duda and Fatima, Lola's talented daughters-in-law; or maybe Yutsa, the wife of Lola's cousin, Fat Albert; or Boka, married to Busha, Lola's godchild. If everyone wanted to go, we had to take a second car.

Getting the show on the road always tested my patience; the women never seemed to be ready. As we drove off, they were still tying their head scarves, while a gaggle of children ran after the car shouting "Buy me . . ." instructions.

More hours passed before the women could find what they wanted. Comparing posted prices that had been slashed and reduced, and then reduced some more, they frowned, haggled and underbid. They fingered fabrics thoughtfully and then moved on, their long skirts sweeping in a dazzle of color down the aisles. These women could spend the entire morning shopping, and sometimes the early afternoon as well, interrupted only by a midday refueling stop at a roadside restaurant.

"We have to take our time. We don't get out enough," Yutsa explained, forestalling my objection to an additional shopping hour as she loaded her coffee with packets of synthetic sugar (and

17

stuffed more packets and napkins into both our handbags and our pockets).

They bought by the bolt, and the price had to be very reasonable, or the fabric unusually wide. "How does this look?" they would ask, intently draping a fabric length around their waists in long pleats with one hand, posing the other above their heads. "Am I dark? Does it make me dark?" they asked, arching their backs and turning to each side.

Woman to woman, yardage was ever the most popular gift. Once, Lola hovered for long minutes over some hand-painted silk chiffon. Finally, she bought one precious yard, at one hundred dollars, for *Chivri* Mileva, the mother of her godchild Busha. "She can make a head scarf," she explained, sighing when she discovered the state tax added nearly another ten dollars to the price.

LOLA DIDN'T INVITE the Kalderasha women to go with us. Or, if she did, they never came. When I asked Katy why, she doubted they would have money to spend. Kalderash men, she explained, earn the money. They buy and sell used cars, trailers and trucks, and like to keep an appreciable sum for a future investment. In contrast to Machvaia, where the woman provides the family income, the local Kalderasha valued self-restraint and thrift, she said, and believed largesse of any kind provokes bad times. But when I asked Lola why Kalderasha saved and Machvaia spent so freely, she commented darkly, "Those people got plenty of money. But they don't have class."

Over the years, I watched her arrive at the local Kalderasha celebrations, armed with her best show-stopping appearance, ready to dance and have fun. One time, pausing in the doorway with her usual aplomb, hand on hip, coquettishly tossing her head, she whispered; "Bette Davis. That's who I'm like. Did you notice? Everybody says so."

By "everybody," of course, Lola meant the Machvaia.

But time and again, the Kalderasha parties failed to meet her expectations. Where was the band? The dancing? The wine and liquor for the women? The opulent tables of meat, salad, dessert— "real food"? Within the hour we usually left "those other people's parties" in my little car, bouncing down the street to better times.

TRIPS TO THE YARDAGE STORE proved so good for morale that Lola instituted a "women's night out." Until this, nights out had always been a male prerogative. "Now we're in America where the women got some rights," said Lola, looking to me for backing. I nodded emphatically. That's how, once or twice a month, I would transport the Machvanki ladies to the clubs while their husbands stayed home with the children.

The men probably agreed to this odd New World development because Lola was an elder and, theoretically at least, could do no wrong. She would always chaperone these events; in those days Gypsy women seldom went anywhere alone. As I think of it now, there was also an element of sporting going on, an intergroup competition. The Machvaia men wanted the Kalderasha to know that Machvaia treated their women well, entrusting them with the sweet freedom of enjoyment.

But I heard a countervailing view, once, when I was sitting between two Kalderasha women at a picnic. They admitted rather grandly that their husbands were crazy about them and so fiercely jealous that they wouldn't let their wives out of their sight. Seeing my puzzled expression, they continued, "Other men," they said, "might notice our 'light skin,' get jealous, cause trouble, fight."

Later, when I told Lola what they had said, one eyebrow curved up like a question mark before she frowned in irritation and ventured another opinion: "Those women are too much with the men. They don't know their own minds."

ONCE, WHEN WE HAD TOO MANY passengers for an outing, daughter-in-law Duda, who couldn't read but who drove like a champion, took a second car.

Because she had begun telling fortunes, we included Duda's pre-teen daughter, Sabrina, backed by a fake ID and carefully made up to look clownishly ancient for her years. Although Lola preferred the Athens Cafe where she knew all the waiters, custom forbade our group from watching the belly dancer's grinding bumps and shimmies in Lola's august presence.

Restrictions of this kind had only a momentary effect on Lola's breezy talent for enjoyment, however, and she readily agreed to go to The Trojan Horse instead. There, amidst the spotlight dusk, Tony Moreno, a young Greek singer, crooned familiar love ballads. "Strangers in The Night" was a favorite, as well as the theme song from *Zorba the Greek*, which he played on his *bazouki*. The women liked heartthrob Tony both because he was a hunk and because he apparently liked, or at least tolerated, Gypsies.

The women began the evening by dancing opposite each other. After warming up, they wove between the other dancers, laughing, commenting, clapping. Boba waved hula hands behind a portly man wearing a pink poinsettia Hawaiian shirt. Duda affected a squat-kneed Groucho Marx Brothers walk and pretended to be puffing on a paper cigar rolled from a cocktail menu. Katy broke spontaneously into a crazy Charleston—she wanted me to know she was famous for her Charleston—while her skinny arm with its sapphire charm bracelet rose majestically above her head.

They insisted I join them on the dance floor and, at first, I was a bit of a stick. For one thing, I couldn't seem to clap right. I always seemed to be one beat ahead, or behind. Still, dancing was a facet—maybe the only facet—of Gypsy life I felt I understood immediately.

I had grown up in a hotel where, like today's young Gypsies who live indoors, dancing was my only regular exercise. I was taught tap, ballet and "oriental" dancing. To redirect some of my abundant energy away from jumping on their bed, my harassed parents arranged for frequent lessons in dance, piano, elocution and voice, all tendered in other people's apartments.

When the women dragged me onto the floor, I found myself moving on my own, getting a sizable rush from inventing steps, following the beat, humming. For a few blissful moments, I felt like I was Rita Hayworth, the enticing Gilda—I have red hair—or my favorite dancer of all time, Suzanne Farrell. She *becomes* the music.

But the spell was broken when the women stopped to watch me, and then became comically awkward as they tried to join me. "That's your style," they encouraged kindly. They wouldn't let me stop, and getting to the end of the set and back to our table seemed to take a century. Lola laid a comforting hand on my arm and reminded me, "You're American. You dance different."

Apparently "different" wouldn't suffice for me because, after that, once my children were in bed I would eagerly put a record on the turntable, turn down the lights, remove my shoes and practice dancing. Studying Gypsies while becoming an anthropologist wasn't going to be enough. I also wanted to dance with the easy exhilarated grace of those who had danced all their lives. I wanted to emulate the expressive moves that bring the inside out and that I recognized as Gypsy.

In the company of Gypsies, there was always an edge of uncertainty and excitement. I was never entirely sure of what to expect from the Gypsy women or how we might be received in public. Whenever, overcome by "the truth of feeling," the women sang along with and upstaged Tony, I half expected to be thrown out and forbidden re-entry.

On one of our nights out, Lola brought along a snack of cold cuts, a fair-sized salami, a full jar of mayonnaise, bread, two tomatoes and some cheese. Seeing what she had unloaded from her snakeskin handbag, I expected the waitress to object. Instead, mercifully, Lola's demand for an order of pickled martini onions "to go with this here on the table" bent the waitress into a spasm of giggles.

Every two or three weeks, I would pick up my Machvanki riders, their giant skirts and petticoats tangling and twisting around them, and head for The Trojan Horse or The Greek Village, another favorite club. During the band's intermission, the women told each other jokes and stories. Fearless and funny Duda would entertain us. She spoke about her arrest as a child bride of fifteen, of how she had been responsible for repaying her new in-laws the expense of setting up her fortune-telling office and of how she and her sister-in-law were "grinding," that is, expediting the flow of cash by allowing no more than a few minutes per client.

"I was doing OK, I was making it." She stood up to emphasize her point, fingers clenched, her small frame shaking with excitement. Then she told how, one day, she had spotted a badge inside a client's jacket and, thinking fast, hummed the theme from *Dragnet* to warn her sister-in-law, who sped out the back door and avoided capture.

Duda's escapade was a world away from my former everyday-housewife-life in suburbia, and I felt a pang of regret that I had never saved anyone from jail or, for that matter, done much of anything particularly daring or outlandish.

But the Machvaia household revolves around the women's *ofisuria* (offices) and their upcoming business appointments. Of course, fortune telling was illegal in Washington State (and elsewhere), and I was seriously impressed by the women's daring, the off-hand way they managed to live with the constant threat of arrest.

The Machvanki were famous among Gypsies as the fortune tellers of renown, "the highest class," and they told me proudly, "We work too. We have careers, like you."

Still dependent on my alimony check, I too wanted to be ready for any eventuality, invincible in the face of defeat. I liked the classy snap of their floor-length skirt hems, the directness of their gaze. In trying to understand them, I found many reasons to admire the Machvanki. I wanted to be like them, to opt for courage and adventure.

WHO COULD RESIST a Gypsy party?! I always had time for parties. As Lola's personal chauffeur, I drove her to the ceremonials, Saint-days, weddings, death commemorations, all the events an outsider is, by Roma rule, not supposed to attend.

Years later I learned from Lola's son, the laughing Miller, that he had explained my presence as required; he told the other tribes, the Kalderasha families, that I was Lola's nurse. He thought it a great joke: "Who would refuse an ailing old woman the attentions of her nurse?" His news dismayed me. At the time, I had mistakenly believed I was gaining in popularity and cultural expertise.

At the parties and celebrations, Lola was given the best seating, the most considerate service. The women paid her honor, beckoning their daughters to our table, waiting for Lola's notice and approval. The younger ones danced for her, ending their best efforts with a nod and bow of respect, their praying hands pointing in her direction. I sat beside the Grande Dame Lola, and proximity counts. That's how I found myself sharing the glory.

At first, I didn't have the knack for celebration. Nothing I owned featured a bare bosom or a tight-bodice with a circular skirt. I tried wearing whatever I could find around my apartment or what could be borrowed from my sisters. But my skimpy India cotton skirt stopped above my ankles, the wrinkles wouldn't come out, the vegetable dye had faded. Multiple pleats were the current Gypsy fashion, fifteen yards in weightless chiffon, and no less than ten in velvet.

The women's shoes with fetishly spiked high heels were indicators of status. My sandals, on the contrary, were designed for walking all over campus. Flat, brown, practical, they left the normally voluble Machvaia women speechless with dismay.

Maybe to avoid the disgrace of being seen with such an eyesore, Katy volunteered to help. I watched while she back-pleated a twelve-yard skirt by hand with heavy double-basting stitches. In the fashion of the day, the Chinese jade-tinted skirt went around me completely and lapped double in the front. The obvious advantage was that I could gain fifty pounds, or get pregnant, and, with minor adjustments, no one would notice. Only an over-sized safety pin held the waist together and, except for this single fastening, the skirt, like a sarong, was essentially open. At first, wearing a skirt without a seam distressed me. But Katy was right, the weight of the fabric held it closed, whether sitting or standing.

Nevertheless my body balked at the new restriction. Accustomed to easy comfort, the weight of the crepe, like a heaviness on my soul, held me down. The skirt clung to my knees when I moved and, when I bent over, the hem would drag on the floor. Sensing my misery, Katy showed me how to set myself free by twirling and dancing. Like she said, the skirt *was* designed for turning and dancing.

A SPARKLING PUBLIC APPEARANCE indicated privilege and status, and was how a Machvanka wanted to be remembered. At that time, gold, *lots* of gold jewelry, was of primary importance. Everyone knew that the woman without it was up to her neck in hock.

I was astonished to learn that their jewelry, more likely than not, was authentic. Each woman seemed to own a treasury of real gold earrings, bracelets, necklaces and pins. Ritual occasions provided the ideal opportunity to show off their quality and intrinsic worth, and to advertise a woman's wearable money-in-the-bank— many Gypsies didn't, as yet, understand or trust American banks.

The recommended look, which came down somewhere between an Oscar contender, Empress Catherine of Russia and a lotto-winning peasant, might best be obtained, I thought, with the backing of my more fortuitously endowed relatives. I put the word out. But my family wasn't into jewelry. All they had to lend me was a discarded wedding band, a class ring and some cheap mood rings that were popular at the time.

I made my first Gypsy blouse from an extra piece of yardage Katy found in a drawer. The fabric scratched my fingertips as I sewed and when I tried it on the intense violet, cobalt and red of the pattern washed my skin out to a pale insignificance. But it looked colorful and Gypsy-like, and it was all that I had to wear, so on it went.

"What's wrong? You don't look right to me," commented Pretty Bobbie, Lola's number-five daughter, who was visiting. We were sitting on the sidelines at a wedding and she became concerned when the metal-threaded ruffles irritated my skin and turned my face and chest beet red.

By then I knew enough to cover over any poignant error or cultural faux pas with a confident affirmation. Exaggerating two or three minor genes from a long-forgotten ancestor, "It's my Irish skin," I lied. (The Machvaia, when they wanted to be complimentary, told me I had "Irish" skin.) No one rudely stared. But, against my back, I felt the eyes of critical appraisal. Several families left abruptly. What was this red disease?

Considering my marginal status, my threat to Romaniya custom and the way most of the women my age wore their hair pulled back and off the neck into a bun, I decided that upswept hair would be imperative. Disregarding the cost, I had my hair done professionally. Any afternoon before a Gypsy party might find me, looking like a sorcerer myself with my elaborately coifed and sprayed "do," seated around a well-used, scratched and wooden classroom table with a group of university students, discussing topics like magic and witchcraft.

Lola never criticized the way I looked. Sometimes when we were en route to the grocery store or out shopping, she would suddenly decide she wanted to stop at Katy's or her son's. Remembering the unsuitability of the canvas Keds I was usually wearing, I often refused to get out of the car. In protest, Lola would stick her face back inside and lift a Maybelline-penciled eyebrow. "*You* can dress any way you like. You're American and free," a remark that always tickled me; to outsiders, of course, it is the Gypsies who epitomize freedom. But I had quickly learned that Lola's opinion didn't always count with the other women, who were unforgiving if I didn't look right.

By the end of my first year of field work, the only material assets I had were hanging in my closet. But I must admit I was having fun playing dress-up and meeting the challenge of acting like a Machvanka.

AT EVERY FESTIVE GATHERING, Lola ignored her doctor's advice and, rising to the toes of shoes with impossible heels, she danced, while others stood in a circle around her, clapping and smiling. She danced "for my life and because I can." She did it to prove her mettle in the scenario of a life in which she was the star, the inspirational muse and the director.

Lola believed passionately in dancing. There were no less than forty rainbow-colored pairs of pumps and sandals in her closet— buckled, bowed and hot to trot. With glowing, impassioned attention, she danced what she called "the old Serbian style," one wide work-worn hand held high and straight as a signal. She danced with stamping, staccato steps, her black eyes glittering over a still articulate, though arthritic, shoulder. She became irresistible, teasing and flirting, clicking her heels, urging everyone to join her.

Dancing suits the Gypsy temperament. Free form, innovative dancing that follows the lead of feeling and the truth of immediate experience is the kind most valued. The people will dance for pleasure, for sorrow, for any reason whatsoever. Years after we met, I watched Katy's now-grown daughter Sophie, a widow at twenty-five, dance out the poetry and drama of a dangerous, difficult death-to-life transition. We were at a Greek restaurant in San Francisco when, following the urgency of impulse and marking the culmination of her one year of mourning, Sophie jumped up to dance. With intricate turns, with graceful reaching arms, finger snaps and sweat, Sophie created one of those dancing memories Gypsies, who live in a heroic time, prize above all others, a "moment to remember."

Katy was pleased and happy with the changes wrought by her daughter's dancing. The following day, Sophie was singing and wearing "Love That Red" lipstick. Two months later, she was engaged to be married.

Gypsies are exceptionally good dancers because they practice. Teenagers work at it for hours, observing themselves with intent absorption in mirrored walls, perfecting the line of the head, the flow of their shoulders, elbows, wrists. New American-style dances are watched, judged and selectively copied. I've never known any of the people who couldn't carry a tune or couldn't dance.

The Machvaia do some of their best communicating while dancing. Women who like me, or who need to tell me something confidential, ask me for the favor of a dance. Men who want to attract my notice will dance where I can clearly see them. The people come to parties eager to reaffirm the value of community and their sense of spiritual connection; to do this, they must dance. The success of any event is usually gauged by the quality of the music and the joy, the physical and aesthetic release, of the dancing.

I WAS TO DRESS UP. Lola had given me orders weeks before. "This is Katy's *slava* (Saint-day). She will make it beautiful." I wore a simple dressmaker blouse I already had and splurged on a slender silver lamé skirt. When Lola got in the car, I asked her how I looked. "OK," she said, then, after another glance, "Kind of quiet."

The inside of Katy's downtown storefront had been transformed, and not just by the rented end-to-end tables. Pageantry and excess were everywhere—the bowls dripping fruit (the real mixed uncritically with the plastic), the red-ribboned bottle of whiskey, the golden pictures and statues of medieval Saints. A blazing three-foot candle, the tallest item on the table, was banked by gladiolas, a waterfall of wheat, a round jar of honey, and secured by a leaning tower of French bread.

The leathery roasted lamb, crowned with flowers and antique coins, wearing near-sighted cherries for eyes, stared at no one in particular. A sheet cake, white with red roses, read *Happy Birthday, St. Mary. Love from the Spiros.* On a springy layer of green celery, my place, like all the others, was surrounded by dish upon abundant

27

dish: several salads, cabbage rolls, desserts, among them the mandatory ceremonial cheese and raisin strudel.

The forest of celery tops carpeting the length of the table brought the outdoors in. Katy explained that the celery was for good luck, green money luck, mostly, to ensure abundant increase of every kind in the days to come.

"But the candle in the middle belongs to the Saint," she explained. "*Slava* is mostly for good health. I took this Saint for Jelly John (her son) when he was sick. Saint Mary saved him. I celebrate Her every year. It's like a promise. A contract. When Jelly grows up, he'll take over his *slava*."

I did my best to pay attention. I tried very hard to concentrate and memorize details, the Old World courtesy of the men, the gentle camaraderie of the women. But a full tumbler of scotch had transformed my absorbent brain into mush. Dimly conscious of many pairs of eyes holding mine hypnotically, and the sweet cacophony of song and conversation, I felt the community connection, the bliss and comfort of sharing and the welcome of unqualified acceptance. Or so it seemed.

THE AFTER-EFFECT LASTED for days. I had some difficulty concentrating on matters of academic theory. Given a taste of the Machvaia genius for parties, I wanted more. I began to suspect that, in terms of an overall life plan, my aerie of books in Suzzallo Library would not suffice.

My first *slava* seemed like an overwhelming success; it altered the purpose and direction of my life. I couldn't say how exactly. Words, in fact, seemed to get in the way. But then, what did Lola mean it was no good? She seemed so dissatisfied with the whole thing.

I puzzled over the way it had ended. We left Katy's *slava* and headed for the Athens Café. Lola's multiple skirts flooded into the driver's side, entangling the pedals so that I had to reach down and keep pushing them away. I could tell she was out of sorts, sniffing at the worn condition of my mini-car's interior, complaining about its size.

The *slava* was "destroyed," as she put it. Why? Not enough people, not enough music. "Ruined!" she snorted. "I didn't even feel like dancing!" How could she say that, I wondered? Everything had been so festive, everyone so gorgeous, and even the arguments had seemed replete with a waggish good humor.

The next day, while serving me leftover lamb, Katy explained, "The Saint knows I tried. But there was too much bad stuff going on." Having failed to find perfection, Saint Mary had apparently kept her distance. So, in fact, had Fat Albert and Busha, Miller's best buddies. They hadn't even bothered to call and explain that they were already drunk at their friend Milanitzi's storefront. The tentative soprano sighs of Luludji, the flower-faced daughter-in-law, hinted that she was planning to leave her marriage—again. And when Ephram, Katy's errant husband, held out a hand that begged forgiveness, Katy shook her head scarf in a firm, flat refusal.

In fact, the previous week had been rife with surmise and suspicion—who had said or done what to whom? To top it off, except for Ephram, none of the Kalderasha, who outnumbered the local Machvaia by ten to one, had even bothered to show up. It was, as I later learned, due to a dispute over territory: the south Seattle Kalderasha contesting the encroaching location of Boyd's newly rented house.

I pestered Katy about perfection. What did she mean? I learned that Saints, being the epitome of perfection, require a perfect party and this is only possible in a harmonious setting. "You start to work hard weeks before. The house must be perfectly clean, the clothes fresh and new, the children bathed, lots of flowers and food. But what matters most is the inside, what you're feeling. Nobody mad. All good friends."

Katy paused, stubbing her long cigarette out fiercely. "We had things right, perfect." With her elbows tensed against her slender waist, Katy's lifted up her palms toward Saint Mary, in pious supplication. "'We had things *almost* perfect. We had the music, but not the dancing. Good music, singing, lots of dancing—that's a perfect party, that brings the people together. That brings the Saints to be with us. That's the happiness and good luck."

Katy bent her golden flame of hair and explained in a dignified and confidential tone, "The Saint wanted to come. We know our Saint likes parties. She wanted to come around, but she couldn't."

The more parties I went to, the more like a musical comedy my life became. The life of enjoyment—recommended by Lola because "when you're dead, game's up, that's it"—struck me as exemplary. The opportunity to sing, to dance, to participate in making a party was too appealing to pass up.

I spent more and more of my free time with Gypsies. I couldn't wait to see what was happening at Easter, Christmas, New Year's, at every celebration. During the holidays in Seattle, after a brief hello, I left my family stranded and went to join the Gypsies. Considering these parties to be part of my research, my family said they didn't mind. But I had begun to internalize the chasm of difference between Gypsies and non-Gypsies. In my heart, in my gut, I knew it for what it was in truth, the beginning of betrayal.

ONE EVENING IN NOVEMBER, perhaps curious about the stranger who was permitted to drive their wives about, all six of the local Machvaia men (five of whom I had seen several times at parties) appeared at my door without notice.

After seating them in a circle at the dining table, I hastily installed Leslie in the kitchen as coffee server and told my son, as official family male and our one protector, to briefly emerge from his bedroom on occasion and check out the proceedings. I don't recall that he did.

To my relief, my daughter, who had spent some time with me at Katy's storefront, performed as splendidly as any Machvaia daughter might have. She assumed a modest air, promptly offering refills, dropping her eyes without speaking.

Fat Albert stood, and swept his fedora in my direction; he played his guitar and sang. Then the men sang together, improvising lyrics, interrupting one another, often pausing to laugh and joke. Boyd kept reminding the others that I couldn't understand their Romani. But the men just laughed and sang some more, throwing in a sentence here and there in English.

They seemed to be having a hilarious time; I had the impression that some of the singing was satiric and a bit off-color. Despite the language barrier, I understood that I was being warned to beware of the Kalderasha men: "Those not so good other Gypsies." Katy's Kalderasha husband, a notable womanizer, was the case in point. I already understood the gist of this message well.

When the jokes got a little too suggestive and Boyd was obviously becoming uncomfortable with their direction, I pointed to the tape recorder I had turned on earlier and told the men that I was planning to replay and study what they had been saying. As a body, they arose politely, bowed in cool acknowledgment of my foresight, and left.

A FEW DAYS LATER, Boyd called to invite me to a party at Fat Albert's. Boyd said a fine Machvaia family had arrived from California for a visit. "Remember Max, who was with us when we sang?" he asked. They were welcoming Max and family with a party, and the party was running out of liquor.

I was sure this was some kind of breakthrough, this relaxing of the usual code of separatist ethics, and, grabbing a bottle of white wine, which was all I had, I gleefully drove up University Way. The door of the little house was open and the music filled the entryway. I negotiated the living room of men in the properly demure Machvaia way, no doubt to their amusement. Lola wasn't there, so I plopped myself down on the dining chair next to Katy.

And that's when I saw him for the first time. He came to the women's table to welcome Max's wife and sister. He bent above me and I couldn't help noticing his sweeping luxuriant lashes, his boyish, burly directness. As discreetly as I could, I asked Old Dinah who he was. "Stevo Polo," she said (pronouncing it *Stayvo*). "He doesn't come around except on the special occasions."

Where had he been during all the Seattle parties and Gypsy picnics the previous summer? Where was he when Katy made her *slava*? Hadn't he been invited when the Machvaia men paid their corporate singing and joking visit? And, if he was, why hadn't he come?

He was outside at the curb when I left, trying his best to start his car, a tired 1955 Chevrolet sedan with a For Sale sign in the window. I explained that my car was parked down the block and offered to drive him home.

We drove and I told him what I, an outsider and a *Djuhli* (as he called American women), was doing at a Machvaia party. "That's good," he said in unaccented musical English. "We need studying. Enough has been written about stealing children. No one knows anything *real* about Gypsies."

Before he got out of the car, he asked politely, while staring intently into a distance someplace behind my eyes, if he might kiss me. Confused and surprised, but divorced by then for several years, I barked "No!" with such explosive force that the car door on his side seemed to fly open of its own volition.

The moment after is like a flag in my memory: the gravity of his stride as he walked away in my headlights, his baggy pants, the cheap haircut, too high and short in the back, that struck me as offensive. Why should I care how he looked?

Desire and fear beat in panic against my chest. How could a man who needed to go on a diet and who hadn't the fashion sense to wear designer jeans possibly attract me? I was a bit wary of men anyway. The women's movement was still embryonic and I was just beginning to realize in what measure men held the high cards and ran the game. I reminded myself of what I had at stake, of how I had managed to sneak into graduate school by the back door by taking advanced classes and proving I could do it, about how I had waited years, my whole life really, to embark on a career. Indeed, nothing was more important to me.

To me, anthropology was both my mission and salvation. I fantasized the bush-whacking adventure of African safaris. I could see myself on expedition in the Amazon, smoking Gauloises, or at the Explorers Club in New York, flanked by polished walnut paneling and yellowing elephant tusks, being toasted and cheered along by my fellow explorers. I was, however, so unprogressive, so much the product of my time that it didn't even seem odd to me that all my fantasy companions were men, men with bushy beards and weather-beaten smile lines.

On the way home from that abortive no-kiss encounter, I resolved to avoid temptation. Besides, involvement with a Djuhli would threaten him as well. Eating with an American woman, being seen in the same car as an American woman, any intimate contact with an American woman—all could mean blacklist by Machvaia, and the other Roma as well.

But what did I know?

THE ONLY TIME my former husband deigned to speak with me was to schedule our children's visits. Yet, here he was at the beginning of the Christmas holidays, the unexpected visitor, hat in hand, waiting like a tallish sad-eyed spaniel. As soon as he sat, he became immobilized, almost as if he had nowhere else to go.

In a panic, I began a one-sided conversation, speaking wildly, inanely, about my schoolwork, the weather, whatever came to mind. When I ran out of topics, the silence was deafening. That's when the phone rang.

Stevo was calling from a nearby tavern. Grabbing a sweater, I announced I had to go out, and ran with relief down the block. By the time I returned, the children were already in bed and their father, poor man, was gone. That was the last time I ever saw him.

I was amazed at how comfortable I felt with Stevo at the tavern. His behavior was courtly, his table manners exquisite, his responsiveness disarming. He told stories, did imitations, sang a bit from a musical comedy, did everything he could to entertain and keep me laughing. When Stevo, the poorest Machvano in town for reasons I later discovered, called for a date the next day, I accepted.

He arrived in his spiffed-up Mafia suit, booming good will, smelling of breath mints and shoe polish. I went to say goodnight to my son who was in his room, entertaining a school friend with a giant three-cheese pizza and word games. "I'll be back early. We're just going out to dinner," I reassured him.

But when I returned to the living room, I found Stevo fast asleep, completely relaxed into the goose down depths of the sofa. I didn't have the heart to wake him. Instead, I looked beyond the style of his clothes and the cut of his hair. I had time to appreciate what I saw: the buff, adorable form; the in-and-out surrender of his breath; the dark, near-black curls; the perfect fringe of lashes resting on his smooth broad cheeks. Sipping what remained of the drink he had left and chewing on the ice, I studied him as intently as I studied the text in my schoolbooks. Fragments of Christmas carols drifted through the half-open window. While the moon slipped through a moving mask of clouds, the radiator tranquilly popped and fizzed.

The exhausted Stevo slept for hours, never knowing we were courting. I sensed the danger, the loss of self, the death in life that is passion, and tried to resist. But it was too late. In the face of Stevo's inspired sleeping tactics, I was quietly, readily wooed and won.

TO A MACHVANO GYPSY, the American woman represents the ultimate possibility of free love. No bride price. No expensive wedding. No ancient lineage and luck inheritance to match. No demanding elders and in-laws to mollify. No grim threat of unending vendettas following a messy divorce. He can disappear without a trace whenever he likes, and America can never find him.

As a free gift woman, a pearl beyond price, I was treated like a goddess. At least that's how I felt. No one had ever cared so much about pleasing me or listened so attentively to what I had to say. The evening that my parents arrived from out of town to visit their four adult children in Seattle, Stevo unexpectedly rang my door bell. I buzzed him into the lobby and went down by elevator to greet him.

It was after nine, the lobby still and empty as a church, the coffered ceiling dark, the table lamps dimmed. He looked at me, his black eyes narrowing with delight. My parents had never forgiven me for my divorce and, to mollify them, I was wearing new silk jersey poppy-print lounging pajamas, an outfit more in keeping with my former role as the standard corporate wife than that of a student, a fieldworker, a single mother. It was my own classic Hollywood movie moment, the one where the heroine appears, perfectly turned out, and the hero is instantly struck dumb with adoration.

I asked if he would like to meet my parents. He hesitated, then refused. "What will you do with the rest of the evening?" I asked, unwilling to break the magnetic force field of connection. "It won't matter," he answered bluntly, turning his great shoulders resolutely toward the door. Before long, our connection had become the crime of the century.

THE MESSAGE OF THOUGHT and feeling danced across Stevo's face. Increasingly, I became beguiled by Stevo's emotional availability—so different from my former husband's, who had worn his work as a protective suit of armor, clanking about like a ghost. And maybe he was a ghost. Barely out of childhood when he was drafted into the Navy, he had had flown continuous years of bombing missions over the Pacific, and had possibly flown too far from home.

To me, Stevo Polo looked like a man, as the Gypsies put it, "full of luck." He was gorgeous, the best-looking Machvano I ever saw. He was, in the manner of upper-class Machvaia, well-spoken. Gypsies tend to have idyllic childhoods and Stevo possessed the panache that results from being an adored only child: pampered absolutely, and given everything he wanted. Maybe all that early love had something to do with the abiding sweetness of his nature. When I mentioned this, his laugh was short and bitter: "Ha! You think I'm sweet?" In light of the harsh realities of his current lifestyle, sweetness was a luxury he didn't feel he could afford.

Gypsies are always advising me; they contend that advice is a good luck gift. Katy must have noticed my interest in Stevo. We were at a Gypsy wedding when she said, within earshot, that Stevo looked like luck, all right, adding "but something is wrong." Something was wrong, all right. I was napping in the library and falling asleep in my classes.

For more than a month, December to January, we sat every night in the row of parked cars without lights that faced Green Lake, still locked in desperate embrace at three, sometimes four, in the morning, necking like adolescents, hour after hour. I couldn't get enough of him.

One day, without thinking, I brought matters to a head. Stevo had parked and pulled me toward him, when I heard myself saying, "I'm not a teenager, you know." Wriggling out of his arms in a fit of conflicted dismay, I grabbed for the handle on the door. "OK," he snarled, spinning the car's back wheels and speeding away. When he said nothing for more than a mile, I thought he was taking me home. But he stopped on the far side of the bridge, at the Hillside Motel. "I'll pay," I offered; Machvaia women pay for everything. "No," he slammed the car door. I could see he was annoyed, or that something was wrong. But maybe not?

That first night a bit too brusque and expedient for my taste; I didn't even have time to remove the go-go boots I was wearing. He, of course, was going home every night to his wife—yes, he had a wife. But what, really, could I expect? I had, more or less, insisted.

WEEKENDS FOUND US MEETING in secret—our time together brief and precious, the car our safe, two-person world—and we mapped the city with our turning wheels. Little by little, he told me about himself, mostly stories about the uncles who were close to him in age, and who had done what he couldn't, being too tender-hearted.

They left their wives, ran away to America. "How do your uncles live?" I asked. "What do they do?" "They have fun, drink, date women, do drugs," was his answer. How tiresome and unoriginal. Nearly every young hippie I knew was doing much the same.

These were the uncles on his father's side, the wicked side as his mother's family saw it. One of them was just a day older than Stevo and invariably cast as the hero of his stories. I suspected they were dealing drugs, although Stevo refused to admit the possibility. Because bloodline and destiny are inextricably linked, he must have seen our relationship as emerging evidence of his own tendency to deviltry and rebellion.

As we drove through the town in one of the aging cars he was invariably intending to sell, I told him of the lackluster days before my divorce, and confided how school had become my escape. Never before or since have I experienced such a lack of reserve or judgment, such a sense of close connection. In tune with the seasons, we spent entire days together, "car days" that were like my training wheels for life.

I learned that music is a benchmark of enjoyment. Stevo often sang his favorite oldies by Sinatra, or Dean Martin, crooning "All The Way" and "That's Amore." When the car radio wasn't working, as was often the case, we sang together, all the lyrics we could recall, filling in the blanks by making up new ones. Whatever he sang, or did, or said, struck me, his uncritical audience, as wonderfully original.

For income, Stevo bought and sold cars. During emergency times, he worked out the creases in other people's fenders. He operated without a business license and any attempt he made to earn money seemed riddled with risk.

He solicited business door to door. As the door of the selected house swung open, his chameleon response always stunned me, his adaptable posture, the way his hat brim automatically tilted to the suitable angle, the originality of his opening gambit, his unfailing panache. I wondered how, without formal training, he got his genius for dialogue and learned to act such disparate dramatic roles. An inspired mimic, I thought. A Gypsy Barrymore in the making, a man who had missed his true calling.

Significant profit hinged on his finding a car that was unused, dusty and for sale at a decent price. Sometimes he introduced me as his sickly wife, a pale and terrified Camille, "unaccustomed," he said, "to such a hard life." Then, with my fists pushed inside my coat pockets to simulate pregnancy, I would walk crab-wise to the house.

True, I was neglecting my schoolwork and acting like an adolescent. But riding along next to Stevo, I had insights and experiences that can't be found in books. I learned to know about the neighborhoods, from one end of Seattle to the other, and how the people in them lived. I grew sensitive to the character and generosity of places, the volatility of human affairs. Some days began with a lift-off feeling, a sun spark on the windshield, the peppy young gas station attendant with a beamish smile, and luck would come our way. Other days, after a fruitless morning, pausing opposite a beguiling view of Green Lake or under a shade tree in the park, we picnicked on our purchases from a nearby Mom-and-Pop grocery: cold cuts, tomatoes, onions, potato chips, sliced bread. We took the time required for the necessary mood change. We kept open to the message of feeling. As the nomadic Machvaia Roma had done, and the Gypsies have probably done for centuries, Stevo and I were looking for omens and possibilities. We were looking for our *po drom* (on the road) luck.

If I was losing my mind, I hoped it was temporary. At first, I didn't tell anyone except, of course, my children; they lived with me and were the first to know. I didn't discuss him, the unlikelihood of him, not even with my sisters. He wanted me; that was my reality. I understood that his shade lived somewhere else with a wife and family. But the insistence of his desire belonged to me.

SOME MONTHS LATER, I met Tutsi, Stevo's wife. I was at Lola's when they walked in. Her black hair was pulled tightly away from her face into a bun and emphasized her sharp cheekbones. A nervous, wiry woman, she was obviously pregnant. She and Stevo had not been there more than a few minutes when she said, "We have to go. We left the children alone." I understood later that they had come to ask Lola to baptize some of their children, but Lola, for reasons she never said, refused.

Seeing Tutsi in person alarmed me. When Stevo arrived for dinner that evening, I couldn't look directly at him. He had mentioned nothing about a child-to-be. My heart splintered into bits as I entreated, "Why didn't you tell me?"

Stevo's eyes went dead and he explained what he called his "bad life situation." Ever since his mother died and he was married at fourteen to a girl he didn't know, crises had dogged him like a malevolent shadow. Born into a notable family, to avoid embarrassment, now he didn't even bother to associate with other local Machvaia, in part because he was as poor as a Kalderash, but also because, more than anything, he wanted to escape the Gypsies, his family and whomever or whatever had cursed him.

It seems that I was his big time opportunity, the indication of oncoming good luck. The luck of the Machvaia man, he said, relates directly to the quality and status of his woman. "The woman makes the man," he assured me most sincerely, folding my hands in his and putting his life between my palms. In the end, it was no contest. Between the misery of wife Tutsi and the misery of Stevo, I found the latter the more compelling.

Single women, my friends without children, were hard for Stevo to comprehend. He approved the young women we passed who were carrying babies or pushing strollers. "Look at them," he would say in admiration. Raising children is the raison d'etre of Machvaia life and, for Stevo, a woman with a child had considerable cachet. For him, as a traditional man, I could see that sexual intimacy was strongly tied to the reproductive results. Once, our passion spent, he propped himself up on an elbow, smirking with satisfaction, blowing smoke rings out his adorable short nose. "You should have been pregnant fifty times by now. You realize that, don't you?"

Irritated by this remark, I was tempted to ask if he thought he was playing slam-dunk. I well remembered the subsequent nine months of backaches, overheating, the chore of providing for a helpless newborn's every need, and had no desire whatsoever to change places with Tutsi.

Considering the bounty of Stevo's passionate attentions, I found it easy to be fair-minded and big-hearted. Did Tutsi love him? That was the main issue to me. Not how many children she already had or that she was pregnant again. If she really loved him, I decided I would be willing to split him half-and-half, twelve hours for me each day and the same for her. But nothing came of my half-and-half decision and no one ever asked for my fair-minded opinion. The cataclysmic events of our lives just took steam, gathering their own inexorable momentum.

IN 1967, SAN FRANCISCO was the place to be. In the halcyon summer of peace and love, flower children lived in the hand-to-mouth manner of old-time Gypsies, sleeping outdoors in the park; or in cars, just as Stevo's family was often required to do whenever they ran out of money. Everyone seemed to be traveling—mind traveling, space race traveling, electric Kool-Aid acid traveling, fieldwork traveling. Machvaia believe luck can be found *po drom* (on the road). When they want to get lucky, they go traveling.

I never found out whether or not Stevo told his wife I was coming with him to San Francisco. If he had, I doubt she would have agreed to go. Poor Tutsi, unaware, was anxious to set herself up in a grab-the-money-and-run business, and to win Stevo back with the profits. She drove the better car, crammed with children, and she got there first. Stevo and I followed in a car that wheezed on the hills, and rattled at the turns.

Once in the green immensity of western Oregon, giddy with the luxury of so much time together, we left the highway and parked. Lured by the jewels of sunlight spinning on the Rogue River shallows, we waded out from the shore, laughing and slipping on the smooth round rocks. Then, finding a level spot, we daringly pitted the tide of hot desire against the river's chilling rush.

Somewhere out of Grants Pass, Stevo's black brows massed together, and he tossed the West Coast map out the window. "We're going too fast, we'll be there too soon," he declared.

We stopped for a beer where our multiple reflections were caught in the paneled bar mirror, image upon paired image. Pleased at the effect of so many complementary couples—all Stevo Polo and Djuhli—Stevo bought a round for the house. To underscore the fullness of his feeling, he insisted on leaving an oversized tip, money he borrowed from me, money I had got from the Department of Anthropology to finance two too-brief weeks of California fieldwork.

LATE IN THE EVENING of our suspiciously tardy arrival, Tutsi screamed and broke a cocktail glass. We were in a diminutive bar in the Haight-Ashbury district, the three of us, drinking Manhattans, a trendy drink for the Machvaia at the time.

Through the window we could watch the scene outside: the swarm of young people (hardly more than children) recruiting passersby with newspapers, flyers, drugs, tie-dyed T shirts or the gift of a single flower. Stevo, in obvious disarray, attempted to defuse the ticking-bomb tension with a diversionary tactic. "Look at that!" he said with an emphatic nod toward the window. Tutsi never looked. Her eyes sparked and avoided mine. She already knew all Americans were crazy.

One minute, clean upturned glasses were hanging in tidy rows from the varnished racks on the ceiling. The next, Tutsi's patience had exploded, and they were hitting the floor in a shattering crescendo.

Stevo pushed me out the door, into the car, and drove away. As we turned the corner, Tutsi materialized right behind us. Grabbing the bumper, she fell. I could see her on the pavement behind us, shaking both fists. I swiveled front and said, with more assurance than I felt, "I think she's okay."

But Tutsi had a gift. The next morning, she tracked us down in a coffee shop four miles away. How did it happen that, out of nowhere, midway through an omelet with chives and sourdough toast. Just when Stevo and I felt blissfully safe from discovery, Tutsi showed up?

She edged into the booth beside me. Her smile switched on and off like a mocking, triumphant Jack O'Lantern. "See!" she pointed at the gap in her teeth. "You did that!" Stevo threw a bill at the cash register and raced out the door. On the sidewalk, he seesawed for a few moments between us, then escaped across the Bay to the lair of his same-age uncles.

Tutsi and I, robbed of our bone of contention, went shopping together for clothes for her children, ate lunch and tried, after a fashion, to get along. But détente wasn't easy. "Mine," she kept insisting, thrusting her injured face close to me. I understood what she meant. She thought she owned him, that Stevo was her property, like her in-and-out-of-hock jewelry, her few pieces of furniture, her many children, her missing tooth.

Our truce was brief. On the phone the next day, she promised to throw acid in my face, to stab me while I slept.

MOST DAYS, I STAYED in a cheap hotel south of Market. The bathroom was down the hall. Until one of the other tenants interrupted by banging on the door, I would monopolize the mirror, practicing defensive disguises, wigs, different postures and gaits. My departmental stipend, about $150, didn't go far, and finally, flat broke, I slept in the rental car and ate day-old doughnuts I got free from a bakery.

My final written report to the Anthropology Department omitted many significant details. I didn't, for example, explain how panicky and disoriented I felt when, midway through that week, all my contacts managed to vanish, including Stevo, Pretty Bobbie, cousin Egi and even Tutsi.

On a hunch, hoping to salvage my research, I haunted the UCSF Hospital lobby for two long days. Then, Pretty Bobbie's mother-in-law, the head of a giant family, was hospitalized for breast cancer, and I ran into several dozen of the Machvanki as they passed through the lobby. Their bad luck was my good; one of them had heard of me. We exchanged gossip. I wrote Bobbie's new telephone number on a paper napkin from the cafeteria, again in my address book, and, as a security measure, once again on the skin inside my wrist.

My final report to the Department avoided mentioning how, angered by Stevo's cowardly defection and the way our traveling good luck had devolved into rubbish, I found myself in the Sir Francis Drake Skylight room, slow dancing with a presentable stranger. We had met in the cable car line and moved on to dinner. I don't know what I expected, perhaps a little comfort and reassurance, perhaps just a little dinner? But soon bored by the tepid big band music, the mannerly restraint of the tablecloth-and-drapery setting, and the predictability of my partner's well-intended remarks, I suddenly remembered another appointment and made my escape.

In my report I didn't describe the picture of Lola, hands-on-hip and young, in the San Francisco police station's album of Gypsies. The police refused to give me a copy. Nor did I complain about the heartbreak when my lover disappeared for eight long days, or confess my relief and joy when Stevo showed up the night before I left San Francisco. He hadn't been home, he said, so Tutsi couldn't have followed him.

I really don't care for poetry readings but, in a perverse moment—by then, I was feeling quite perverse!—I made him go with me to one. The air in the crowded room curled with heavy incense, sitar music and second-hand dope smoke; within minutes, we were stoned. Stevo was horrified. He was always trying to protect me, like he did his children, from the danger of drugs.

TRAVELING WITH STEVO, I learned to pay attention to the good and the bad of luck. Machvaia luck, rather like karma, is an incipient power that colors human experience. But Stevo's good luck mostly rested in the past, and too often escaped him in the present.

In the end, it was Lucky Star Lola who taught me the most about how to get luck, how to keep it. When she moved to a new address, she liked to say, "I'm going to look for my luck," meaning she intended to look for her luck *po drom* (on the road).

She always expected the move to be easy, but it entailed more than rolling up the Wilton rug, folding the tent and packing the car. Lola owned a truckload of furniture, gadgets and clothes, and each move proved to be a massive effort. She would call to say, "I don't know how I'm doing it. But I'm doing it." I got the impression that the faster she moved, the more likely she was to run her luck down.

In return for the promise of half her psychic reading profits, her son Miller helped out, marketing her services with ads in the local papers and on the radio. If I didn't hear from her for days on end, I knew she was out there somewhere, on expedition for her luck. Once I dreamed she was stomping along the Alcan in sequined heels, a hitchhiking woman of nearly seventy, flinging the end of her feather boa flirtatiously after the dust of the passing drivers.

In time I learned to listen for the querulous moment that her luck began to slip, when the neighborhood lost her vote of confidence, clients didn't honor their appointments, the doctor failed to render satisfactory service and the city police ordered her to take the little palmistry sign out of the window, her electric and telephone bills went off the map.

Although getting another phone without established credit was invariably hard, it was not as hard as sitting beside a silent phone at night, wrapped in a silk-and-goose down quilt, curtains drawn, wondering what was going on in the houses of her many daughters. Bills in the mail had little reality anyway. "They don't care," she stormed, filing the envelope under a sofa cushion and plopping down on top of it. For Lola, the commercial always took a backseat to the personal. "They send me this bill I can't pay and never call to see how my family and me are doing."

Lola traveled for business. She traveled for the sake of traveling. She seemed to enjoy nothing as much as riding in my Volkswagen, the wind on her face. First thing, as we drove away, Lola would roll down the car window. Leaning out to converse with the pedestrians we passed, as well as the other drivers, she would inquire about the quality of their lives, their health, their names, where they lived. She offered her uncritical admiration of their children.

I drove her everywhere, all over the city, and sometimes state to state. Clutching the handle on the dash with one hand, pointing and gesturing with the other, she tried to orchestrate our passage with a chorus of fierce commands, "Stop!" "Turn!" "Look at that!"

Traveling, even days of traveling, never tired her. She always seemed unable to accept that I had had enough. At the end of a long driving day, still two hours away from our destination, I complained that my eyes ached from the glare of the oncoming headlights. "How can you be tired?" she'd ask, abandoning her scanning-eagle position on the edge of the front seat. "You've just been sitting there all day." I had to veer the wheels a bit and fake a close call before she'd let me stop. Lola usually chose the motel, the largest and most luxurious one possible, preferably with a crown or some indication of royalty on the logo. She paid all the bills. When I protested the cost, she promised, "If you spend it, you make it. You know that's my way."

One low-key evening when we were watching a musical on television and drinking coffee, she suggested we drive to Vancouver to see the Royal Canadian Mounties with their red coats and horses, and their songs (like an old Nelson Eddy movie). Later, she suggested we go to Puyallup for the Fair, and then another time, to Tahiti. "Where's Tahiti?" she'd say. She was always full of fresh ideas for traveling. "We could do *that*," she declared.

From Lola, I heard the high-risk stories. Even she had been impressed by an adventuresome cousin who transported her entire family, even the daughters-in-law and the grandchildren, to China. "Someplace in China," Lola explained. "What year? How would I know that?" They arrived to find a war they didn't expect and no other Roma to assist them.

"They nearly had it. They nearly starved." Lola emphasized her point by stabbing the air with her needle. Pausing to build suspense, she added that the cousin had been a lucky woman: she bought a pair of winning raffle tickets with her last few dollars and the winnings got them safe passage home.

"Is that true?" I asked, stunned by a story so spare of detail that my imagination went into a frenzy of supplementation.

"Of course," Lola responded furiously, raising her head from the ten yards of skirt she was busy hand-pleating and wounding me with a glance. "That's my family. I know what happens in my family."

EVEN STEVO TOLD a traveling story that ended in a windfall of success. One summer, he said, he had found his good luck near Bonners Ferry, Idaho. "We were somewhere backwoods and we had it so good there, you couldn't imagine. Tutsi and I were broke, the children sick, a church was feeding us and the only house I could find had no curtains for the windows. So I got poster paints and painted big palmistry hands instead. The children messed them up immediately and all you could see were the fingers. Still the customers came. We had two folding chairs and no table. I kept the children in the bedroom."

"Tutsi felt so bad, so embarrassed for the customers to see her in such a shabby state; she wasn't even polite. That's when the Americans began to beg to get their fortunes told. They said she was a witch. So, naturally, she agreed. The more the place looked like a nightmare, the better the customers paid. I didn't believe it before that, but luck can be found anywhere."

I traveled too, of course. My traveling began as Lola's driver and continued with those musical weekends in the car with Stevo. I took extended trips—I regarded them as anthropology, at least in part—with Stevo, with Lola, several times with Katy. I learned to rely on intuition and let the road give me directions—which way, where to stop?—following the flow, following the line of least resistance.

Stevo explained it best one evening in Seattle when he was tuning my son's twelve-string guitar to a minor Eastern key (an adjustment that drove Colin crazy when he found he had to tune it back). I asked how he had managed to get the money for our dinner.

"I drove north for awhile," he said. "And then I came back to town, went over to Alki Beach and got the feeling to go north again. That's where I made fifty dollars, fixing a pop-out fender. I knew I would; I had the feeling. It's an extra-sympathetic feeling. That's how I live."

THE YEAR AFTER the broken tooth episode, I drove Katy from Seattle to San Francisco. Each minute we spent on the road, Katy became more paranoid.

The Romaniya laws are strict; they forbid a woman to travel anywhere alone, and this was Katy's first time on her own, the first time in thirty-something years she was without the company of her family and the authorized protection of a male. Legally speaking, traveling with a non-Gypsy was tantamount to the crime of "running away." I knew all this, but suspect I took some pleasure playing with the rules.

This time I was financing myself and intending, again, to do fieldwork. Katy had plans for a secret vacation. I had been telling her about our family vacations, the camping and fishing trips we had taken when my children were small. When she wistfully admitted, "I never had a vacation," I felt the unfortunate need to rectify the situation.

The trip began light-heartedly. But by the time we reached the state line, all the vacationing spirit had flown. Katy kept checking out the passing cars, jumping up and then crouching down; "Look! I think that was Roma! I think they saw me!" she'd exclaim. Exasperated, I tried to assure her that no one was likely to recognize her riding in such a funny little car while wearing black sunglasses and a floppy face-concealing sun hat.

But fear made her frantic. Our anticipated walk on an Oregon beach proved disastrous; Katy saw Roma behind every dune. Plans to detour for a leisurely day of lake country fishing had to be abandoned. The third endless night, we arrived in San Francisco and looked for a cheap motel. Exhausted, we settled for one on Lombard Street that exceeded our budget.

From the chenille edge of one twin bed, I stared across the chilly linoleum floor and shivered. Poor Katy stood in the doorway, biting her lip and wrapping both arms protectively around her suitcase. "What do you think?" Her voice wavered with alarm. "Not too good," I answered from my heart.

Avoidance and escape are standard Gypsy policy. We got our money back and hastily drove off. What could that cold, colorless feeling have been, other than a ghost? "Something happened there," Katy confided. "Someone died, or suffered."

She called home that evening. Her children were hysterical. Rumors that Katy had been kidnapped, murdered or, much worse, had run away were already crisscrossing the country. Ephram's wealthy brother in Tacoma had managed to interest the police in the curious case of the "missing heiress."

I drove Katy to the airport. She flew off into the night to meet a sister in Los Angeles, pretending to have been there all along.

Luck warns and then re-directs.

I KNEW HOW ANTHROPOLOGY fieldwork should be done. You took a bi-plane, then a boat into the continent's interior; you airlifted supplies and hired a porter. You pitched your tent at the edge of the village and soon, perhaps the next morning, began to establish rapport with a person of some local consequence who was happy to teach you the language. Optimally, this agreeable contact became a loyal friend and helped you collect information about the local indigenous families and their systems of kinship. With the kinship charts in hand, you could begin to fathom who was who and what was going on. Without them, you were in the dark; no telling to whom you were speaking. After a year or two, confident you now knew the ways of the foreign village even better than the village in which you had been born, you returned to America, holed up in the library to mull over the ordeals, triumphs and insights and the unresolved musings of your experience. Then you wrote your anthropological analysis. Simple enough.

I had what seemed a likely situation. Without much expense or difficulty, I was already comfortably established: bed, kitchen, typewriter and table in the middle of my Machvaia "village." Stevo, when he was available, was usually an arm's-length away; Lola and Katy were each ten minutes by car; Yutsa and Fat Albert, Lola's cousin, no more than three blocks; Duda and Miller, Lola's son, about a mile; Lola's godson Busha, and whatever newcomers came to Seattle to make their fortunes, never seemed further than fifteen or twenty minutes. Moreover, we all spoke the same language, one that was mutually intelligible and into which their Romani could easily be translated.

It was a very small village, of course. But the extended families of those in my village were only two states away and I never doubted that as soon as I finished school, I would expand my village into Machvaia home territory.

But my situation was not as simple as I had supposed. Among Machvaia, rights of primacy and ownership are strictly observed. Customers are the fortune teller's livelihood and, as the people saw it, I belonged to Lola. My talking, eating or dropping in on anyone else was regarded with suspicion. Even my developing friendships with Lola's children could be construed as their attempts to steal my driving services away from their mother. For this reason, I never seemed to have much luck with interviews.

The language Romani has no word for *friend*; instead, a person is defined as in or out, family or not, *vitsa*—of the tribe—or not, Gypsy or outsider. But, to Lola (and, of course, to Stevo), I was never an outsider. Lola was my adored and constant companion, and several times she reassured me: "There's no difference. I've given the matter a lot of thought. Americans and Gypsies, we're just the same."

I didn't appreciate, at the time, the novelty of Lola's thinking. I didn't understand the militant power of the Romaniya laws that guard their separation from outsiders. Not until I moved from Seattle, which Machvaia regarded as a wild and wooly frontier outpost, and moved to the orthodoxy of California did I feel the severity of these rules.

Lola treated me like family. She treated my family like her family. She gave us gifts, made demands, offered advice and wanted to discover everything about us. There was no constraint to her kindness and no limit to her expectations. After she met my parents, I heard her brag to her daughter. "I went to their party. The mother is nice, beautiful. The man is important, big, you can tell. They liked me. She's got a beautiful American family. And," she nodded encouragement over the phone receiver, "she's my company. My everyday company. She drives me everywhere I want to go."

When she hung up, I hastened to correct her. "That's not true. I can't take you every day." But she didn't seem to hear. She believed in exaggeration and the power of suggestion.

Lola was my nemesis, my hair shirt, my Pied Piper; charming, but not without faults. I swung between outrage at her calls, which might number ten a day, and abject adoration. Her emergency style of command was hard to refuse; the funny thing is, I had never before been amenable to orders.

Just as in the first weeks of our acquaintance, Lola, the dear and entertaining nuisance, called me day and night for rides. Confronted by the force and multiplicity of her requests, my excuses sounded pitiful and unimaginative. Eventually I learned to tailor them to circumstances she could accept: the needs of my children, the requirements of earning an income, and failing health (never, of course, mentioning the existence of Stevo).

Those first years of graduate school, my children and I lived in a two-bedroom apartment in a venerable, high-security hotel. One evening, to avoid driving her to a party, because I wanted to spend a few quality hours with my son, I complained of a headache.

A short time later, there was a knock on the door. Lola had come to the rescue by cab, paying the fare with the Gypsy advice "that is better than money." She had talked herself into my locked lobby and risked the danger of the elevator up to the sixth floor: "Ooo, it's too high here!"

She came prepared, with a fat purse full of proven remedies— "These are my favorites"—none of which she could identify, but which she insisted I down with water.

I had never expected to conduct my fieldwork by car, by *sitting* in the car, by constantly driving my car, and an old one at that. I couldn't take notes while driving. I couldn't ask questions and, if I did, distracted by Lola's demands, I couldn't remember the answers.

But, Lola's insistence won the day. I would drive obediently to Katy's with a cardboard suit box full of frosted doughnuts and a strawberry cake to share. Sometimes we made a number of emergency stops in fifteen-minute meter zones while she paid her bills, angrily, in small and grudging doses. Once a month I took her to a doctor with unfamiliar initials after his name.

"What does he do?" I asked.

"He massages and listens. That makes me feel good."

While she received this nurturing treatment, I sat in the car, studying, the windows rolled up to blot out the traffic noise.

I drove her to Porter-Jensen, the jewelry store where she made minuscule payments on her layaways. As patiently as I could, I waited for her to admire the jewelry, the china clocks, the hand-painted figurines, in each of the lighted cases. All the while, at the back of my mind, loomed the matter of my professional goals and family obligations. All I seemed to do was drive and wait.

Was this fieldwork or just hanging out? As I see it now, the distinction doesn't matter. Everything, be it fieldwork or hanging out, held the valid possibility of a lesson.

Lola and I passed long slow hours sitting side by side at Katy's storefront. We took turns crooking a finger, calling in the fortune telling customers. I well remember the color and feel of the sofa, the daylight through the glass and, on the ample window apron, the plaster backs of the church store statues, a large thirty-inch statue of Jesus, a similar size one of Mary and the gilt-framed Byzantine print of a pale and wan Saint Anne.

Katy's storefront had no tub or shower. So, at Lola's urging, I would pick Katy up, take her to Lola's, and wait while she took her weekly bath. Katy would soak, wash her hair, luxuriate in the steam, fix her face and finally exhaust Lola's patience. "What's going on in there? You think I'm Elizabeth Arden?"

KINSHIP CHARTS ARE the *sine qua non* of fieldwork. The next year, when I began traveling to California by myself, Lola realized the awkwardness of my outsider/enemy position and relented.

"Tell them you know Lola and Bahto and they'll treat you right," she suggested. (She was wrong.)

"But how will I know who they are?" I whined in frustration. That's when she urged me to hurry home and get my notebook so I could write down "about the families."

She had a lot to say, beginning with the pioneer ancestors, and, simultaneously, to keep her hands occupied, to maintain the flow of memory, she sewed together a dress. "I don't need a pattern. I make it up as I go," she insisted.

Sewing, she explained, was an art; each dress had to be a little different than the one before. She held the material against her body, shoulder to waist, and then waist to hem. Suspending the garment high above her head, she sculpted the dancing edges speedily with her scissors. "Tukano John married Mileva. They had these children," she said as she zipped up the seams on the Singer portable and measured again. "Pisadi, that was the oldest, Nino, Milano, Djorji Bango, Marko; the girls were Keka and Pisa. I think there were more."

I was there from five to midnight, during which hours Lola did more than just sew and talk. At six, she cooked and served an ample four-course dinner. An hour later, she brought out a bowl of potato chips, another of corn chips and a platter of maple frosted doughnuts. A little later, she offered me soda pop, tea, coffee. When I refused, she chastised me with that sorrowful look I always found so compelling. "Eat!" she ordered. "You'll get sick if you don't eat."

By ten, "to keep us going," she suggested chicken-fried steak. Food, as opposed to the stereotypical anthropological hazards—cannibals, a hostile government, dysentery or malaria—proved to be the major hazard of my fieldwork. Before midnight, she presented cubes of cheese and cucumbers, sticks of celery, pickles, peppers, slices of brown bread and tomatoes, some olives and fresh parsley. Where had it come from?

This was precisely the kind of food that I liked to snack on. But it was certainly not Lola's daily fare. Suitably impressed, I obediently ate everything on the plate.

FINALLY, INEVITABLY, I WAS called to the office of my committee head. A gentle and accommodating man, a valiant listener, he gave me the impression that he wasn't in full agreement with the committee that was recommending I finish up quickly by switching to library research. Although they appreciated that Gypsies were a difficult study, I was, in their opinion, taking too long for my Masters.

Maybe they had begun to suspect I was going native, which was criminal then, but now is a valid method of research. Back-lighted by the small leaded window over his desk, the kindly Professor Harper swiveled in his chair and offered his encouragement. "You could save all the fieldwork material you have collected for your doctorate," he suggested.

"But there's nothing in the library," I countered, without thinking. Then, remembering his undergraduate thesis had been about Gypsies, "Other than your work, of course."

He didn't contest my statement. But he couldn't have agreed. Earlier, to help my research, he had handed me his personal card file several inches thick, a bibliography of Gypsy publications, one to each 3 x 5 card. I skimmed through his sources.

Most of those I could find were so fantastically romantic, so remote from serious research with any particular band of Gypsies, that they gave me a headache. None of the recommended authors was an anthropologist and most treated the world's Gypsies, despite their dissimilar histories and the distance from India by a millenium, as if they were one big extended family. The Gypsies I knew were keen and vocal about the differences.

When I showed the Machvaia women a picture of Carmen Amaya, the famous Spanish Gypsy dancer, they expressed their disapproval of her hiked-up skirt and bare thighs, and either doubted she was really a Gypsy or disdainfully put her into a rank several degrees lower than theirs with this dismissal: "Thank God, we don't know her."

Regarding what they called "those other kinds" that they had heard of—the non-Roma American Boyasha, the American Romnitchels, even some Kalderasha—the Machvaia were careful to avoid any contact.

All I knew was that I had a passion to understand human behavior. I wanted to understand the Machvaia Roma, I wanted to be with Stevo, I looked forward to seeing Lola that night at dinner and learning the latest gossip. And the best part about all these activities is that one automatically involved the other!

After my pressure-of-time interview with Harper, I felt the Department nipping at my heels and tried to expedite the data-collecting process, but Lola was of little help. Perhaps because she was trying to confirm herself as American, my equal and of "no difference," she usually refused to answer my questions. Or maybe it was more that she was my elder and direct questions showed her disrespect.

Stevo was my salvation. He was eager to teach me how to behave correctly and to answer whatever questions I asked. He wanted me to know he was a "good man," not a flake like Ephram, also known as Playboy, Katy's errant husband. One time, he held my fingers and promised, "This is all true. I never lie to you." Another time, he took an oath in husky Romani, holding me captive with the stabbing ardor of his eyes: "Whatever I wish for myself, I wish for you," adding, "and let my words reach the dear Lord's ears."

Unable to respond in kind, I tried to immortalize the moment by writing his words down phonetically and illustrating them with a tentative pencil sketch of his broad-cheeked Slavic Gypsy face.

Yet, I knew I needed a woman's point of view. For some time, I had been desperate to interview Katy. She was a marvel: she thought before she spoke; she never said she knew something when she didn't; and she was my age, so I was permitted, according to custom, to be direct in my questioning with her.

But I couldn't contend with her daily schedule. Katy had to earn a living, keep an immaculate house, attend to her ever-present children (who didn't go to school), entertain drop-in visitors and answer the phone, a major interruption. The calls were usually from the local Kalderasha women. They liked to solicit her advice on matters of policy regarding their husbands and difficult relationships with their in-laws. They called to discuss the local gossip, sales and bargains, doctor's appointments, questions about their health. Like the other women, I wanted Katy's considerate advice and attention, but she seemed as unavailable as if she were on the moon.

That's why, when I had nearly finished the outline for my thesis and wanted to cross-check my results, I invited Katy to dinner at Seattle's Trader Vic's. Picking her up one weekday afternoon, I noted that the evening had promise: she was on the alert, wearing pretty pointy-toed pumps instead of her usual comfortable, backless Chinese satin slippers. At the restaurant, lulled by the mellow cadence of Tahitian music, tranquilized by fancy platters of finger food and drinks ruffled with paper and match-stick parasols, I finally had Katy's devoted attention. Perhaps she understood the significance of her obligation when she read the prices on the menu. At any rate, she answered every question. The fact is, we had a lot of fun. The evening ended in a two-person drinking orgy. I don't recall driving home.

The next morning I found several notebook pages carelessly stuffed into my jacket pocket. On the first page, plainly written, was posted all the vital, corroborating thesis information. The rest was indecipherable. I studied the scrawls for clues. I tried to recall the gist. But the magic of those inebriated hours, the scribbled key to the mysteries, was still in Polynesia.

Over breakfast and across the table from my son, I lamented the loss of all that critical material and found him unreceptive. He couldn't believe I had spent so much money from our modest alimony-child care budget. I tried to explain that Gypsies like parties, and a party was the only way I knew to lure Katy away. He could think of better uses for our money. He went to his room and slammed the door.

I HAD BEEN WARNED about the Gypsy men. "No good," Lola promised, "none of them. Ephrams, just like Ephram."

Katy's husband, Ephram, was notorious for "not paying attention to his family." At the Laundromat, while her clothes were flopping arcs of suds behind the round glass door (and Katy's zealous use of Clorox was tweaking painfully at my nose), Katy lit a Marlboro Gold and admitted wryly that she "wouldn't mind if he were average. But he goes out beyond the limit." Later, Lola matter-of-factly summed up Katy's domestic situation: "My daughter stays home with the children and her husband bumps around."

Even I was indirectly affected by Ephram's "bumping." Several years into my study, Lola admitted that Katy had initially suspected I might be related to the girl/woman Ephram was dating at the time, maybe an aunt come to find out "what kind of family would let an old man"—Ephram was maybe thirty-five and already a grandfather—"go out with a child of seventeen." Pity for the child and the child's family was apparently the reason Katy didn't lock the door or kick me out.

"We were sorry for you," Lola said. "If you were related."

In his bumping mode, Ephram would disappear for weeks and return whenever he liked. "No. He's not here and I don't know when he will be back," Katy would say into the phone, which only served to publicize the scandal. I knew Katy was a proud woman. Once, when she answered the phone with "No, he's not here," I ventured to ask, "Are you all right?"

Without hesitation, Katy assured me she certainly was and, furthermore, that she couldn't possibly be jealous. In her mind, Gypsy and American women were basically so dissimilar that competition between them would never be an issue, a remark that puzzled me for some years until I better understood the nature of the Gypsy/outsider separation.

I really hated taking sides. My weather-vane sympathy veered in the direction of whichever one I was with, Katy or her husband. Ephram, a Kalderash Rom who resented the superior status of his wife's Machvaia family, was anxious for me understand the nature of his problem. He described a lost time when he had had everything: money, an impeccable reputation, a used-car lot, a ranch style house on several acres. Then he hired an American bookkeeper, a pretty divorcee with a child, and fell in love, falling from grace, falling from the status of big to little. "Happening once," he said, "made it easy to happen again and again."

"I didn't mean to make trouble," Ephram admitted, striking a disarming note. "I just wanted to find out how the other half lives." Precisely what I was doing was my thought. To conceal the sudden rush of empathy I felt, I hid my face over my writing.

Despite his appearance—small, slender, swarthy and with the smart face of a ferret—Ephram had a deadly effect on women. His success issued mainly from the sincere regard in which he held them, his whole-hearted devotion to their pursuit, and a killer's instinct for capitalizing on any sign of vanity or vainglory. He certainly had my number.

He would call when I had despaired of ever fitting the Gypsy puzzle together. In a voice pulsing with concern, he'd ask, "Is there anything you want to know?"

It was not my intention to learn so much about Ephram. But he was a marvelous informant, sharp-witted and uninhibited. In negotiating the nether region between worlds, his and mine, Ephram had already worked out so many answers that he could, at times, anticipate my questions. He would cross his legs straight out to show off his alligator shoes, and place a diamond-ringed hand on his knee where it caught the light. With the delight of the connoisseur, he explained that contact with outsider women was forbidden and the penalty, "the worst."

Ephram was an altar boy at the shrine of the forbidden. Gleefully patting my hand as I scribbled notes, he enthused, "Ugh! Dirty all over!"

Did he mean *me?* Did he ask for the scarf I was wearing as a souvenir? Could he be planning to use it to weave a spell? I wasn't sure why I refused him. But I was wary and took care never to be alone in Ephram's company. When we met at restaurants, I drove my own car. When he came to my University apartment, I made certain my children were in evidence. I suppose those monitored meetings were a kind of game. I always knew they couldn't last.

The minute I was careless and met him in an empty house, he negotiated me into a corner and pounced with the abandon of a jackpot winner. This struck me as so unlike the romantic image he liked to present that I forgot about tact. My uncontrollable laughter drove him away.

The incident struck me as fairly inconsequential. The next day, however, during a seminar, something had triggered the memory of Katy's despair: "It's war. He's not going to stick with me, and he's going to try to take away my children."

War has sides. So which side was I on? Hoping I sounded indignant, I called Katy between classes to complain about her crazy, kissing husband. It wasn't easy to tattle, particularly when I felt at fault. My mouth was dry as ashes, but I dialed the phone. I certainly would never have called an American woman with such a challenging bit of information. But on Katy's wavelength, so often the reverse of mine, tattling seemed politic.

Immediately, the infamous story about the kiss-and-tell Djuhli circulated through the community. I was astonished to find that my status had improved. Now, my appearance at public events was welcomed with a smiling exchange of gossip. I had gained something I hadn't expected: the favor of reputation. Not an illustrious reputation, certainly. But the people do love stories.

When Ephram phoned for an explanation, I told him that I hadn't wanted to take the chance he might tell his wife. I said I had noticed he was jealous of the relationship between me, his wife and her mother. To my astonishment, he offered a grudging appreciation. "Too good is no good," he said. "Now you're getting mean like a woman should be."

Apparently, meanness was regarded as a womanly virtue among the Kalderasha. Bred to the opposite ideal, I had some difficulty recognizing myself as mean. In any case, that was the end of my meetings with Ephram.

Lola had warned me that Ephram was trouble. She said, "Ephram lies to you. You can't trust anything he says."

"I know that. I try to check what he says with others. I've heard you stretch the truth a bit at times too." I had heard her tell white lies when she wanted to flatter and please.

"Well, if you don't lie, you can't live," Lola retorted. A long pause. "Now I'm going to tell you the truth you should know. Gypsy things are *secret*."

Despite this discouraging news, and despite the loss of Ephram as informant, I still had Stevo and Katy to query. Fieldwork was full of surprises. My reluctant kiss-and-tell report had bonded me with Katy. I learned that, in many ways, she was the opposite of her mother. For one thing, at difficult moments, Lola called for the help of *O Devla!* (Oh God!), whereas Katy complained to *Prikadja!* (Bad Luck!). As Katy often pointed out, more sad than sardonic, "A human person is both an angel and a devil."

Katy lacked the sunny optimism and easy warmth of her mother—or, for that matter, of all her sisters. It wasn't hard to see why: she was only a tomboy child of seven when, knocking a pan of frying potatoes off the storefront stove, she burned her arm and side and spent months in a Sacramento hospital; in her teens, she ran away with sister Boba, returning in shame when she found she couldn't make it on her own in "America." In keeping with Machvaia custom, she and Boba were given to the first Roma that asked for them.

Katy's family of marriage proved to be "a family of pickers" and, after a week in the fields, sick and sunburned, she went home to her parents. Bahto immediately gave her away again, this time to Ephram's out-of-state family.

Nowadays, no family would punish a daughter in such an unfeeling fashion. But then, it was part of law and custom, and considered the honorable and necessary thing to do.

EARLY IN MY STUDY, I found myself at a Kalderasha wedding in the Eagles Auditorium Hall. The formally dressed crowd was milling about and I was watching with amusement a precocious pair of dancing sisters, not yet five, mimic *The Supremes*. Stomping, wiggling their little arms and buns in synchronized motion, they frantically mouthed the lyrics to "Stop in the Name of Love."

But I was bushed; I'd been up most of the night studying for an exam. Relieved to spy an unoccupied bench against the wall, I crossed the dance floor. When I sat down, the room fell silent. As I remember it—but could this be?—even the band stopped playing. The hushed circle of turning backs told me I had broken a sacred rule.

The bench I had sat upon was really a low table. Gypsies, like their north India forebears, remain obsessed with matters of purity, defilement and related washing practices, which separate activities of the lower body from the upper.

"Will they have to throw the table away?" I asked in distress.

"I doubt it," Katy's oldest daughter answered, sarcastic. "They'll probably just give the table a different name."

Back at the storefront, in consideration for my feelings, Katy studied the pepper plant I had given her and avoided my eyes. Aware I was likely to make the same mistake again, Katy began to explain: Americans don't keep the separations, upper body from lower, purity from contamination, and are not regarded as being auspiciously clean. Americans, she said, are dirty all over, "indecent," as she put it. The hard fact was that intimacy with outsiders—touching, dancing, eating with them and most particularly sleeping with them—was forbidden to orthodox Roma Gypsies.

The very next day, I bought two sets of soaps and towels. How could I remember all the rules, or discover which rules had been missed, if I didn't follow them myself? To offset the handicap of being the only outsider at the Roma celebrations, I wanted the personal satisfaction of knowing I was, in a manner of speaking, superlatively "kosher."

Of course, in a few months, despite the proper use of soaps and towels, from the technical standpoint I knew I had absolutely, in the *marimé* sense, destroyed poor Stevo. He appeared totally fearless, however, at least in my presence. The only thing that he really seemed to care about, and that was still intact at that time, was his public reputation.

Defilement, as it happens, was my thesis topic. I was loaded with material, both written and experienced, and was an expert on the *marimé*.

ACCORDING TO THE GOSSIP, Katy's husband hadn't been "good" in the way that is recommended. So it was that, being a woman of decision and purpose, Katy followed him when he went to visit his American girlfriend. By some manner (through the window?), she had seen them together, the girl in her slip, and a woman in her underwear is hard evidence.

A Roma court was solemnly assembled. The men represented the three local Roma tribal kinds, one Machvaia, two Kalderasha. Bahto, Katy's father, spoke for his daughter. He opened by complaining about Ephram's escapade, citing Katy as eyewitness. But the meeting was over as soon as Ephram threatened, "You all go out with other women. If you black ball me, I will report everyone in this room."

Now it certainly wasn't true that *all* the men were seeing women other than their wives. The local Kalderash men worked very hard, buying and selling cars. I doubt they had the time, energy, funds or imagination to date American women. (In fact, according to the gossip, only one had a girlfriend.) But since no one could be sure what their relatives might be doing, the men didn't care to take the matter any further. Katy was indignant when Ephram got off with only a warning.

The next I heard, Ephram had been given a government grant and was running a small grocery. However did he manage? Could charm and promises have sufficed as credit for a man without an acceptable credit history or American business experience, and who couldn't read or write?

Katy and the children would have nothing to do with his folly, and to offset the isolation of running a business that was open all day every day from nine to six, and to encourage his customers to linger, Ephram converted the grocery's stockroom into a bar with a sofa, chairs, a television set and snacks. Then, he called everyone—relatives, friends, me. "Yes, open house every day," he promised. For several months, Ephram's winning showmanship triumphed over his inability to read labels or to write supply orders. Once he even managed to enlist the help of my son (whose heart is as soft as a Gypsy's). But payment in canned food didn't hold my son's interest and he refused to return the following day. Inevitably, the shelves became alarmingly depleted. The brass spring bell that welcomed arriving customers froze into silence.

Ephram's store was only a few blocks from Lola's apartment. One afternoon when she ran out of coffee, I walked through the store, front to back, and there was no sign of him. It was the beginning of the end. I took a tin of coffee and left the money on the counter. Soon after, the electricity was disconnected. Katy and I hurried to serve our families tasteless meals composed from the packages of vegetables swimming in the freezer.

The old ways and the ancestors had been vindicated. America's style of success was clearly not designed for Gypsies. Over the hill and gone again, the susceptible Ephram found what solace he could with a pretty teenager who was unemployed and available. Katy called, and I ran to help. Together we pried open the door of the abandoned grocery and loaded the last of the canned goods into my Volkswagen. Several trips later, we had moved everything into her attic, enforcements for the hard season coming.

That finished it for Katy. She refused to take him back. "I can't have him here anymore. He'll bring me and my children a bad disease."

Some months later, Ephram stopped by Fat Albert's for a visit. Albert wasn't home, and his wife, Yutsa, served Ephram coffee from a cracked cup. The cup told Ephram he wasn't good enough to be treated with the purity and respect due an orthodox Rom. From then on, and for several years, to prevent further embarrassment, Ephram avoided any contact with his people. The power of the women of America to defile, and the Roma to confirm that power, had finally taken effect.

The Machvanka is expected to tell fortunes with or without a license or a sign. But Katy said she had "lost heart for fortunes." In a fit of ethical logic, she decided she couldn't tell Americans how to live when her own life was a chaotic mess. Lola and I helped her move to a tiny leaky storefront in the Farmer's Market area. Then Katy took to her bed.

Luludji, the costly daughter-in-law with the soft round face of a Persian miniature, returned to her family in Florida. Katy's oldest son, Barney, once again single, moved to board with his father's brothers who, he said, were only a little crazy, not entirely, like the rest of his family.

With raccoon-circled eyes, Katy collapsed to bemoan her losses, personal and financial, and held a recumbent court. Crowds of women in sweeping skirts bustled in to show their support, shaking their heads. On the coverlet at her feet, coughing and wheezing from endless colds, lay the youngsters, Julie and Jelly. The store was a hushed, shades-drawn ward of the fallen, the sick and the suffering.

I was unsettled by the ordeal. I didn't dare admit to myself the similarities between Katy and Tutsi's situation. I refused to see myself as the instrument of a betrayed wife's torture. Instead, I took my guilt out on Katy. I thought, "this wasn't the tower of strength I thought I knew." I was so upset that for several weeks to hide my emotional distress, I stopped taking her phone calls. I didn't realize she was soliciting sympathy the only way she knew, that she was reminding everyone the missing Ephram was the villain. I didn't anticipate the difficulties she would eventually encounter as an unmarried woman without the protection and support of a Rom.

POVERTY REQUIRED KATY to apply for public assistance. She asked me to be there and I watched helplessly as the social worker's probing insinuations reduced her to tears.

For more than a year, the feeling for celebration never sparked in Katy. Neglecting the rituals that protect the family's health and luck meant that bad luck had a field day. Katy tried to learn to drive and wrecked the borrowed car. When she turned on the gas heater in the storefront, it exploded, burning off her eyelashes and scorching the wall.

In time, Lana, Katy's favorite daughter, eloped with a lower-class Rom. She was returned in shame when the boy's family couldn't afford the bride price. Poor, delicate Lana pined away. Katy had no choice; she gave her back, at a very low price, and somehow Ephram ended up with the money.

Like suds in grease, Katy's good luck slipped away and disappeared. The result of Ephram's bumping around was precisely as Old Lola had predicted. "If you don't live right, stay home, attend to business, take care of each other and show respect for the family, *Prikadja* happens," she said of the Demon of Bad Luck. "For the man and woman to be good with each other, that will bring happiness, good health, good luck and money. All or nothing. That's the way it happens."

WHENEVER HE MANAGED to get a bit of money, Stevo liked to take me out. But black, at that time, was considered bad luck for Gypsies, and the only short American-style dress I owned was an all-purpose black silk. Dipping into my small savings, I managed enough for a simple yellow-and-rose printed organza shift.

I wore it, one fateful night, to High Balls, a trucker's tavern. The male attention I received pleased and excited Stevo. But, not knowing quite how to handle the novelty of this development—it would be reason for war at a Machvaia party—he suggested we leave. Before we had the opportunity, however, he noticed Tutsi at a distance through the window. And, before I could ask how she knew where we were, he ran out the back door, shoving me in the other direction, shouting, "Go! Go!" My escape was a bit delayed owing to my stiff new ankle-strap shoes and a wistful uncertainty about the nature of our drama: was it comedic or tragic?

Tutsi caught me by the hair in the parking lot. As she pulled and tugged, I grabbed her hands and tried to hold her away at arm's length. I could see this confused her. "Fight!" she yelled. "Why don't you be a woman and fight?"

I might have explained that I didn't know how to fight. Or that I so disliked violence I never allowed my children to watch anything violent on television. Or that, as this was the age of peace and love, she should get in step with the program. Or that, although flooded with anger, I wasn't angry at Tutsi. In my thoughts, she verged on divinity—an avenging angel, perhaps—by reason of being Stevo's wife and the mother of his children.

Instead, I was suddenly furious at the out-of-sight Stevo Polo for putting me in this ridiculous position. Did he expect me to resolve the dilemma of our triangular situation by defeating my rival in battle? After calling me everything she could think of, disgusted by my lack of fighting mettle, Tutsi climbed back into her car and one of her teenage sons drove her away. She was still muttering.

STEVO OBVIOUSLY WANTED Tutsi and me, the woman of obligation and the woman of choice, to get along. Of course, if we had, his life would have been much, much easier. In an earnest attempt to legitimize our unholy threesome, he began escorting us as a unit into the American milieu with which he was most familiar, taverns. Like the Gypsy he was, he announced his dual allegiance with a formal public appearance at a tavern where he was well known. And like the hip American he was trying to become, he alternated between us, pushing in our chairs, bringing us drinks, treating us with equal and solicitous regard. While he played pool in his shirtsleeves, his wife and I served as audience at an adjoining table.

One memorable evening, he pivoted under the garish Tiffany-style lamps to proudly model the new tweed jacket Tutsi had bought for him. Then, he carefully folded it and laid it over the back of the chair. My plan was to ignore him and pay special attention to her. But Stevo kept looking my way.

When, nonchalantly, he switched his pool cue into the crook of his muscular left arm, my mouth went dry with longing. Reading my thoughts, Tutsi whipped a pair of scissors out of her purse and began cutting the sleeves off his jacket. When he didn't respond, she stood and shouted "Fuck you!" in Romani and English, over and over. While she cut the jacket into vertical shreds, I sat dumbfounded, wondering how she could do that, to cause Stevo the least bit of public embarrassment or displeasure.

My life became increasingly unbelievable. I hurt my back, and he insisted on bringing Tutsi over to my apartment to give me a back rub! Was this a specialty of hers? Apparently not; she made herself a pot of tea instead. I wondered what had gone on at home between them. Was this a ruse on Tutsi's part to see where and how I lived? Or was it the acid test of her capacity for suffering?

That evening seems as unreal as a scene out of Kafka: Stevo on the sofa, brooding; me on the single bed in the living-room corner, beetled on my back; Tutsi at the dining table, her tea forgotten, saying God knows what in a flow of Romani that cadenced louder and faster. Stevo didn't bother to translate, but I got the message that she was upset. Finally, worked into a rage, she opened the window and sat halfway out, shouting in English to attract the world's attention.

"Murder!" "Help!" "Fuck!" "Djuhli is a whore!"

When that didn't stir us into action, she began to swallow handfuls of sleeping pills she had the foresight to stow in her sweater pocket. I supposed she was trying to equalize the pity situation: my back problem against her death.

While Stevo drove Tutsi to the hospital to get her stomach pumped, I tried to explain to the manager of the building that my unfortunate visitor was mentally unstable and had taken her medications out of sequence.

The next week, still banking on a happy home with a peaceful pair of wives, Stevo suggested I come over for dinner. I could hear Tutsi in the background, screaming "Fuck you, the whore," and understandably felt a bit tentative about going.

But Stevo reassured me, "It's Tutsi's idea. You'll get to see all the children."

Answering the door, he ushered me to a chrome and red kitchen set in a living room otherwise empty of furnishings. One of the boys was crying loudly, out of control, in a bedroom. Tutsi, busy in the kitchen, leaned around a cabinet to joke about the possibility of me moving in and becoming part of the family. "Easier housekeeping! More cooks! Drivers!" I tactfully agreed, aware of Stevo watching us, pleased to have us all under the same roof and not arguing. But, in light of our recent history and the children's worried expressions, I kept my eye on the door, my bag strap over my shoulder.

To hope our war might ever resolve into domestic bliss was incredibly naïve of Stevo. He really wasn't equipped to deal with our situation and, when Tutsi seated me at the table, he suddenly began to sing a love song to me. He sang the song start to finish and in full voice, in front of his entire family.

At first, I thought he meant to offend her; their relationship fed on contention. My cheeks pinking, I glanced in alarm at the solemn faces of the children standing around the table, boys mostly, some nearly men as their people think of men. I didn't know what I should do.

Mid-song, I realized the musical statement was not only addressed at me. He sang from the passion of the moment. He sang from the truth and strength of feeling. The song was given voice with the brutal honesty that inspired Carmen, knowing she could die, to confront Don Jose and confess to his face that she loved another. Stevo apparently hadn't considered the consequences—consequences and delayed gratification are not the Machvaia people's strong point—and he looked stunned when Tutsi screamed. A few hot words passed between them before he aggressively pulled me down the stairs to his car. As we drove away, the new domed barbecue that had been cooling on the porch above us sailed alarmingly close to our front windshield and smashed resoundingly on the pavement.

THERE WAS NOTHING UNDERSTATED about Tutsi. She had tolerated me only long enough to size up the situation. Loud and clear about wanting revenge, she now set out to get it.

Firebrand Tutsi was relentless, a wizard at discovery, and she kept me on the move. She swore she would kill us, chasing us down the freeway in one of the second-hand cars Stevo intended to sell, squealing the brakes, banging bumpers and doors and ruining the body. She followed us down alleys and over bridges, making U-turns so sharp and fast that I expected to see her screaming children fly out the broken windows.

The year that began with the sleeping pill episode, I moved five times and got evicted three. Relocation inevitably followed the awful sight of Tutsi tearfully beating on my door, shouting obscenities, ripping off her clothes; and the equally awful suspicion that she felt obliged to endlessly repeat the performance. That peripatetic year involved the cost of broken windows, broken locks, the loss of my rental deposits and the repeated labor of transporting everything I owned—loads of boxes, clothes, furniture and books—up and down the steep narrow staircase into and out of my sister's dark, unlit attic. I looked for apartments with quick escape routes, with windows on two sides, and back doors into alleys. I ordered unlisted phone numbers in another name, and painted my gray car arctic white. Fine tuning my defense, each apartment I rented was smaller and cheaper, and each carload a bit lighter. I discarded furniture, camping gear and memorabilia from the past—even my precious but cumbersome *Oxford English Dictionary*.

Tutsi, too, moved constantly. She gave me hard lessons in what conveniences I could do without, some of the same lessons, I expect, that she learned daily. It was what Gypsies call the hard luck times.

AT CHRISTMAS, THE ALWAYS resourceful Tutsi invited my sisters, my son and several of his hippie student friends, who already knew Stevo, to her house for "Gypsy dessert." They went because it was the Sixties and they saw this as the opportunity to restore the affectionate balance of the world. "To keep in touch," Tutsi requested phone numbers, including mine.

After that triumph, she called my family daily to holler and complain about the wanton woman who had ruined her life. My sisters changed their numbers and were more cautious about sharing the new ones. My daughter, who was back with me for the holidays, answered my phone and heard Tutsi out, too stunned and too polite to hang up on an adult.

But calling me names didn't change my feeling for Stevo. Nor did his nightmarish home life change his feelings for me. "Before," Stevo admitted, "it was only a matter of wanting. But now I'm used to you."

He cut down somewhat on his drinking, exercised, lost weight and became even more attractive. I liked him either way, lean or chubby. His arching eyebrows, his face was always dimpling and peeking into my thoughts. "Yes!" was the organizing principle of our universe. Our partings were a hairsbreadth from unendurable. They put a sharp cathartic edge on the time we had together.

RUNNING AWAY FROM THE GYPSIES, known as *nashlimos*, leaving Gypsy law behind, is a serious crime. Still, Stevo had mentioned running away before. But how could I take him seriously, with the empty bottle of scotch at our feet on the floor of the car and his words slurring into each other? He told me his master plan: Canada wasn't far, and he was sure he could make us a modest living there washing dishes in some unobtrusive diner. I noted with a pang of fear how critical it seemed that he work some place where none of the Gypsies could find him, and realized that the Gypsy nation, which was supposed to be the subject of my objective study, had become suddenly, invasively, much too near at hand.

He suggested running away again. Seattle is the city of rain, not snow. But snow it did and, after drinks, liar's dice and billiards at O'Banions, we opened the door at closing time to the bite of icy-faced winter. When we reached the car, laughing, slipping, the battery was dead. Our only option was to walk the several miles to my basement apartment.

The night had clouded and obscured the moon. The stores we passed were closed, all the houses dark, the streetlights pallid against the enveloping white. We sang and shouted; the falling snow muffled the sound. Snow was up our noses and in our ears, wrapping us up. Snow stuck to his elegant lashes and drifted stars onto his hair and shoulders. While brushing them off, a little heap thumped on my face from an overhead wire. "Oops," he said, and stooped to kiss me.

"We should have met years ago." He said it over and over.

We arrived at my apartment soaked through to the skin. It was that difficult year of many moves and my son, in disgust, had gone to live with my sister. I was temporarily installed in a deep dismal basement where the prefabricated shower stall was just big enough for one. Until the tank ran out, we took turns under the modest spurt of hot water. Then we dashed for the single bed to warm up, competing for the quilt my mother had providentially sewn from vaguely familiar pieces of the velvet coats and dresses my sisters and I had worn growing up. Snow drifted over both the high basement windows, cutting out the night and sealing us in. Before or since, I never saw him look so happy.

"We have to run away," he said. But I didn't answer; I wasn't entirely certain what running away entailed. Did he mean we must leave behind the city and all we knew? Didn't he realize I was in the middle of a graduate program and my son was still in high school? Stevo, in fact, had even bigger obligations: a wife and, at that time, seven children, wild and mostly boys, reared on emergencies and long odds and with a knack for crises. The other Machvaia families I knew, those of Stevo's generation, were relatively modest in size, three or four children on average. Large families seemed a workable unit in the old days when Gypsies traveled *po drom*. The people would set up their tents in open fields and meadows where their children were free to run and play, and do whatever children will do until they get exhausted. Then, I am told, ten or more children were never any trouble.

These days, most Machvaia families I know live where their customers live, in cities. City children must be watched, amused, dressed up in shoes and bribed to good behavior. Their parents suffer from what might be called urban Gypsy paranoia. Having seen, as they say, "everything" about the perils of the American life on their television screens—drugs, beatings, shootings, rapes, kidnappings—they are afraid to send their children to public school, to a playground, to a movie or hardly anywhere alone. Stevo's posse of boys, always quartered indoors, tended to become restless and ungovernable. They ruined the rental plumbing, tore down walls, wore the finish off the hardwood floors. No sooner had a landlord discovered the extent of the family's destruction than they were shooed out the door and would, once again, be homeless.

"What, another child?" I hissed, outraged each time he confessed to their being another baby on the way. "You can't take care of the ones you have." Stevo and his wife had scarcely enough to feed and clothe themselves, least of all their constantly expanding family. Staggering under the blow of lost expectations, I stopped counting when, as the years passed, it became seven, eight and finally nine—nine children for a quarrelsome couple who didn't live up to the Machvaia ideal involving charity, parties and money for good times, and who failed the standard for acceptable, civil Machvaia behavior. Only the wildest and messiest Gypsies in town, a family from another tribe, would allow them in the house.

Lola had said it. Success and luck requires that both Machvaia partners work harmoniously together. First, the husband finds a likely business location and advertises his wife's fortune telling skills by passing out flyers, making the necessary arrangements for a neon sign, calling the local phone company and placing the reader's telephone number in the Yellow Pages. Then, the wife prays to the Saints for kind-hearted customers with a significant amount of cash to spare. Hostile and angry—much like I was becoming—Tutsi couldn't work. She had too many children underfoot to pause and concentrate on reading palms. They survived as best they could—poor, often sick, crowded and contentious, always looking for a new address to escape the bills and to avoid paying the rent or because they had been forcibly evicted—on monthly checks from Aid For Dependent Children and Stevo's cheap car sales with little profit.

When I asked what they did about birth control, Stevo testily refused to answer. But, another time, he told me how his mother had grieved over a series of miscarriages; maybe he thought he was doing Tutsi a favor, keeping her pregnant. That early summer,

Stevo avoided further mayhem by the usual Gypsy means: escape. Taking his family, he made the necessary arrangements for a business place, an *ofisa* in Idaho.

He flew back to Seattle, his first time in the air, to visit me. Arriving penniless, he borrowed my little car to go look for another. He called Tutsi every few days. He said he had to tell her what to do. "I would leave her if I could. But she has nowhere to go and no one, not even her family will help her."

Seasonal fortune telling was their habit. In the fall, they returned to Seattle and would leave again the following summer. Whenever they returned with a little money, they blew it on diamonds and gold jewelry, new clothes and cases of Seagrams. Within a month or two, the jewelry would be traveling into and out of the local pawnshops. By Christmas, the family was signed up with several charitable organizations for free holiday food and toys.

Sometimes on impulse or under duress, Tutsi left Seattle without him. She took all the children and whatever car was available, driving badly and without a license. The children suggested directions. The one that could read would call out the road signs. Tutsi invariably headed for California and stayed with her saintly brother. But the size of their combined families strained even the warmest welcome. She usually wound up selling the car, or wrecking it, and hysterically calling for help from some cheap motel.

Stevo swore he wouldn't pay attention: "She's out of money. She did this to herself. Let her figure it out." But after a few days and a few more distress calls, he would concede that she had won. He'd pawn a gold ring and go south to save them.

One unforgettable afternoon, it started to rain big drops and we stopped on a lovely cedar-lined street to wait it out. He said what he had on his mind: "She's crazy, you know." Rain washed over the windshield and my dreams ran for cover. "She's crazy as a loon," he repeated.

He didn't ask for pity. He just wanted me to know. "I can't leave my children. She wouldn't know what to do." He was right and I had to agree.

LOLA'S EX-HUSBAND BAHTO died in 1968 at, Miller guessed, around eighty, which was unusually old for a Gypsy. To finish my thesis, I had deliberately isolated myself from the Gypsy community. I missed Bahto's funeral and all the important rituals—except the last. During that period, I never had a phone of my own or called Lola to explain my absence. Driving her anywhere was out of the question. I had hardly a moment for Stevo. With Tutsi chasing me from one rental to another, I was running for my life.

My son and I had been forced to give up our comfortable, sixth-floor apartment, which had become the after-school hangout for Colin's many hippie friends. Senior year is a bad time to change schools, lose friends and, quite possibly, lose your mother. But Colin responded in his usual creative fashion, and insisting on his half of our alimony check, he went to live on his own. I know, although he never complained, he must have been disgusted with my instability. I permissively thought some karmic radar would keep a wise child on target. But the expense of maintaining two households made for even skimpier lifestyles. Colin had to scramble, living with a friend for a time and with one of my sisters for a week or two, in shared houses and apartments. He really believed in fraternity and the equitable distribution of goods and services, and I never heard him complain. I treated him more like a revolutionary hippie compadre than a dependent, and so much faith in a lad of seventeen now strikes me as poignantly naïve. In truth, I was a terrible parent, a bad example, and I left Colin little choice but to grow up fast.

By the end of that mobile year, my daughter, who lived with her more conventional father and who had never been much of a rebel, dropped out of college, became a platinum blonde and opted for adventure. She married a glamorous older man who flew all over the world. Their apartment was conveniently close to the Sea-Tac airport.

WHEN, MONTHS AFTER BAHTO'S funeral, I finally arrived back on Lola's doorstep, she was justifiably upset. At first, the Old Lady refused to speak, lashing me with angry glances, slamming doors, complaining loudly about "farewell fair-weather friends." But that didn't keep her from offering me the courtesy of coffee.

Soon she was telling me everything about the funeral—who came and who didn't. Miller and Boyd, she said, "made it so beau tiful." Fruits and sweets were piled high everywhere; flowers, too. She had ordered a little bower made out of red roses for the head of Bahto's "box." Although music is forbidden at Machvaia funerals, she had proposed a more festive send off, with a big brass band and a New Orleans-style funeral cortege pulled by plumed horses. But Boyd, her oldest son, had refused on the grounds that "it would be show-off."

She had dressed all in black, the forbidden color, for the occasion. Clutching the black chiffon dress up to her chin so I could see the effect, lifting her forehead lines in question, she asked me what I thought. When I assured her that black was indeed her color, pleased, she returned the compliment. "You wear black good, too. I've seen you."

I knew I was forgiven when she hurried me off to the bedroom to show me all the clothes, perfume and jewelry she had acquired during my absence.

Bahto's death left his family in a morass of conflicted feelings. As he was dying, he had refused Duda the blessing that is so critical to the luck of the living. He had refused to make peace with her before it was too late. Lola predicted "fears" for her daughter-in-law. "I said to him to 'Wish good things for your family, for me and your children. Do it now. You know you are dying.' And he did except for Duda. When Duda asked him for forgiveness, Bahto looked away. We felt bad for her."

It seems that Duda and Miller had left Bahto in charge of their children for several weeks while they partied in Florida. Bahto wasn't well and he phoned them to come home. Instead, the pair took a side trip to the Bahamas. To my mind, Good—Time Miller seemed more responsible for their delay than Duda; after all, Miller was supposedly "the boss." But I do know a daughter-in-law is the family member with the lowest status, and the one in the family who usually gets the blame.

When Miller and Duda were away in Florida, Lola had suggested I might stop by to see how Bahto was doing. He was already ill and frail, although I didn't know how ill he was. I found him looking a bit lost and lonely, erect and rather formal in his chair at the far end of the living room. He was the only Machvano I ever met who remembered the old days in Serbia and I had a lot of questions. When I asked how his life had changed, he was abrupt but helpful, explaining that in Serbia the winter holidays were cold with snow and wind, and the holiday preparations more difficult and time-consuming, starting weeks and weeks before. Proudly, he declared "*There* we were Grassnaria, the People of the Horses. But Serbia is mostly poor farmers and mud." I always had difficulty imagining Bahto, with his small clipped mustache, his French-cuffed striped shirt and the impeccable crease in his trousers, in a muddy rural setting.

It was even harder to imagine Bahto as a hostile ghost. Nevertheless, despite the best of intentions and even after the formality of ritual, between the living and the dead unsettled affairs can prove upsetting. For nearly a year, Duda's myriad terrors followed her through the house.

Concerned and curious, I called often to check on her. She never had more than a moment to talk, however. Breathless, she complained, "I'm cleaning it and cleaning it. I've got someone helping. I'll keep cleaning it until the house feels good again." What helped a little was re-decorating Bahto's bedroom, adding fresh flowers, the icons from the shrine, and buying new drapes. Telling fortunes in his bedroom helped even more; a keen nose for business had been their primary area of agreement.

But the haunting continued. A man who looked like Bahto, slight of build, dapper and bow-tied, was seen waiting at the bus stop on their corner. During the night, while the family slept, pots and pans flew out of the cupboards. The cleaning lady's small daughter was heard talking to someone in the bedroom. Was it Bahto? Duda had terrifying nightmares. Then the house burned down, and the trouble stopped. Firemen blamed the wiring. The family blamed the dead man.

The facts were hard to ascertain. Perhaps there were too many possibilities. I told Katy about the rumor I heard that her brother Miller had started the fire to collect the insurance. She answered evenly, "Really? Well, the ghost wants it, I suppose, and you do what you must."

THE FIRST TWO *POMANI*, or commemoration ceremonies, for the Dead Man, Bahto Mulo, were offered in California. But the third *pomana*, the one-year event, was held at a community hall in Portland, a few hours away from Seattle. I was ecstatic when Miller called and asked me to help. Miller, his *Chivro* (Miller and Duda baptized two of his children) and Boyd cooked and ladled out portions in the kitchen; Duda, Katy and I served.

Not ten minutes after we set out the food on the long thirty-foot table, the guests began hurriedly filling the boxes we had provided with the remaining fruits, desserts, the hams and roasts, the bread and the giant floral arrangements. Surprised by our guests' sudden and seemingly rude departures, I complained to Lola who was busy cutting into her chocolate mousse with an over-sized spoon, "Why was it over so soon?"

Taking a bite, she sniffed in disdain that "those people," referring to the vanishing Kalderasha, "must be afraid of their own shadows."

"Ghosts," Katy explained, handing me another damp towel to wipe up the table. "Gypsies are afraid of ghosts." And then, with sarcasm, "Gypsies are more afraid of ghosts than anything."

That's how I discovered that those present at Bahto's *pomana* had been required to eat with the entire host of the Roma dead. To glorify the dead is to glorify the living. The dead have enormous powers to protect and promote their living kinsmen. The Machvaia can call on their dead ancestors during emergencies, assaults, territorial challenges, threat of jail-time and whenever a patrolman stops them for speeding. The Dead Ones protect Roma law and custom and are known to easily take offence. There is no escape from the dead.

With our living guests gone, Duda, Katy and I ran from one end of the table to the other, collecting the garbage into body-bag-sized black plastic sacks. Pieces of cake with one bite removed had slipped to the floor and mixed with the chocolate eclairs, spilled soda pop, squashed grapes, mashed potatoes, peaches and partially eaten paper plates of food. My fingers kept gluing together; there was no time to wash. The hem of my skirt dragged in the sugary mess. My shoes, popping, sloshing, stuck to the floor, holding me back. "Hurry!" Duda urged. "We only have the hall until eight."

During Bahto's post-death year of travel, when he was "visiting all the people and places he loved," he made the customary appearances. Lola saw her former husband three times, once in his coffin in her living room while she was painting glitter on the heat register, and twice in her dreams. She thought that was the right and reasonable number: three. Bahto hadn't appeared angry or asked her for anything, Lola said. The nature of luck depends on the disposition of the dead, and a Dead One who makes a request is considered a very bad omen.

I rated the living-room episode as different from the dreams. But, at my suggestion of "a vision," Lola bristled.

"What are you talking about? A vision! Well, if it was, it's the same thing. I saw him. Each time. The first time, I was painting sparkles in the living room and he showed up in his box. There!" She pointed emphatically at the center of the room.

"What did you do?"

"Nothing. I lit a candle and kept painting."

Later that night, Miller knocked on the door of our motel room to thank Lola and Katy, his mother and sister, for their help, and to give each a gleaming American five-dollar gold piece. Hurt that he hadn't included me, I walked to the window in my stocking feet. Looking out, concentrating on the car lights that were sweeping through the night, I tried hard not to care. Just moments before I had felt part of the family. But no, Djuhli was still the outsider.

STEVO WANTED ME TO understand everything about his prospects. The only son of an eldest son, as well as the first grandson, he held a prime position in his father's large extended family. Gypsies tend to indulge their children, and he had been lovingly cosseted and spoiled. Because luck tends to run along bloodlines, his expectations had been great. Once, as he said, he had been a little king, adding, "The best expects the best."

We were in the Washington tri-cities area. Driving around over a hot summer weekend and looking for a suitable car to buy, he told me about his mother, Yelena. A somewhat delicate red-haired woman, she always dressed in silk satins and crepes, even when she scrubbed the kitchen floor, as he remembered. The first daughter-in-law in her family of marriage and abusively overworked, she was required to cater to ten men and men-boys. Only in her early thirties when her doctor said she hadn't long to live, and with concern about Stevo's future, did Yelena buy her son a first-class wife.

"She was a beauty, tall, like you," said Stevo, changing the gears before he reached over to slide me closer to him on the seat. Reassured by my hand on his knee, he allowed he had been in public school at the time, maybe, he guessed, in fifth grade.

An eleven-year old groom for a bride of eighteen! I suppose it showed how it shocked me because Stevo, embarrassed, immediately tried to change the subject.

Although he refused to admit the possibility—"I was big for my age"—the boy Stevo had been considered too young for the connubial duties of a husband. While he attended grade school, his wife helped with the fortune telling, did the housework and, as is the duty of Machvaia brides, kept his mother company.

But then there came the trauma he could barely recount. For reasons no one bothered to explain, his parents were arrested; his mother, as he learned later, for attacking the police and destroying property; his father for, as the people tell it, "breaking The God's laws."

Child Stevo was taken away to live month after month with a Catholic, non-Gypsy foster family. Years after the episode, after the emotional wounds had scarred into a deep-seated defiance, Stevo found that his mother had gone berserk when she had discovered her husband in bed with the new daughter-in-law. Stevo's wife had been, of course, immediately retrieved by her natal family.

Mother Yelena died when Stevo was only thirteen. Before that, because of his shame, Romero, his father, was refused admittance to Machvaia events or orthodox Machvaia homes. He was declared an outcast and *marimé*.

He tried to take Stevo with him. He asked him to a bar for a man-to-man talk, and invited Stevo to join his exodus to America. Stevo refused. In a sense, Stevo had already tried America and failed—the alien foster home, grade school, Boy Scouts, Catholic piety and prayers—failed in everything, in fact, except athletics. For several of his young years, Stevo worked out at the YMCA with "the enemy," bulking up his muscles, trying to grow up quickly.

Bad blood is known to travel in families, so the people are meticulously careful when arranging marriages and designing the luck of the future. Stevo, although anxious to be transformed from boy to man, had already earned a reputation for stubbornness which, coupled with his father's criminal reputation, now made him an unlikely prospect. No bride price was forthcoming from the uncles on either side. Although Romero would eventually earn a reasonably good living gambling, while he was still learning the skills necessary for his new lifestyle, he was too impoverished to jump-start his son's career. Eventually, Stevo was married to Tutsi.

But, without the customary bride price, he was indentured to her family.

He had no kind words for Tutsi's parents and I could tell that the humiliation still rankled him. As Tutsi's in-house husband, lacking the prestige of authority that usually exalts the male, he was treated like a low-status daughter-in-law. Eventually, Stevo would manage to persuade his wife to abandon her parents and to strike out on their own. But corporate sharing is how Gypsies survive and, without their families' support, the couple was left to their own devices. Over the years, on the grounds that "they weren't there when I needed them," Stevo, like Tutsi, refused the help and advice of blood kinsmen. As a consequence, the isolated couple had no one to furnish financial backing, no one to share telling fortunes or emergency child care, no one to offer them a territory or a business place—no one, I couldn't help thinking, to advise them on the reasonable size of a family.

BEFORE I KNEW GYPSIES, I never thought much about luck. But now, I began to realize I had always been pretty lucky. My life, as a whole, seemed to proceed according to some fortunate plan. For a time, the only child in a hotel full of adults, I received a rich bounty of affection, admiration and attention. Smiles followed me wherever I went. Each Christmas was resplendent with gifts. I particularly remember one, a set of ivory and silver fruit knives, which to my chagrin my mother hastily put away, explaining that knives were not toys. Flattered to receive so obvious of an adult gift, and wondering what it was you do with fruit knives, I watched where they went. Ever doubtful that adults knew best, I sneaked them out of the closet and studied them. Their silver ribbon backs gleaming, couched on white satin, they were four perfect mysteries, alluring, dangerous, sharply beautiful and, to my mind, wholly useless.

In time, I was blessed with the sisters who became my permanent support. At nineteen, I married comfortably. Much of my married life, I did what I liked to do: I read books and went to school. I had two healthy, handsome children. Even my divorce was cushioned by a modest alimony settlement that included the money for college for each of my children as well as some graduate school money for me.

As a result, I was more or less ignorant of tragedy and hard times. Unlike Stevo, I had been buffered from the violence of economic need. In truth, I artlessly thought of my life as a series of happy endings. But what Stevo's and mine might be, I could never let myself imagine.

Screwing up my courage and without mentioning names, I once asked Lola what a bad-luck man could do to get lucky. And she, perhaps intuiting who it was I had in mind—she never showed me the disrespect of mentioning him by name—assured me that luck is contagious and suggested he get next to the good-luck people, study them and find out how they do it. The Machvaia are there to help each other, she explained. Wanting to be near a lucky person confers honor and worth to the advantage of both parties. That was what Stevo was trying to do, I guessed, in getting close to me.

He knew what he wanted: another woman, another job, another life. Our evenings together moved from a trucker's tavern on the noisy freeway to another, quieter street near the University, a place with leather-padded booths called O'Banions. There, pool cue in hand, Stevo held court while I watched. Struggling to find the way to be a man who was neither Gypsy nor Machvano, he devised another identity, Dr. Emacio, a visiting Professor of Foreign Languages. He bought a J. Peterman-style outfit and buttoned the sexy shirt that formerly fell open to his waist, Belafonte style. He began to surprise me with multi-syllable words I hadn't known he knew.

Of course, fooling college kids provided a man of his gifts with little challenge. So he took to fooling me. One evening, when the pool-game bets had escalated into the hundreds, I broke into worried tears. His fellow player, a young bespectacled accountant who consistently stopped at two beers, took me aside to explain that the pair were in cahoots. "Your boyfriend Emacio and I are just pretending to be big-time gamblers. At the end of the evening, whoever wins always gives the money back."

After a year or so of pool at O'Banions, the more confident Stevo dropped his alias and became himself. Gypsy Steve developed quite a popular following. But when he drank too long and too much, his congenial charm turned into a savage belligerence. I would watch the Neanderthal glower develop as he demolished a friend or acquaintance with snide remarks. The next day, he wouldn't remember any of it.

He tried a role he thought he already knew, being a father to my children. When my son reached driving age, Stevo gave him an aging Oldsmobile and warned him to fix the brakes. My son didn't listen and, several months later, slid into another car at a busy intersection. Stevo took back the car, sold it and, to my son's eternal annoyance, failed to split the profit.

Because I disappeared for days behind the ivied walls of the University, Stevo manfully tried to come to my rescue, to see for himself what I was up to. I arranged for him to attend one of my seminars. He came in the guise of Dr. Emacio, and he assured me he found the experience "quite interesting." But after a two-hour documentary and the subsequent discussion of the topic—spear-wielding, lightly clad and colorfully feathered Papuan natives—he assured me he had seen quite enough.

Stevo went with me to a dance that the Anthropology Department sponsored. He showed up in a business suit and tie, sporting a high-powered haircut, and looking solidly prosperous. Everyone knew American Gypsies were the subject of my studies, but apparently no one except my friend Darleen realized my escort was a Gypsy. We didn't stay long. I hadn't anticipated feeling quite so torn by divided allegiance to two worlds, or so worried about the possibility of an insult to either.

To a Gypsy, restaurants, taverns and nightclubs are a kind of neutral ground in the war between purity and defilement. Stevo felt entirely comfortable taking Darleen and me out on the town. I think he felt as successful as he ever would, walking through the door of the jazz and blues nightclub with a woman on each arm. To him, women were a scarce and valuable commodity; the beginning of good luck, the balance of the world, was honored in the union of the sexes. He considered my unmarried female friends as incomplete as a car without wheels or a working engine. He was always noticing and remarking, "A woman alone? What a shame and a pity." On the whole, he treated me like family.

He said he didn't think he could make it to my daughter's wedding. But, for the Machvaia, auspicious beginnings portend the character of the future, and community support has everything to do with marital success. That's probably why he arrived early, a half hour before I did, and stayed for the eight-course reception supper.

Like me, Stevo was continually challenged to keep the two parts of his life viable and separate. At home, he was the boss, or knew he was supposed to be. But where did he stand with me? He could barely endure the sight of me talking to another man. One night, at the birthday party of a fellow student of maybe thirty, the host asked if he might kiss me. Stevo, not understanding the rules of the game, jerked my arm and drove me home in a cloud of ill feeling. On the way, he complained that no well-bred Machvano would ever have insulted his respect in such an insensitive fashion.

His sense of manhood was both fragile and complex. Going through the snapshots I intended to paste in my album, I usually chose the ones that showed him smiling, and he invariably preferred the ones in which he was not. I think he admired, indeed wanted mightily to be, a man of intractable fierceness. Perhaps fierceness fit his difficult domestic life. But his personal tendency toward me was much more tender. I know he found me incredibly naïve. He never said it to my face, but my sister tells me that he often referred to me as his "little girl."

IN THE END WE WERE DOOMED, I suppose, by that difference of luck between us. I represented much of what Stevo had always wanted and been led to expect. He initially saw me as the lucky royal goddess who lived on the sixth floor of the golden tower. He said I was American and free while he was the victim of his birthright. "It's quiet here," he would say with wonder. "Nice," gesturing at the extra unused towels on the bathroom shelf.

His appreciation of my world put me at a disadvantage. I was always trying to make up for the bed he went home to that smelled of diapers and sour milk, and for what he perceived as my easy life which, by then, didn't seem that easy to me. Wanting to salvage the promise of the first son of a first son, I did everything I could to protect his abused psyche from further trauma. To avert additional disaster, I gave away a little of my birthright. For the firmness and security of his arms, I risked the welfare of two families, mine and his. Once, to explain the inordinate dimension of my feeling, I turned to my son and rashly told him I loved Stevo more than anything else in the world. I can't remember what came before or happened after or if I even said it. The words just protrude cruelly out of memory like the glyph on a Mayan tomb, bizarre and puzzling and, after all these years, with the smell of blood and the ruin of sacrifice.

While waiting for my thesis to be approved, I moved again into a new apartment. I hung orange-juice colored curtains to "bring in" the sun and, in exchange for a few not unpleasant duties as manager and gardener, I got the apartment for half the regular price. Whenever the sun escaped the clouds, it would flash across the surface of the goldfish pond outside my window, projecting waving watery finger-lights against my ceiling. I had to keep buying new goldfish for the pond. In the middle of the night, two noisy raccoons would hang over the cement edge and snare them up.

Sometimes Stevo would invite men from the tavern for an evening of poker. Occasionally, he had too much to drink and stayed overnight. On those nights, I hardly slept at all. Transfixed by his proximity and warmth, I would lie awake to listen to the inspiration of his breathing and the soft shoe swishes, the plopping clog and shuffle, of the rain.

My sister Nancy married Patrick, one of our drinking cronies from O'Banions, an impoverished Irish poet with a black goatee and soulful eyes. Nancy looked sensational in silvery tights and a Mary Quant micro-mini dress. The pair had, of course, scripted their own poetic vows, with quotes about union and unity from Kahlil Gibran. But Stevo wasn't listening. He kept squeezing my hand and whispering "I do, I do." With an answering squeeze, I responded with a heartfelt, "Oh, yes. Me, too."

Another sister, Joan, was living with a talented but as yet unrecognized artist who painted realistic watercolor landscapes. Upon graduating, she got a job teaching high-school art on an island in the San Juans. But the small town school board disapproved of their live-in relationship. She had to marry the red-bearded artist in order to be able to support him.

Economically speaking, life was a challenge for both my sisters. Our parents had always believed that the proper duty of a man was to provide for his family. They never approved of our unorthodox taste in men—a poet, an artist, a married Gypsy!—each ten to fifteen years younger than we were, none of whom could be depended upon to earn a living wage. Looking back, I believe that we were destined for those tender-hearted young men who represented our escape, who brought us out of the closet of middle-class convention. They challenged us to discover the missing pieces of our capabilities.

IN THE CUSTOM OF GYPSIES, Katy blessed my apartment: "I pray this apartment brings you happiness and luck." Maybe that was why it was lucky: Tutsi never discovered us there. Katy also mentioned that my new place "really lacks something special," and dropped the subject. The way she said it—quite serious and dipping her strawberry-blonde head away in dismissal—I knew she would consider me mindlessly stupid if I asked her to explain. After she left, I carefully reviewed my notes until I had figured out what she'd meant. Her storefront home had a personal shrine that she cherished; mine didn't.

It seemed that Katy might be right. Those Saints that have been "taken" to protect a family's good health are known to be especially effective healers: that's why you celebrate them at *slava* and light a candle to them each Sunday. After receiving my Masters degree, and a year into the doctorate program, I had been diagnosed with cervical cancer. The hemorrhage began after an otherwise unremarkable evening of drinking at O'Banions. On the way to the hospital I had to laugh at Stevo's cornered response when, suspecting I had become devious enough to enlist his sympathy through suffering, he called me Tutsi by mistake.

Getting a Saint seemed a reasonable idea. I could certainly benefit from a boost of good health. But where could I find one? Katy had already explained that the acquisition of Saints must suggest evidence of The God's intention. They should appear in a serendipitous fashion, be discovered in a closet during a move, be handed down through the family or be designated somehow as a windfall gift.

A Saint for four dollars certainly seemed like a gift. This one was life-size and painted in strong colors on a sturdy board. "Saint," as I called my new-found icon, caught my attention with the surprise of her electric gaze, her dimpling cheeks, her over-sized gold-painted halo, the ornamental roses nesting between her big bare toes and a cleavage that looked friendly and available. Saint's obvious passion for life and preference for color reminded me of Lola. I could hardly wait to tell her.

I discovered Saint in a most unlikely spot, at St. Vincent de Paul, a dilapidated second-hand warehouse that extended on piers over Lake Union. I had taken Lola there only once. She had a powerful aversion to the place because of the water flowing underneath, finding it deep, opaque and dark. "I can't see the bottom," she cried, moving quickly away from the edge of the dock. Lake Union was apparently full of Gypsy kinds of pollution and other terrible things she refused to describe.

When I called Lola, I tried to avoid mentioning Saint's point of origin. But Saints, I learned, are so hardy as to be practically impervious to defilement. "Where'd you get Her?" Lola demanded to know. Then, after my hesitant admission, she responded resolutely, "That can't hurt Her."

As soon as I said that the Saint "has your look, kind of jolly," Lola didn't let me finish my sentence. Instead, hanging up without the courtesy of good-bye, she rushed over the two blocks to my apartment by taxi. Flouncing in, housedress over her poinsettia patterned negligee, hair wrapped and tucked for the shower, she immediately assumed command. Saints are authorized to be treated with an exquisite consideration, and Lola had come prepared. Handing me a package of rope, she ordered me to tie the lady Saint to the top of my Volkswagen. But first I had to wash my hands with ample squirts of Ivory dish washing liquid and pad the back of the board with paper towels. Clearly, Lola had misunderstood the purpose of my purchase. Yet, how could I refuse? Saint had obviously been destined as a gift for Lucky Lola, not for a nonprofessional like me.

The trip to Lola's was quickly negotiated. She had recently moved into a red brick apartment, one long and one short block from mine. During the ride, we each held a side of the Saint to keep it steady, one arm out the window and Lola, chanting anxiously, "Slower, slower!" When we got Her into the apartment, Saint was placed in the back corner of the living room where the sins and shames that surface on the television screen would be deflected away from Her 100-percent pure line of vision. To welcome Saint's arrival, Lola poured us each a glass of V.O. whiskey. She lit St. Anne's three-foot candle. When I asked how she knew this Saint was Anne, she admitted she was guessing. But we both knew that Lola was better than good at guessing.

In an effort to protect her luck, Lola usually preferred not to think or speak about anything unpleasant. But the advent of a Saint as sizable and significant as this inspired fresh confidences. That's when she told me a bit about the time, after her divorce, when she nearly went "out of my mind," moving from place to place searching for good luck. "There's nothing worse than when the cupboard is bare and the children are crying for food," she confessed. In her misery, she had somehow lost her precious statue of Saint Anne, as high as her knee, all gold and fourteen carats. Of late, a fortuitous dream had sent Saint Anne floating toward her in a cloudless sky. An omen of a Saint returned? Amazement mixed with her delight. Cultural surprise, I realized, could be a two-way street. This miracle came from me, the American Djuhli, the outsider.

DURING MY LONG BOUT with the serum hepatitis I contracted from a transfusion, the boon of alimony money ran out. Forced to abandon the doctorate program, I began to teach at the local two-year colleges.

I taught cultural and physical anthropology part time at six different colleges in and around Seattle. Unaccustomed to the sound of my voice, uninterrupted, I longed for the encouragement of student response and did whatever I could to provoke classroom discussion. One topic proved a sure-fire catalyst: Gypsies. My students came alive, sitting up in their seats, wide awake, at the mention. Gypsies? Here in America? Where? Could I bring one to class?

With some trepidation, I broached an invitation to Lola. When I bribed her with the promise of a ride to a future Portland party, she agreed and arrived wearing her favorite dress of the moment, the bubble gum-pink, as she called it, with the circular ten-yard skirt. For such an important occasion, she had added a pink feather boa which, with inspired timing, followed the movements of her shoulders and arms. The smell that shot off the aureoles of tiny fluff from the boa was the result of enthusiastic applications from the many bottles on her glass bedroom tray.

Standing still was not her forte. In lieu of her usual tasks at hand, she paced to and fro by the blackboard, brusquely negotiating the weight of a swinging handbag loaded with pills, cosmetics, money, jewelry, gum for herself and candy for the grandchildren, her black ringlet ponytail of Jezebel curls bouncing and tossing at each turn. As she paced, she studied my class without seeming to, those quick liquid eyes sizing up the situation's prospects. Lacking experience at this type of encounter, she watched me for cues and then, taking note of the captive desires behind the solemn faces, tried to set them free with a few improvisational dance steps.

Just like the time I had placed a mike and tape recorder between us on the kitchen table, she grabbed this opportunity to formally address and thank her American public. In keeping with the oral tradition of her people, she announced that everything she said was true, "the story of the world." Explaining that her mother always told her America was good to Gypsies, "full of gold and good for living," she added that American people had always been good with her, so she was always good with them.

I was pleased to present my class with such a superior specimen, a BaXtali from a distinguished family, a Gypsy I could guarantee to be genuine or, as she put it, "100 percent." But it was a mistake to subject the Machvanka, who invariably treated me like her daughter, to the insult of interrogation. My students were taught to insist on answers. They were inquisitive and vocal and encouraged to think for themselves. The first question was "How old are you?" and it dumbfounded Lola. In her mind, numbers were always relative to the situation and she really hadn't a good idea. "I remember a lot of war," was her evasive response. The next question, "How many people in your tribe?" nearly put her out of commission. After a pause, Lola offered, "Just enough. The right amount." Questions about marriage and children involved sex, a taboo topic: "We don't talk about that." She had come expecting honor and respect for her age, the welcome of friendship and, possibly, a bit of adoration of the kind that her idol and mentor Bette Davis always seemed to invite. On the drive home, although I apologized most sincerely—and Gypsies are experts at recognizing insincerity—her silence was deafening.

Long before class time was over, she wished the class well, and insisted I drive her home "this minute." Before she left, she handed out her business cards and advertising handbills, some for Sister Ruth, some for Lili Marlene.

How did my class judge Lola? A con artist or entrepreneur? Did the charm of the bubble gum-pink work as well as it had the time she called a car agency for a demonstration ride, alighting curbside from the latest model directly in front of Katy's storefront. I can still hear the driver's startled laugh at Lola's sudden exit and her husky command, "Yes, you can stop here. This is my daughter's place. Yes, this is a fine car, and I will bless it. May you be extra lucky and sell two dozen today."

I KNEW STEVO AND I couldn't compose a life of any substance out of drinking in a tavern and looking for cars. He needed his children as much as they needed him; I couldn't imagine Stevo without them. But I had begun to believe in serendipitous outcomes, and my lover came by as he liked, as he could, and the sight of him, the fevered moment of his return, was what I lived for. I thought, well, why not? How can it last? What does it matter? But for now, there is only this moment, and this is all I will ever want or ask for.

I had always been lucky. So, I thought, maybe some miracle will resolve these niggling domestic complications of a wife and too many children. Or maybe I can learn to live without him, later. Much later. Maybe he will be gone soon, sooner or later. On the other hand, maybe the sooner the better. Or I might leave for the Continent to study and live with the Gypsies in Europe. The truth is, I was deliberately vague in assessing the future. It was a barely conceivable gift to wake up each morning and know that I might see him. A greater gift to know he couldn't stay away. After all, I was a graduate student/teacher who had lived her life in books, and he was a Gypsy who never finished fifth grade. What did we have in common? The next question was, what did we not?

Eventually, Stevo began dividing his favors between us, spending several weeks with one, and then with the other. But when I was on his schedule, he usually drove home each evening. "Not to Tutsi," he assured me, "to the children."

Although too proper to use the word *sex*, his meaning was obvious: If a woman (meaning Tutsi) was unsatisfied physically, she might be hell to live with. He brought the subject up several times to make sure I understood the message. He was planning to sleep again with his wife.

It couldn't have been easy, with their ongoing vendetta, to make the transition from Tutsi to me, and back to Tutsi. Whenever he called, I could hear Tutsi screaming in the background, "Fuck you, the whore!" She thought she gained ground by turning the children against him.

Children are what Machvaia live for; they are considered life's greatest blessing. But all those children didn't seem so advantageous to me. Whenever he arrived at my apartment, I had to leave him undisturbed for long minutes, until his spinning head slowed down. The transition was a ritual: lights down, feet up, eyes closed.

It was my luck to find merit in Stevo, and to inherit Tutsi along with so many of his other pressing needs that mine seemed trivial by comparison. It was my luck to become brave and interesting, more from necessity than by choice.

WE WERE INCREASINGLY CARELESS and unaware. Nothing turned our minds from each other. Despite the damning evidence of Ephram's case, which I was still feverishly running through my mind for loopholes, I felt we were safe. With each passing day without gossip or scandal, it confirmed for me that a coterie of angels— I visualized plump and Kewpie doll pink Botero angels—were fielding our defense.

One night, a bit drunk, we threw caution to the wind. Sometime after midnight, we stopped in at a popular all-night eatery next to the house where Fat Albert lived on University Way. We had just ordered Hasty Tasty hamburgers when Albert's wife, Yutsa, without makeup, a coat thrown over her nightclothes, rushed into the diner.

Flustered, avoiding our eyes, she announced to the room at large that she had a boy at home with a fever, and that's what required her to be in this ridiculous place at this awful time, buying aspirin. Lucky for us, either through good will or self-interest—a shame affects the tribe as well as a family—Yutsa never gave us away.

In the official sense, our infamy remained a secret for several years. One reason may have been Tutsi's lack of favor with the other women. I doubt I would have dated Stevo if she had been among the Machvanki who accompanied Lola and me to the clubs. More to our advantage, I would guess, were the requirements of respect. The local Roma preferred not to insult my illustrious sponsor, Phuri Dei Lola, with the ignominious information that her companion/nurse was behaving badly. After several years of deliberate public blindness, I would bet that everyone in the area, with the exception of Lola, either knew about me and Stevo, or suspected as much.

Then Zorka, beloved mother of the thirteen adult children in the southern Seattle Kalderasha family, died. Her first death commemoration was scheduled for the Knights of Columbus Hall. I had become so overly confident from those free-loading years of gratuitous good luck, so focused on reviewing my notes, that I failed to remember that death is the time of forgiveness, the time when Tutsi's errors—she had been banned from Kalderasha storefronts for drunk and disorderly behavior—might be overlooked. But how could I have anticipated our fairy tale's unfortunate climax when I was up to my teeth in denial?

Tutsi came to the commemoration with Stevo, of course, and as soon as he saw me, he angled away from the crowd and dashed to the kitchen. From there, highlighted and framed in the serving window, round-eyed with anguished delight, his mouth opening and closing like a gasping beached salmon, he stared directly at me. What was he doing? Didn't he realize the blatant obviousness of his behavior? Until that alarmed moment, I had never imagined that he could stupidly fail to show the Machvaia penchant for public perfection.

As dinner was served, I noticed that Machvanki Duda and Boba were avoiding the table. Wanting to be correct, I pulled my chair over and joined them against the wall. But, ignorant of my misdeeds, my companion Lola insisted I come back to the table. That's how Stevo and I ended up eating together, 20 feet apart, an outrageous flaunting of our transgression. With each overconfident mouthful, we cast shame on the memory of The Dead One. With each brazen lift of the fork, we ritually defiled all those people.

That same evening, Stevo was called to trial by the Kalderasha. But the swift delivery of justice was handicapped by the fuzziness of the facts. His accusers, Zorka's sons, had begun legal proceedings by erroneously claiming that Stevo and I had arrived at the feast together. Then, unable to provide the necessary evidence, they refused to attend the trial. When questioned, Tutsi loyally swore that she and Stevo had arrived and left as a couple. Stevo wasn't chasing around, she insisted. He was home every night, shoeless and in his shorts, watching television. I doubt she was believed. But she was the only vocal and willing eyewitness.

For Roma, eating and drinking are matters of purity and honor. During trials, votes are cast by drinking, or refusing to drink, with the defendant. Hoping for clearance, Stevo drove to Tacoma to test the hospitality of Ephram's famously successful older brother Milanitzi. It was after midnight and for nearly an hour he sat at the curb, shame-faced, until he was noticed. Then, Milanitzi invited him in and gave him his vote of confidence by sharing an indigestible saucepan of boiled-to-black Gypsy coffee, ritually prepared.

But Stevo hadn't the heart to solicit any more drinking opinions. During the year of many moves, there were days we had repeatedly driven past both Albert's and Miller's houses, carrying eye-arresting carloads of my belongings. Damning evidence, and undeniable.

Nor, in terms of trying his luck, was Stevo willing to face the righteous wrath of Zorka's sons for his part in ruining their mother's death commemoration. He lost all taste for Gypsy events. When I asked, one evening, why he hadn't gone to a local wedding, he waved away the possibility. "Never mind," he retorted. "I didn't feel like going."

I COULD ONLY GUESS what would happen next. Taking Stevo as my lover had been taking a crazy chance. I now assumed that the damning publicity would hamper any further fieldwork and might even cost me Lola's friendship. I expected to feel the sting of disdain and, quite possibly, the fury of rejection. Instead, Lola never mentioned the incident and continued to take me with her wherever she went.

Except for a comment by Milanitzi's son, a slow lad in Tacoma whose remarks were frequently an embarrassment to his family, and another time, during an especially intimate moment with several of Stevo's aunts, to this day no one has ever shown me the disrespect of mentioning Stevo, the forbidden subject, to my face.

In fact, after our crime became public, the Machvanki seemed unusually warm and solicitous, inviting me to their houses, asking, with concern, "Did you eat today?" Perhaps they were relieved it hadn't been their husbands who suffered stigma. Perhaps they felt a little sorry for the headstrong Djuhli who ignored their best advice about staying clear of Gypsy men. Maybe I seemed more human and understandable, having revealed a character flaw or two. Or maybe I became more Machvanka, being required to deal with the lordly demands of a Machvano on an ongoing basis.

Tutsi and her angry thoughts, however, worried Katy. Soon after the strain of the trial, we were sitting in her storefront window. I was getting better at reading minds and could tell Katy had something on hers. That's when she shyly handed me a small packet of incense sewn with loose stitches into a drawstring pouch. "It's pure tree tears," she said. "Wear it next to your skin at all times. You understand? For protection."

For a brief moment, I couldn't imagine why I might need protection. Then I remembered Tutsi screaming, "I'll get you!" Curses, I had been told, result from the emotional force of "strong thoughts" and are guaranteed to work, particularly those involving the dead. I was quick to assure Katy that I appreciated her concern. But the elixir of love had damaged the synapses in my brain and I wasn't really worried about Tutsi's "strong thoughts." (Perhaps I should have been. Stevo apparently became susceptible to witchcraft. The next year he had an operation to remove a sewing machine needle that had mysteriously pierced his buttock and migrated to some depth.)

What did it mean that I, the outsider, was tolerated, and the insider Stevo was not? Why was I lucky while Stevo was rewarded with more damage to his hard luck life? Now, as we drove through Seattle, one of us hid from the view of passing cars by lying full-length in the back seat. The need to hide made me feel like cheap and damaged goods. Finally, reluctantly, I was forced to acknowledge that more than the possibility of poison in his coffee or Tutsi stabbing him while he slept, Stevo feared the public shame.

HE'D NEVER BEEN to a musical comedy before. I took him to see *Man of La Mancha*, which put him into such an expansive mood that he wanted to hang out in the lobby and get to know the theater public. "Your people," he said affectionately. "You look like these people to me." For his sake, however, I'd become quite paranoid in crowds and so apprehensive about discovery that I hurried him to the exit and kept the usual fair distance between us on the sidewalk.

Inspired by the character of Don Quixote, Stevo liked to sing "The Impossible Dream" as he walked through our garden apartment, getting dressed all the way. He would hum the song as he rummaged through the newspaper, searching out the recent Want Ads. I could hear him in the shower, reaching happily for the high C.

The Machvano with the apricot skin wouldn't leave me for reasons of defilement. But I was beginning to find it hard to ignore the obvious, that the power of Roma rule and Machvaia bloodlines was absolute and unforgiving.

But why admit the hazard when the resolution seemed so easy? Together, Stevo and I explored the possibilities. What our encounters lost in spontaneity was offset by the sweet perversity of our pleasure, the mutuality of our pain.

FOUR YEARS AFTER WE MET, Stevo said he had something to tell me that I wouldn't like. His sons were growing up and he needed to teach them the business. The weekends we had spent together, looking for cars—those two and three idyllic days by ourselves, often out of town—were over.

That was one of the very few times (really, considering the many provocations) that I cried in his presence. Normally, when he was with me, no matter what was going on, I seemed to become airborne, soaring on endorphin highs.

Without him, my focus on the weekends turned to Katy. Her new midtown storefront was only a half-block from the Public Market. Fronting onto the noise and congestion of pedestrian traffic, the store was a magnet for passing customers and also an attraction for the Roma. Gypsy men stopped for Katy's coffee and conversation and to bring her the Gypsy news. They came by because they were curious to see for themselves how she was faring as Seattle's one-of-a-kind, live-alone bachelorette.

The store, barely bigger than a dollhouse, ran front-to-back in a quick succession of undivided areas: window-shrine, bedroom-sitting, dining-kitchen, with a half-bathroom as big as a minute tucked in the rear corner. Only the window area facing the street had the privacy of a partial plywood partition. She and her kids were a good natured family of six in one room, and the way it was done was with tolerance and good manners.

Behind the store, Katy gardened. Hidden from the street side view was the wedge-shaped backyard, four by eight, banked by the sides of adjacent buildings and blessed with an occasional hour of noon sun. That's where Katy put house plants to drain, hung out her hand wash and, on a little dirt hill, encouraged the seedlings she planted from the fruit she had eaten and from starter plants gleaned from other people's gardens.

These modest beginnings were Katy's delight. As a child, she had spent summers on her uncle's and her grandmother's farms and she believed in the virtue of the freshly picked. She was always telling me to stop the car so she could capture a prize apple, a peach that was ripe and growing. Some years later, we would be threatened with arrest for picking a few tomatoes from a farmer's field in California.

Katy often slept until noon; I didn't dare call earlier. Her daily schedule was cued to the activities in the adjoining taverns. While her neighbors were hauling beer and mopping up spills, Katy swept her carpet. Afternoons, the sound of the tavern jukebox pierced the wall, and we would try to guess the names of the tunes and recall what we could of the lyrics. By sundown, shouts of laughter and pounding booms from the bass-heavy music would compete with whatever television program Katy was watching. As the evening advanced, tavern fights spilled out onto the sidewalk, and the trip next door for cigarettes and sodas became unnerving. In the early morning hours, departing drinkers leaned heavily against the storefront's loose front window glass while Katy continually warned the children to stay clear of the glass. At night, Katy's courage sometimes turned to panic. She would call to say she needed a house, that storefronts were no place to raise children. Sometimes, she called after midnight and woke me up, proposing that I drive her to her mother's. Katy never quite got the hang of calling a cab or taking a bus the way Lola had.

But during the day, Katy and her family were fearless. Even Baby Jelly could persuade a drifter off. One time I watched him, dimpled and pudgy and barely five, kicking and pushing a man's knees and shins: "Now you go. My mother said so. You get out."

Katy's Gypsy children were learning to make the most of opportunity. At the produce stands, a few words of spiritual advice might be exchanged for a pile of salad greens. An elderly pensioner might be persuaded to trade a pound of coffee for a home-cooked meal. Baby Jelly John, brush in hand and smile in place, lugged a heavy shoeshine kit up to the corner, where he did a thriving business. Little Julie skipped around the block, looking for change on the sidewalk, stuck in parking meter slots or loose in pay telephone boxes.

I remember life as being always lively at Katy's place across from the Market, all those visitors, the constant quest for meals and money, the challenge of bathing in a plastic two-foot tub, the insecurity of the rickety window glass, the Mardi Gras variety of the streets. Clear and rare days were a special delight, Elliot Bay stretching to the horizon, the magnificent snow-capped Olympics in stately procession. The sun would stream through the storefront window, forming a beacon of brilliance that shot into the windowless rear of the store, drawing us up to the front, to the light. On sunny days, all Seattle liked to go to the Market. On those blissed-out blue-sky days, the streets and sidewalks would be packed with cars and people. I would have to park several blocks away from Katy's and walk.

AT FIRST, AFTER EPHRAM'S departure, Katy had no heart for fortunes. "I can't tell people how to live when my own life is such a mess." But eventually, "because I have to," Katy went to work. In exchange for a particularly effective reading, a street artist painted a pretty sign, *Spiritual Reader*, on a piece of cardboard. In keeping with the tenor of the times, the sign sported Life Saver-colored ribbons, giddy scalloped clouds and a childlike Peter Max rainbow. Without advice from her lawyer, Katy bravely propped the sign up in her storefront window. Luck was on her side. The sign worked fine. And for reasons she never knew, the police were kind enough not to bother her.

As a child, Katy had been the family tomboy. Her sisters recalled how she tied her full skirts to her knees with string and climbed trees higher than her brothers. Once she borrowed her neighbor's motorcycle, and drove it recklessly into a tree. At sixteen, she ran away with a younger sister and got a job as a roller-skating waitress at a drive-in. She said she really liked the white cowboy hat she wore on the job, which lasted a "long time," about a month.

Swearing me to secrecy, Katy would propose adventurous trips to Oregon and California and other forbidden places. Then she usually chickened out. We attended a lecture at the University where she met the world-famous Gypsy authority, Walter Starkie. But on the way home, she admitted the futility of the episode: "So what? Nobody I know knows him."

Sometimes, after her weekly bath she donned a pair of slacks and we played a game of beginner's tennis on the court across the street from her mother's. The court was entirely visible from the street, and I know of no other Machvanka who has ventured such a bold athletic move as public tennis.

When Ephram disappeared, he had taken the bride's gift she had been adding to since their marriage, which consisted of all her savings. Katy had been married into the Kalderasha people her entire adult life and, like them, was not the least adventurous with her money. She had given the matter considerable thought and declared that "fortunes are not like a weekly salary." Without any hint of criticism of her mother, to whom she owed inordinate respect, Katy had the habit of laying aside a half portion of her earnings in consideration of a future rainy day. As she explained, darkly, "You never know what might happen."

LOLA BOUGHT, THREW OUT and raced to town to buy again. She said she did it for her "good living," bought whatever she liked. "That way, I never get jealous." She believed spending was like giving, and giving was good for her luck. As she said, "I spend it and double it. You have to spend it to make it."

I remember one time when we were in the Bon Marche and I hesitated over a purchase. Lola impatiently offered this incredible advice: "You don't know which sweater to buy? Why not get one in each color."

For Machvaia, spending is sharing and sharing is an indicator of the state of one's luck. If I admired something Lola wore or possessed, she would triumphantly insist I keep it. That's how I wound up with a ring I never wear, a ring that is really a watch, rhinestone-studded and with a lid that opens to reveal a hidden poison pill compartment.

Money unspent is unactualized. Money passed around becomes meritorious. Generous gifts, alms for the Roma in trouble, unforgettable ritual celebrations, unstinting hospitality (the kind that lasts for days)—these favor a good reputation, public respect and move both giver and getter to the auspicious dimension. To the Machvaia, money in the bank does not make you rich. Money requires the benefit of an audience.

Even I had something to share. The moment she saw my new earrings, gold-washed tassels swinging from golden knots, costume jewelry earrings I'd bought to make me look more Gypsy, Lola took a fancy to them. She liked them well enough, in fact, to ask for them. How could I refuse? Placing them hesitantly on her palm, I said, "If you want, you can borrow them." She wore them every day and to suggest she give them back seemed crassly materialistic. I learned about giving the generous gift through the ambiguity of that experience, the mixture of pleasure and pain, magnanimity and desire. Those earrings had been my favorites. Over time, as the tassels fell off, their ultimate value became the sharing, and I could no longer imagine why it had seemed so hard to part with them.

By temperament, as the product of fat-cat comforts, I am more like Lola than her daughter. Katy spotted my spendthrift tendencies early on and decided to save me. With admirable finesse, she proposed I dye my hair in the sink like she did. I could put a few dollars away, she pointed out, by quitting salons that dyed my hair red and no longer enduring the torture of hot air dryers. Trying to help, she suggested that if I played my cards right I might get a little more money from my former husband. As evidence of her interest in my welfare, whenever the customers had lined up in the front room of her storefront, she encouraged me to spell her at giving readings. Once, when my parents surprised me with a check for my birthday, I offered to buy her dinner. But she had something more practical in mind. Leading me to the window of a nearby pawnshop, she pointed out a ten-dollar gold piece dated the year her mother was born, or the year she may have been born—Gypsies evince little interest in dates—insisting I purchase it "for the luck of two birthdays."

Katy was right about the gold piece. The coin has proved a multiple blessing, appreciating to many times my initial investment. It has gone into hock during financial crises, been worn on a box-link chain during job interviews and vastly improved the credit of my appearance at the more important Gypsy events.

MY SOCIAL LIFE WAS NOW limited to Gypsies. Indeed, the Gypsies seemed diversion enough. I learned to pay attention to the ever-changing climate of feeling and how the day was going, to pause at the storefront door upon my arrival and not to interrupt.

As Lola and her family continually obsessed over *baX* (luck) and, as luck is contagiously epidemic, to ensure my welcome I made every effort to arrive with a peaceful and untroubled heart. Otherwise someone, usually Katy, would take me aside and insist on knowing what was wrong.

This reading of minds and moods relates directly to the women's phenomenal success as psychics. A girl's training begins early. Once when there was a roomful of visitors, I heard Katy caution little Julie: "Put your mind with the baby's. Understand him. You should know what he is thinking. If he falls, it will be your fault."

Of course, each unmarried year added to Katy's social pressure. Without the tempering effect of marriage, sexual powers are believed to run amuck. A woman alone and in her physical prime was, from the standpoint of the other women, a toxic hazard. To reassure them, to keep their friendship, Katy spent hours on the phone calling Seattle, Tacoma and Portland, reminding the Roma that she was the victim, not the cause, of Ephram's neglect. A compelling example of a single-woman's success, she was even more of a threat—an affront, really—to the men. They feared their beleaguered wives and daughters might become corrupted by Katy's example and get the idea to escape to another situation, run away, marry someone else, or—worst luck!—move into their own apartments.

An incident in Tacoma brought Katy's difficult situation to my attention. We went to visit Ephram's sister, who was recovering from an operation. When we arrived we found only men, Ephram's brothers and nephews, in the lobby. Ephram's brother Coco said something insulting. Immediately, she advised me to walk in front of the seated men with her and turn our backs. In the world of the Gypsies, just turning around could immediately empty a room.

ALTHOUGH SHE WAS NEVER resigned to spending her nights in the noisy storefront next to the tavern, I think Katy made a remarkable adjustment to living alone. She even admitted she was beginning to feel lucky, and that she was seeing "good things" in her dreams. I knew her life was looking up when she announced plans to celebrate the *slava* of St. George, the one her sons inherited through their father's bloodline.

One warm afternoon in May, in a large, cheerful banquet hall with windows overlooking Elliot Bay and a marina with hundreds of furled sails, she made *slava*. The entire Seattle community came, including troublemaker Ephram. Ephram came for reasons that were as convoluted as he was: revenge, threat, boredom, perversity, *slava* rights, perhaps sheer hubris.

Just as everyone sat down to eat he arrived with a young American woman. A turn of heads rippled around the table, and the seated guests were stunned when they recognized the outsider as their local AFDC caseworker. Government regulations require that those receiving Aid to Families with Dependent Children not exceed a given limit of property and cash. From their frantic response, even a confused anthropologist could see that most, if not all, of the Roma attending were AFDC recipients.

Terrified that they might lose their monthly checks, the people panicked. I saw watches and antique jewelry disappear into pocketbooks. Half the Roma escaped down the hall. A few retired to the bathrooms. Afterwards, I heard them agonizing over the possibility there were spies in the parking area who were taking notes, making a record of the high-rollers who had arrived or left in late-model Cadillacs. A visiting Machvano, amused at the pandemonium, remarked that Ephram was the primary entertainment in a town with few features of interest.

Katy was incensed. "You saw that? He tried to sit next to me at the table!" Ephram's notoriety puffed a little smoke and just as quickly vanished. Soon after that, the people stopped discussing him. "He is nobody," they said.

INITIALLY, LOLA HAD MANAGED to hide whatever fear she felt when riding in my little Volkswagen. But on our travels around the city, Lola would periodically tense and grab the little handle on the dash, and I would wonder why. She was, I began to realize, leery of drop-offs, steep hills, the water's edge. When I negotiated the University Bridge with its see-through cement railing, she tended to panic. "Pay attention!" she would command. "This is an emergency! Careless. That's your real name. I'm going to get out of this car, jump out, if you don't stop."

In truth, traveling had a dark side for Lola, and her evening phone calls made me realize she was not, as she claimed, "afraid of nothing." Each evening, immediately after the 6 o'clock news, she was on the telephone reporting on earthquakes, renegade icebergs and what the Channel Five weather man had to say about high-pressure systems, satellite photos and the Celsius report. Anxiously quoting him word for word, her voice trailing off, she would entreat, "What do you think? Isn't that terrible?"

Whatever concerned the elements, no matter how distant—storms, stranded climbers, missing ships at sea—held Lola's rapt attention. The slightest temperature change, the least gust of wind might preview a coming misfortune. Always alert for omens, she would call to warn me. The world was her neighborhood and inclement weather an invader. Sickness, disease and other disasters arrived with bad weather. Bad weather meant bad times.

This likely related to the days *po drom*. When she was small and criss-crossing America with her family, winter's snow and mud would often hold their wagon fast, sometimes for weeks. Then she and her sisters had to stay put in order to stay warm and dry, rest-less prisoners under their layered down comforters.

At first I couldn't understand her panic. Changes in the weather and natural catastrophes on the other side of the world were matters of relative insignificance to me. My own childhood had been spent indoors, protected from the elements with radia-tor heating. Attired in tight white kid gloves, the overly warm con-straint of a woolen bonnet, the flapping nuisance of lined galoshes—these were my escorts for forays down the sidewalk. How easy for me to respond with calm and absolute conviction, "Oh, it's nothing. Don't worry." To hear me say it was nothing was probably one reason Lola called.

Before eight in the morning, Lola would be at the window with her coffee, thoughtfully studying the sky. Was she waiting for an advance of Gypsy premonition to tell her how the day would go? Was she contacting The God, the Ancestors, Saints, the Sun and Moon, those spiritual deities who make their home in the sky?

Lola was appalled by the first Apollo landing. The sight of the astronauts in their Pillsbury Doughboy spacesuits bouncing about, disrespectfully boyish and weightless on the moon's bleak surface, was an experience from which she never quite recovered. "How do they know they should do that?" she implored, her fleshy half-covered shoulders slumping away from the television. I had no answer that could possibly calm her. Until that moment, I had considered the astronauts to be as admirable as the Knights of the Round Table, the risk-taking pilgrims of the century, extending the boundaries of the known world like elastic.

After that, she liked to remind me that man's intrusion into outer space was wreaking havoc with the weather. "Oh, this weather is terrible," she would say. "Summer and it's raining. They shouldn't do that. They should know better. It's because they're always doing things they shouldn't with the sky. They don't care." "They" might be any forces in America she didn't comprehend: NASA, the government, flying airplanes, flying missiles, flying saucers, smog.

Large, opaque bodies of water were known to be the preferred environment of the Devil, and also could be a cause for alarm. We were in an Oregon gift shop when she glanced out a window and the sudden sight of rocks and giant waves made her jump, knocking a conch shell lined with shiny peach nacre to the floor. Angry, she muttered something in Romani I couldn't make out and that she refused to translate. Picking up the shell, I remembered that luck can be found anywhere and decided to test the theory. "What if," I teased, "some of your luck is really in the water? Miller has a powerboat and he usually catches his limit of salmon and halibut. Remember how you told me luck tends to travel in families?"

"Well," she lifted a wry penciled eyebrow, flipped an impatient curl with a head swing and strode archly to the door. "My curses never make damage anyway. They usually fall back on top of my house."

I must suppose that Lola eventually lost a little of her fear of water. Her last apartment, a block from Lake Union, framed a clear view of the lake from her red brick doorstep. I had noticed the For Rent sign and called Miller to tell him about it. Perhaps she simply didn't need to look in the direction of the water. Indeed, she seemed quite pleased with her new location. "I like the neighborhood, and it's on the bus line." She was there until the end of her life, during which her red rose-shaped Christmas lights circled her street-side window all year long. Whenever a customer called she would cheerily tuck the phone under her chin, continuing with the task at hand, and ask, "Can you come over now? No, I'm not busy. I'm on Eastlake, the place with the lights."

THE PROBLEM BEGAN one Christmas, a dismal and dark winter day. I was waiting for Stevo to call. To afford more space in my small apartment, I had tearfully hung the tiny Christmas tree upside down from the hammered bronze chandelier. The inverted shape of my life, I thought morosely. Wracked with self-pity, my gaze followed the swimming motions of the tinsel glittering in the fir branches. The thought of dragging myself out of the chair to attend my family's holiday party paralyzed me even further.

So still and stunned was my despair that a pregnant mouse insouciantly sauntered by my foot, carrying a pecan in her fat cheek. Searching for further mouse-like evidence, I found a shoe nest in the closet with a tiny store of salted pecans, and, with the shoe in my palm, I had a sudden insight of lost expectation. I recognized the poignancy of feeling unwelcome. I had no authorized place in Stevo's life, no claim to his company or his phone calls, no legitimate public standing, no power greater than a mouse's.

I had been reduced to pathetic fragments, smashed to bits by Stevo's calls that gave me news about which child was sick, what had gone wrong followed by sweet honey estimates of when he might come over or crushing reports that he hadn't the money for gas. Something had to give. Anxious, sick with longing, I couldn't stand the city when Stevo was out of town—the incessant rain, myself without him, the quick pity of my relatives, the isolation of books, any type of music, even the kind I liked.

The Christmas with the mouse initiated a fresh resolve. I left the city of rains. The Machvaia, meeting and studying the Machvaia people, remained my most unfinished business. I would look for my luck *po drom* and finish the Machvaia story.

Before I made my break, the pile in the center of my living-bedroom grew and grew. There were two round Chinese baskets packed with shoes and bedding and kitchen equipment, a 3×5 metal file box for reference cards and a box of field notes, an antique standard typewriter, a small lamp for reading and an unwieldy double-speaker radio. All this, plus several duffel bags of clothes to accommodate my two personae, a Romani language dictionary, one address book listing Gypsies and another listing non-Gypsy friends and the friends of friends.

Taking my good-byes by stages, I packed and repacked, and talked about leaving. But I still didn't know when. The truth was, I was not at all certain that I would be able to go, and less certain that I could stay away. It meant giving up my part-time jobs, my only source of income, just as I would be giving up any future Ph.D. prospects. It meant leaving behind my supportive network of friends and family, and even my little love nest with the restocked fish pond and the water movie on the ceiling.

I was waiting for fortune to find me, waiting for the morning that my bones got the message to throw everything into the car and just leave.

Finally, the morning came. Pulling away with a load so high that it dimpled the fabric ceiling of the Volkswagen, something— maybe the shock absorbers!—squealed in outraged protest. I tried not to listen.

THE FACT IS I NEVER said good-bye to Stevo. Maybe I had in mind that he might follow. Maybe by leaving that way, I hoped to stir him into decisive action. I am pretty sure I was putting him to a test.

When I had known him only briefly, Stevo proposed running away, the only solution, it seems, that works for Gypsies. "Leave with me now and we will never look back." I wasn't sure what he meant. I doubt that he knew either. Now, I would run away by myself.

But it was mostly longing that launched me on my journey south. The longing to understand Stevo's people and, through them, him. The longing to leave the unresolvable behind. I had already practiced traveling—with Stevo, with Katy, with Lola. This time I intended to go all the way to Los Angeles, the ceremonial home of my tribe of choice. I had in mind a leisurely expedition in the poetic vein of Richard Halliburton, the early twentieth-century travel writer my sisters and I had read growing up.

Driving down the Pacific coast in my Volkswagen, I would look for "Psychic" signs, "Palmistry" signs, and search out the direction of my luck. I would follow my nose, throwing myself on the mercy of intuition and the undiscovered, trusting myself, like Lola, to the kindness of strangers. I was hoping to justify my growing investment in the Machvaia people. *California Dreamin'* was in the air, so I drove there.

Was it hard to leave Lola and my family without the security of a research grant and travel again to California? Not really. What is hard is wanting what you know you cannot have. Gypsies have a word for this kind of all-consuming hunger, the "fasting disease," *postarniko* it's called.

"Gypsies are always wanting what they cannot have," Lola said, solemnly.

"It's the same with Americans," I answered, speaking from fresh experience.

THAT YEAR, SUMMER SEEMED as reluctant to leave as I had been. Field after field of abundant grapevines curled and spiraled out, reaching for invisible support. The heat of northern California valleys made me drowsy. My car had no air conditioning and, by noon, the wind on my face felt dry and oven-hot. I scanned the horizon for places to park, green oases, the umbrella shade of Monterey pines and spreading oaks. To stay awake, I overdosed on coffee.

For days that turned into weeks, I followed the highway near the ocean, exploring the beaches and sleeping in State Parks. Young hippie hitchhikers dotted the roads, and I liked to pick them up; I often stayed overnight wherever they stayed. When I said I envied them the lightness of their loads, they said they envied me the happiness of knowing Gypsies.

Smiling at the passing motorists, enlivened by the quickly shifting scenery, I sang loudly over the roar of the engine. In the confines of my little car, if I rolled up the windows, my small soprano voice resounded operatically. My Gypsy friends advised me to find the feeling in the song and let it out. They reminded me of voracious fledglings, mouths open wide, singing with everything they have.

As the hot afternoons wore on, I tried to remain awake by yodeling. Sometimes I practiced screaming, so I would know my own scream. At first, I had no scream at all. My pre-divorce days, evenly uneventful, had failed to bring it out. Tiring of that, I might work on my French accent which, as I recalled, had once been much better. Mouth-twisting facial exercises amused me for a while. Discovering some Double Bubble at a gas station, I blew bubbles and chewed gum with noisy uncouth abandon.

At times it seemed nothing could dampen the delight of my traveling. At one point, a highway patrolman followed me down a hill and stopped me at the bottom of the grade. "I clocked you at seventy."

"Fantastic," I gleefully responded. "This junker doesn't usually do over fifty-five."

He paused. Under his wide hat brim, I detected the suggestion of a twinkle. Jamming the citation book back into an inside pocket, slapping the hood of my car with the flat of his hand, he motioned me on.

During those five months on the road, besides applying for jobs at the colleges I passed, I tried to find and live with the Gypsies. I was lucky with Lola's sons and daughters. They had married into nearly every important Machvaia lineage and gladly shared the unprinted gossip of the Machvaia Daily News. All of Lola's children welcomed me warmly, all except Boba. Back in Seattle, on a visit to see her mother, Boba had been like all her sisters, hospitable and friendly: "You must come see me when you get to California. You must come stay with me."

But here in Anaheim, her great eyes wide and bright—was it with fear?—she met me quietly at the door and declared she couldn't ask me in. When her sisters told me Boba never went anywhere anymore and never invited *anyone* into the house, I returned several times to Boba's in concern. The last time, an ambulance was screaming down the driveway. In a panic, I followed.

When I reached the hospital, a pale and subdued Boba, her head scarf fallen in nervous neglect to one shoulder, sat in the emergency waiting room. She had discovered her son Duke, the bonny prince of that unhappy family, sprawled on the bathroom floor, bright blue and unconscious. She, her husband and I sat for what seemed like hours, until the examining doctor called us into the hall. His language was technical, but I understood that Duke was brain dead and his coma terminal. Boba, however, had not the least idea what the medical diagnosis meant. My first anguished thought was, how could I tell her? My second was, why should I?

Those who announce bad news are suspected of causing and wishing bad luck. Instead, I escaped decision by fainting. When I came to, Boba was awkwardly trying to help me up.

AFTER THAT, BOBA wouldn't leave me alone, insisting kindly, "You must stay until Duke gets better." She explained my presence at her house as required: "She cares so much about my family, she overdoes it." Word traveled fast: "He's pretty bad, all wired up like a stereo."

Someone from each Machvaia lineage came to the hospital or the house to discover for themselves what was happening. They came because Duke was the first young man of the Machvaia kind to die of a drug overdose. "We don't allow drugs," they'd say. "He comes from a nice family. Why didn't the elders, the grandparents, tell him to stop?" The shame brought upon the tribe was of mutual concern. For what happened to one of their sons might happen to them all.

Boba's house, no larger than a generous-sized trailer, quickly filled up; one night I counted fifty women, sleeping hither and yon on the carpeting. As the resident "help," I bedded with Babyface, the household's tiny industrious daughter-in-law, the wife of Duke's brother. Her young sons crowded crosswise at our feet, we were one wall of flesh against the fleshless—the ghostly visitors from the Other Side—defended by shared warmth from the terror of memory, all of us together in the sagging double bed. Every night, frightening dreams woke Babyface from an uneasy sleep, and she would poke me in the back with her knee.

"Are you awake?" That was my cue to get up to look for "those things," as she described them, that might be lurking in the night. "Can't see a thing. Everything is fine," I would reassure her as tumbling back into bed I booked a hopeful passage on another sleep escape. Then, again, the knee and the urgent whisper, "Are you awake?" And I would know the ghost was back.

After a week of cooking and serving and answering the phone, dizzy, desperate, feeling my age, I resisted the knee. "Don't worry. He's not mad at you. I know it," I would mumble, clutching at my corner of the bedclothes.

Although Duke's drug habit had torn the family apart, I had always considered him in many ways to be the most promising lad of that estranged, embittered family; the best-looking, the most like his mother. The fateful day of his collapse, as I found out later, Babyface had the bad luck to argue with him about "nothing," as she said.

But maybe it was something. Machvaia believe that dying angry, without the ritual of forgiveness, can turn even the best tempered person into a fearfully vengeful ghost. Baby insisted on keeping the light turned on all night and required my company on trips to the bathroom where Duke had overdosed. Although not a particularly clever girl, through enterprise and necessity she became marvelously resourceful. I know this because once, after the knee, after getting up to find "nothing," Babyface asked me something about disease and addiction that pushed my teaching button, and I was chagrined to find myself, upright and wide awake, explaining something about the genetics of human evolution, while she snored softly on our king-size pillow.

THE DAY DUKE DIED, some of Lola's daughters and I went shopping for flowers, long dark skirts and gifts for Duke's "box," as the people called his coffin. "So he won't be lonesome," Katy made little handkerchief dolls representing each member of his family to put in his box. To keep Duke company we sat up all night at the funeral parlor, stuffing ourselves with black coffee and indigestible desserts.

After the weeks of sketchy sleep, I struggled to remain conscious. Hoping a little physical activity might wake me up, I volunteered to go into the darkened chapel and check on Duke's candle. That's when, in the middle of the center aisle, I paused, feeling an awesome and transcendent presence which I took to be the ancestral ghosts spiriting their way past me to the coffin, coming to welcome Duke, the newly Dead One. "Feel us. Don't try to see us," they soundlessly said. And that's what I did.

Boyd drove us to the burial. First we stopped for flowers and the cold lunch we would eat on the grave. Then our car full of grieving sisters turned sedately into the cemetery, now a city populous with the living.

That's when I first saw the Machvaia nation, saw them in the way I had never imagined, more than two dozen different groups, elegantly dressed and posed with a fine theatrical sense of limb and profile beside the massive gravestones of their family tombs. It didn't occur to me at the time, but I now think that having heard about the headstrong Djuhli who was writing a book, the dramatic staging may have been deliberate. I had been alerted before I left Seattle. Duda had told me to prepare to be impressed.

The Machvaia of Los Angeles, she said, were all "beautiful people, beautiful parties, beautiful times." Never, among Gypsies, would I see "so much blond hair, fair skin, white teeth and smiles, on such pretty people: shoes from Italy, dresses from Paris, the best singing and dancing."

Machvaia tend to intuit worth by first impression. They recognize good luck by the evidence of happiness, glamour, beauty, wealth and charisma. But, that day, I looked tragic. I knew I did: all the mirrors had been covered in the house, but I had seen the damage at the store when we went shopping.

Two weeks of losing sleep and weeping with the mourners had left my face blotchy red, my eyes discolored and swollen. For years I had fantasized meeting all these people, fantasized a regal appearance and an empathetic welcome. But when my moment of truth arrived, I would have given anything to vanish.

After the picnic, I hid in the back seat of the car with Boba, the grieving mother of the Dead One. Curious about Stevo's Djuhli, Stevo's paternal aunt came over to greet me. She sailed into my blurred field of vision like a cheery mirage and tried to start a conversation. But the circuits in my brain had come unplugged and I stared at her dumbly. The exhausted bride of Frankenstein could neither think nor speak.

IN THOSE DAYS, Motel 6 really was only six dollars a night. I splurged on the recovery of two days and nights of undisturbed sleep and technicolor dreams—oh, how the Gypsies filled my dreams!

Then I was back on the road, drifting from household to household, wherever I was tolerated. A month after the burial, I was staying with Katy's cousin Suzi in Van Nuys. Suzi lived on her

Lola's daughters fishing below the Golden Gate Bridge.
"We didn't catch anything."

Lola and Carol—1968.
(photos by Margaret Hollenbach)

Baby daughter Zoni calls from NY threatening to leave her husband.

Even sad, Lola danced.

Fortune telling: "a gift from The God—so we would have *something.*"

Rose in front of
Barbara Miller's *ofisa*.

The Lee and Todorovich wedding in the 1920's
Lola's husband Bahto is second from the left.

Katy's Market storefront, with a Peter Max "Spiritual
Reader" sign, housed a family of six in 1972.

Katy's joyful, successful *slava*.

Fatima's *pomana* in 2007—offerings for the Dead One.

Goodtime Miller at Katy's *slava*, 1979.

Miller's *pomana*, 2003. Brother Boyd "took the suit" and painted the picture of young Miller.

Boyd and Fatima at home in East Los Angeles, 1998.

Welcoming Zoni to San Francisco with drinks, jokes and gossip, 1972.

Lola's daughters: Boba, Pretty Bobby, Katy, 1981.
A day in Old Mill Park.

Carol the *Djuhli* (American woman).
(photo by Joyce Crews)

Lola's great-grandchildren smile for the camera.

own in a stucco bungalow and, to keep her lifestyle hidden—in those days, a Machvanka living alone was reason enough for ostracizing her entire extended family—she couldn't advertise or give readings. This left her with the novelty of leisure time.

Weekdays, while her son attended grade school, we danced, played records, shopped and talked. I had heard similar stories before, but listened with sympathy to the horror of her two marriages, incident upon incident, the lies, the fights, the trips to the hospital.

Suzi's lover dropped by several evenings a week. He wasn't pleased to find me there: "Don't look at me too hard," he begged. "I don't want you to remember who I am." I was perfectly agreeable. "OK. I've forgotten your face already."

One evening, the pair was louder than usual and woke me up. The sounds they made, like happy children chasing and playing, triggered the memories of what I had run away from, and what I was determined to forget. The following morning, on my way to the supermarket for groceries, I found myself heading north for Seattle.

I NEVER ASKED STEVO'S permission to extend my work to California where stories of reputation are critical. I just saved a little money and left.

Stevo refused to comment on my escapes to California or how, as the only outsider, I made him the focus of further gossip as the word went around the room: "Who is she?" The frequent answer, of course, was "Stevo's Djuhli." Clearly generous and even-handed, he never faltered from a proud sense of Gypsy justice. He didn't question my passion to meet his people or try to discourage me from learning all I could about them. He said life is short and style important. "You do what you must."

I had very little first-hand experience of the world as a dangerous place. But the primary job of the Machvano is protection, and Stevo did what he could. He trained me for defense by lecturing me on topics like the advisability of locking my apartment door and checking to see if the stove was off. He taught me to be a safe and considerate driver.

By the rule of his people, the female is the provider, providing children, service and money, all impossible roles for me. Except for my three years of teaching, I was practically untried at earning an income. Fieldwork headed my list of expenses. I would work, save and then travel. Our mutual shortcomings required that we be unfailingly tolerant of each other. Stevo gave me freedom because he had no other choice. I gave him freedom for the same reason.

SEATTLE WAS KALDERASH TERRITORY and the Machvaia, being few in number, lacked clout and security. Nearly all their important social events, including politics and courts, required travel to California.

As her children grew older and some of the Seattle Kalderasha began to hint at future weddings, I heard Duda say, "We have to get out of here. Sabrina might run away with one of *them*." As it turned out, each of the Machvaia families in Seattle eventually returned to California and to the kinsmen who possessed the same knack for generous good times.

Exasperated with Ephram's playing around, his brothers began to pressure Katy to take him back. Secretly and reluctantly ("because then I'll be all alone") Lola arranged for Katy's marriage to a California Machvano.

Miller was the Seattle family "boss," but Katy didn't ask his advice. Instead, Lola arranged the marriage and received the fifteen-hundred-dollar bride price. Katy's new husband came to get her and, by the time Miller heard the news, Katy was already in Oakland. When I called, she was cooking stuffed green peppers.

Stevo and I never discussed the possibility of his moving to California. Perhaps it was Tutsi who lit the match. This time, returning from Suzi's in Los Angeles, I learned that Stevo hadn't been hanging around the way he usually did, picking up tidbits of news about my whereabouts from my sisters. I had to call Katy in Oakland. When I asked about Stevo, she apologized, "I'm sorry to tell you. I heard he's here, in San Francisco."

BACK AGAIN IN SEATTLE, my sisters helped me get a summer job supervising Work Training employment counselors. Five months later, I had saved enough to make another trek to California.

Katy, whom I now considered a good friend, invited me to Oakland where she lived with her new husband King. A bit overwhelmed by her new situation, she complained she hadn't been around "my people," as she called them, since adolescence and was having difficulty matching names to faces. Even worse, like a very young girl with little status, whenever anyone asked who she was, she had to prove her legitimacy as a Machvanka in the most humiliating manner, by referring to her famous parents, Lola and Bahto, and sometimes to her long-dead grandparents on both sides.

Katy was obviously glad to see me. Within an hour after I arrived, she was showing me around her yard, the fruit trees and flowers, calla lilies and tiny nodding lilies of the valley. I stayed for months in her roomy two-story house, and through the leisurely days, patterned my schedule to hers. We shared our innermost thoughts and feelings and keened into the texture of each passing moment.

In the twenty-first century, there is little time for gossip, parties or for traveling. Festive occasions with hundreds in attendance and three-day weddings are few. There is less keeping up with the Gypsy Joneses and more concern with earning a living. But the 1970s and 1980s were easy-money time and the heyday of the public ritual life for the very sociable Machvaia. Community events were what we lived for. We were either shopping and getting ready for a party or reviewing the last one attended.

I was relieved that King seemed pleased to have me around, and no less willing than Katy to ignore the rules and sponsor me at local events as the lone Djuhli. We went to all the Bay Area parties and were always on the lookout for cheap, wide material that could be made into the dresses that were constantly being worked up at the dressmaker's. We knew our appearance upon arrival would be thoroughly critiqued. King and the boys were no less vain, fussing over their hairdos, shoes, matching accessories and the overall effect they had.

Whenever I was sick or out of town and missed an event, I experienced a wistful sense of waste and letdown. I construed history as a series of unique and irreplaceable moments, *these* particular people at *this* particular place and time. I loved the *vitchera*, the pre-party night before, the anticipation, the build-up of excitement and, the next day, the carefully orchestrated costuming and make-up, and then the sense of destiny as we arrived.

Entering the hall, I would pause to check out the seating and, as a security measure, address myself courteously to the most reputable and elderly women present. I was aware that, as a Djuhli (an American woman) I represented the accumulated tragedies of the past and the inequities of a Gypsy's life in America. Against this, I counterposed my admiration and affection for the people I greeted. Being the fortune tellers of renown, the great Machvanki sensed my sentiments and responded in kind.

I tried to look agreeably lucky, a role I would play again and again. Whenever my reception seemed somewhat tentative, Katy came to my defense, quickly announcing that I had baptized several of her children (although I hadn't). Godparents must be treated with exemplary respect in the Roma world.

KATY HAD BROUGHT TWO of her children to California: Julie, twelve, and Jelly John, ten. King's daughter and son were a year or two older.

To Gypsies, matching is important: matching powers, making things even, keeping like with like. But, as it turned out, the two boys were of vastly different temperaments. King's son, the street smart Fonzie, went to school in a tough urban neighborhood, while Katy's Jelly was still his mother's dimpled stay-at-home darling. But the girls got along beautifully. One reason was the sweet and generous nature of King's daughter. Since her mother had run away with a younger Rom a few years back, Big Girl Pinkie had been in charge of the housekeeping and the cooking, and served as the primary caretaker of her younger brother. Without a trace of hesitation or resentment, she had relinquished these roles to her new stepmother. In my opinion, the success of those first years of Katy's marriage to King had a lot to do with Pinkie.

She once told me, with more wisdom than I expected from a girl so young, "I don't want my Dad to be alone when I get married."

WE SELDOM LEFT the house before noon. Katy's toilette required endless hours of preparation. Perhaps because in the past Katy had so seldom had access to a proper bathroom or any reason to meet a deadline, years passed before she was able to expedite the process.

Dinner each day was in the mid-afternoon. King often cooked his specialty, American hamburgers with onion gravy, for our lunch. King said he understood Americans, having worked a good many years as cook and counter man in a fast-food restaurant. Because of the novelty of this type of work from the Gypsy standpoint, the Machvaia gave him a derisive nickname, The Hamburger King.

Bear-like, good-natured King seemed excellent husband material. He indulged his children; he took us shopping, to get food stamps, to cheap movie matinees, to the hardware store where he purchased useful items like drill bits. He never complained when we asked him to drive us for long visits to Katy's California relatives. I figured Katy would never have to worry about King "bopping around" and running away and spending Katy's savings on good times, the way Ephram had so often done. King was too invested in real property.

After Katy insisted he quit his American job, King spent his days converting the double garage on the alley into two tiny apartments, which he immediately rented to Latinos. Delighted with the easy income, the kitchen was remodeled into another rental and King threatened to start on the rest of the house: "We don't really use the sun porch."

King's efforts to pay bills on time and keep a credible credit rating didn't impress Katy, however. She complained, to me and to the world, that King was overly cautious. For one thing, he never ordered drinks all around for the house. The Machvano's role is to spend, the woman's to save so that he can, and Katy, thrifty herself, found King's frugality excessive.

One birthday she had to apologize when he offered to take us to dinner at the nearest McDonald's. She insisted we drive a mile or so farther to the relative luxury of dinner and dessert at Denny's.

Things were not always right between Katy and King. A peace-loving man, he could never find the justification for an argument. Whenever his equanimity threatened, he disappeared into a double-feature movie, returning late, after the family had gone to bed. That left the volatile Katy with yards of wisecracks and sassy rebuttals wound tightly inside her head.

SUMMER CAME AND it was time for Jelly John's Saint-day. Dresses were ordered and matched with accessories, food was bought, guests invited and arrangements made for where they would stay.

We cleaned and washed, replaced some of the furniture, painted the porch and worked outside in the heat. One day, when we were vigorously polishing the large front window glass, Katy paused, laid her rag on the sill, and voiced this belief: "The most important place to be clean is on the inside. What matters most are our thoughts and feelings."

Ritual, and particularly the *slava*, is only effective in an ambiance of fellowship and good feeling. We began the process weeks before, working at harmony with a will, trying every way we could to please and, as the Machvaia put it, "satisfy" one another. As Katy said, "No bad words and no bad thoughts." She seemed particularly solicitous of King.

That July, I learned what a truly effective *slava* was all about: a musical comedy performance, properly orchestrated with music rhythmic and loud, the liquor ample, the changes from singing to dancing and from dancing back to singing, artful and well-paced; the mood inspirational, the company compatible and lovingly-inclined. When intention matches desire, the result can be euphoric. That's what a *slava* is intended to create, euphoria.

At Katy's perfectly realized *slava*, everyone drank, laughed, took turns singing and crying; understood or not, table songs appear to be unbearably sad. When I asked Katy to please translate what the men were singing, she admitted they actually only knew a few of the words and the rest must be Serbian. Then, an introductory phrase in a minor key lifted the company to their feet, and we danced by lines, young and old and in couples, matching eye to eye, beat to beat, no one left out, every effort met with a response.

The music was provided by the family's sizable collection of vinyl records. But the catalyst was the people, family and visitors, fat and thin, light and dark, some pretty and some not. We danced until we were the stars and the chorus, until we were the cities of gold. As the beginning light of dawn shot through the window sheers and onto the carpet, no one wanted to say good-bye, to break the spell, to leave the people they loved and always wanted to be with. It was a successful series of what Machvaia most want to achieve in this life and are heroic about collecting: unforgettable moments.

The people say that no one has a better time than Gypsies. As Lola had once announced years earlier, smiling and pivoting blithely on her new marabou-covered mules, "See! We're the happy-go-lucky Machvaia."

121

"We know the Saint wants to party," Katy had explained. "Like us. So if everything goes perfect—no fights and no long faces— She'll come."

On this particular occasion, the Saint, gladdened by good times and ecstatically entranced, just like us, wrote a special thanks in the *slava* candle wax, a modestly suggestive figure of herself sliding down the candle's side. Katy said that the Saint was probably dancing.

AT KATY'S MARKET storefront in Seattle, I had been much too fastidious to try my hand at telling fortunes. I could hardly imagine gazing intently at the palm of a customer who reeked of stale sweat and sour beer. I couldn't tolerate the humiliating attentions of Myrna, a smirking crazy lady who often slept in alley doorways. She would surprise us, barreling into the store and then screaming the Devil's name in our faces!

My inclination was always to kick her out. But Katy's oldest daughter, who was no great hand at fortunes, had the wit to listen, the patience to transform hate into docility, and she made the old woman a regular customer. Not a paying customer, of course, but Myrna had her uses; she could carry messages and run errands.

The Machvanka has to put up with all that, I thought. Lucky for me, I don't.

But to justify my frequent Saturday visits, to provide some parity for the meals we took together, I learned to beckon the customers in, to line them up and delay them in the front until the fortune teller in the back was ready.

In the north, Katy had a steady and lucrative business. No win the south, as the returning prodigal Machvanka, she was eager to establish her worth. With a little persuasion, she got King to quit his job and help her out. He was somewhat reluctant, owing perhaps to inexperience for the wife who had left him had apparently not been much for telling fortunes. But how could he refuse when the new wife asked no more than what is generally expected? So, he ran ads in the local paper. At Katy's insistence, he reserved her a booth at a weekend fair. And, of course, being unemployed, he was now available to keep her company—"better than being alone," Katy assured me—while she waited for clients.

I LIKED TO LISTEN to the women at their work. Their readings might begin in quite a predictable fashion:

"Make a wish."

"I see for you . . ."

And then shoot off in unlikely directions. I would say that the aura of sincerity is the major message of the Gypsy reader. Machvanki are good listeners. They often give clients who are poorly motivated the impetus to go out and get what they want.

Over the years, I have met all kinds of American people, some with advanced academic degrees who told me in wonder about the Gypsy who had correctly foretold what would happen in their future or what had happened in the past, or had given them inspired advice about how they might solve an unsolvable problem.

Most of the time, the reading relies on what the Machvanki know best, human nature. The women pay attention to their own responses and feelings; they focus on joining minds and hearts. They wonder why Americans don't do this. Understanding oneself and others is the measure of Machvaia IQ.

Despite all that listening over the years, whenever Katy or one of her sisters invited me to join them, I had to ask them what to say. Their answers were no help.

According to Katy: "I can't tell you that. You must have your own words."

"Say what you are thinking and listen to the customer," said Pretty Bobbie, Katy's younger sister. "Put your mind with her mind."

"You just say what you feel," is how Zoni, Katy's youngest sister, put it.

If I did that, I thought in a panic, I would tell the client to go home and forget it.

NON-GYPSIES OFTEN QUESTIONED me about fortune telling. Was it a racket or on the level? Morally reprehensible or altruistic? Could the Gypsies really read the future? The answer, of course, is that no one can read the future with certainty. Nevertheless, the willing customer's future is usually read in the following astute fashion: "If you keep giving your boyfriend money, you won't have enough for your car payments, your children or me."

As to the accuracy of Gypsy predictions, the Machvanki mostly talk about the more successful readings. Duda admitted, "Sometimes I'm psychic, sometimes not." Once Katy called to tell me about a client who longed for a baby, but who had been pronounced infertile by her doctors. If the woman gave her a thousand dollars, Katy told her, she would do what she could to help.

The client came back later, pregnant, and asked if Katy could make the baby a girl. "So I said, if I prayed for her and she had a girl, she owed me another thousand. And that's what happened. She just came by to show me the new baby and gave me cash."

The ability to invent a living, even at times a very good living, with little except wit and intuition seems to me (and sometimes to the Machvanka) an astonishing thing. Opening several pocketbooks and dumping dozens of bits of paper and fabric onto her peach satin quilt, Katy once admitted it was "craziness in a crazy world."

Propped on our elbows on her bed, we studiously assessed the value of each piece of jewelry and tucked the piles of change into paper rolls. I asked her how much of her efforts might be considered hanky-panky work and Katy admitted, in her usual direct fashion, "I don't know how I do it. Or why it happens like I say."

Lola had another explanation: "It's a gift from The God to the Machvaia. We're born with it."

For Gypsies, money is the dynamic behind cause and effect, good days and bad; it makes the mystery tangible. Old hands at survival, and often suspected of black magic, they are not averse to exploiting this notion and any mystery for cash. But they themselves believe that success at telling fortunes must be based on something more pragmatic. The possibility that there might be anything truly supernatural involved would scare them to death.

Money, however, is not the only acceptable form of payment. Housework and items in trade are equally welcome. For long-term clients, the Machvanka usually provides friendship and advice in exchange for a regular service or income. Clients of this kind are the women's money in the bank. They can last a lifetime, longer if the client dies and leaves the bulk of her estate to her psychic.

Belief in the success of fortune telling colors the popular gossip. No matter how a family makes a bit of money—selling a house, a daughter, a car, collecting old debts or collecting on insurance—the oldest Machvanka in the house and her facility for telling fortunes is likely to get the credit. The women constantly discuss matters of business: offices, customers, advertising, and, in the best capitalist fashion, charge whatever the market will bear.

ONE TIME WHEN PRETTY BOBBIE was visiting her mother in Seattle, the waitress brought our orders, and Bobbie paid for her meal with words of warm concern. Presenting a business card in exchange for a cup of coffee, Bobbie inquired about the young woman's course work at the University and about her boyfriends. "I see that you are a gentle, good-hearted person and you mean well. You want to be a lawyer? Not enough good people are lawyers. I will pray for you."

Leaving The Husky Café in a haze of good feeling and one client richer, Bobbie, Katy, Duda and I all felt productive and imbued with self-worth. Of course, Bobbie knew a lot about lawyers; she had married into a family with perpetual legal problems. But, considering how remote her world was from universities, and that I had an undergraduate degree in psychology and she did-n't, the absurdity of my situation struck me like a deck of collaps-ing cards. Here I was, trying to observe and understand these peo-ple, and they were reading me as well as they read this waitress—like a book. Or better, since they don't read books.

IN CALIFORNIA, THE INVARIABLE question the Gypsies asked me was whether or not I told fortunes. "You can do it," the women encouraged, the implication being not that I couldn't, but that I'd rather not. "It's easy."

Women I just met assumed I would be good at fortune telling. Strangers offered me the opportunity of a chair in their storefront windows, a corner of their territories, the rule being that I was to split the profits. Lola's granddaughter, the glamorous Sonia, said I had the "right look." Sonia advertised in the *National Enquirer* as the "Original Sheba, from Egypt," and gave readings over the phone. I didn't know what to do with her compliment. I couldn't see how the "right look" had anything to do with her success over the telephone.

Lola was the only Machvanka who never pushed the issue. Hav-ing met my parents, she had correctly surmised they didn't approve of fortune telling.

Of course, my official purpose wasn't to tell fortunes. My inter-est was Machvaia custom and how these people behaved in social groups. But I could neither emulate the women's efforts nor explain what they were doing. Each time they paid my share of the night club or restaurant bill "because you only have a job and not much money," my Whoopee cushion of self-esteem would sigh and deflate.

Besides, there was this stalemate: if I couldn't give advice for money, how could I support Stevo in his accustomed lifestyle no matter how inelegant it might be? What would we do for income when Tutsi was chasing us from city to city? How would we manage to run away?

On the other hand—my mind kept doing these mental push-ups—I occasionally gave lectures on the topic of Gypsies and had a certain responsibility to my students. What if one answered a Psychic Reader ad and discovered that their teacher, the advocate of the rational, had taken to practicing the occult?

I HAD ARRIVED IN THE BAY AREA without a job prospect, but with every intention of remaining. Katy welcomed me warmly with the usual meals and entertainment and acted as if my arrival was her felicitous luck. As is customary among the people when a new woman visits, she generously offered me the chance to tell fortunes.

Katy's family often slept through the morning. But the day of the Fremont Fair they woke up early. All the children were going, including Katy's stepdaughter, Pinkie. Pinkie had explained to me privately that she really wanted to become a Beverly Hills real estate agent; "I'd know how to do that. I could sell houses to the stars." In the meantime, on her way to more glamorous employment, this would be her first time out, her first attempt at fortunes.

When she confessed some anxiety about advising older women, I considered the odds. Pinkie had inherited the gift. But I had the advantage of two relevant degrees and a compendium of life experiences. I was also a bit concerned that as a non-paying guest I might put a strain on the family's hospitality. The timing seemed right for me to take the plunge, and Katy's logic was unassailable. Annoyed by my continuing questions, she had already explained; "You won't know how until you do it."

The morning was cloudless and not too warm. During the long drive, Pinkie and I sat hip to hip in the back for the comfort of contact. Big Girl Pinkie tossed her long black curls and handed me half of her sticky Danish along with a damp paper napkin. Then she managed to buoy up my flagging courage with this remark: "We can do it because we're going to do it together."

When King arrived, he steered the car into a likely spot near the entrance, then took command, hauling out the two un-ironed bed sheets that separated our space into three topless booths. He unpacked pillows for the kitchen chairs. He nailed up a sign scrawled with marking pen on a torn piece of cardboard, *Mother Mary, Spiritual Reader.*

He turned on the portable radio and began to wave and shake hands and invite the passersby to pause. "This is your lucky day, good people of Fremont. Today we have *three* Mother Marys, and one of them is from far away."

The more we snickered at King, the more outrageously he behaved. People stopped to watch him and check us out. As I led a young man to the other side of the sheet, Katy whispered a final bit of advice about not thinking too much, a warning that might well have put me out of commission if I hadn't already been deaf and numb with panic.

By noon, the steady flow of clients kept my misgivings from spreading to epidemic. None of our clients, as it turned out, were older women or, for that matter older men. They were mostly Latino; all of them were young, although not as young as Pinkie. "How do you tell fortunes?" my second Jose asked me.

"I see pictures in the air around you." Immediately, what I said was true.

So, I learned, fortune telling was mostly guessing. Sometimes it seemed like inspired guessing. Even I, the unbelieving novice, apparently guessed a two-digit number correctly. "That's it," my customer said, so eagerly agreeable that I will never be sure. Like the Machvanki I had overheard, I found myself advocating familiar values to my customers. But mine—regular exercise, loyalty to friends, positive thinking—were different than theirs.

When I ran out of inspiration, I resorted to an old Machvaia standby. "Your family is still in Mexico? Here, take this little charm. It will keep the loneliness away."

How to explain exactly what I did. Intuition, ESP, psi are words some of the younger, hipper women use. Normally, however, the Machvanki make no distinction between extrasensory perception and ordinary thought, between intuiting what to say and saying whatever comes to mind. Learning is by emulation and doing, not by prescription. The women do what they must.

"I did it," Pinkie sighed in relief, spraying us both with heady spurts of *Miss Dior*, a gift from a client who was short by several dollars. "The Americans believed."

We discovered too late that two of our clients were boyish plainclothes detectives. The events of that day, I was informed, had been observed by telephoto lens. Now permanently filed away in a database somewhere, they are available to the judgment of steely eyes should any of us ever apply for federal or state employment. We had been discovered practicing the infamous black arts, selling advice to those who want a quick five-dollar fix of comfort or inspiration, and who haven't the appreciation or the money for more credentialed help.

On the way to jail to be fingerprinted and photographed, Pinkie and I were a little frightened, but still rather proud to so quickly achieve public enemy status. We were, in fact, not the least bit depressed to be transformed, our first time out, into confirmed practitioners of an ancient profession that, I assured her, may have begun with the oracle at Delphi. We did, of course, regret not having had our hair done professionally, for the mug shot.

But Katy was not amused. "I'm divorcing you! You're no Machvano! Where's our license?" she screamed at King from the police car. When she learned he had no lawyer lined up either, only the closing door and the dispatch of the driver kept her from tearing King into shreds. After the initial outburst, a bout of high blood pressure sent her to bed for a week of sedation during which her voice would hardly rise above a whisper.

I HAD EVERY REASON to believe that Stevo knew I could find him in San Francisco. After all, hadn't Tutsi taught me how to track a prey? Hearing his name mentioned at a party, I moved my chair in closer. A Machvanka called Hrita was complaining that Tutsi's storefront had opened only two blocks from her on Mission. "That's too close. Her children run out in the street and grab my customers."

She must have wanted me to know. She looked me directly in the eye and mentioned Tutsi's general location at the same time that she handed me a doughnut.

I told Katy and King that I was going into the city to look for my own apartment. King's soft voice objected, and he wagged his Grecian Formula head in concerned dismay. "Why do you want to leave us? Why don't you want to stay?"

Katy said nothing, but I saw her glance at my dressy pumps. I think she knew what I had in mind. I never wore high heels except to parties.

I decided to take the bus. But the walk from San Francisco's TransBay Terminal soon cramped my arches, and I wished I had worn a more sensible pair of shoes. At Fourteenth Street, a giant neon hand glowed in a second floor window and, for a moment, I thought I had found my objective. But such a gaudy sign was clearly out of Stevo's price range.

Venturing on, I passed pawn shops, a yardage goods, a Woolworths, a store displaying white bridal gowns and frilly christening dresses and restaurants filled with wonderful tomato, cumin, and coriander smells and Latin music. With each step I became more self-conscious, an over-sized bumpkin with fiery feet. I worried about running into Tutsi. If she found me in her neighborhood, would she pull my hair? The hair on the side of my head which she had pulled in the parking lot has never grown back entirely.

Standing behind the narrow trunk of a palm tree, the only cover available, I pretended to read a newspaper. Gypsies say you must remain entirely calm to become invisible. But really, I felt desperate. A million critical eyes seemed to be watching, aware I was up to no good. If I was spotted, I could imagine Tutsi inventing an emergency that would spirit her family to some remote bunker, without a phone line, from which Stevo would never manage to escape. Unaccustomed to such paranoid thoughts, trying to look every way at once, I stumbled into a low metal mailbox and cut a gash in my knee that required all the loose Bandaids in my shoulder bag to cover. That was enough adventure for the day, I decided, and headed back to the bus station.

Passing a boarded-up, abandoned movie theater, I remembered the first time Stevo and I went to a movie. Because Stevo had said he liked Zero Mostel, I chose the musical, *A Funny Thing Happened on the Way to the Forum.* As we sat in the dark, I could feel his turmoil and excitement and thought it might be sparks from our developing, not yet consummated, relationship. But it was more, as he admitted later: it was the first time he had ever sat so close to a woman not his wife, or even been to a movie with a woman for that matter. He was jumpy, and he kept glancing my way in disbelief. As we left, I asked politely if he had enjoyed the film. He could only stare at me wildly, uncertain, I would imagine, as to how he really felt.

THE NEXT WEEK, BACK in San Francisco, I parked on Valencia and bought a black wig at a wig shop, shoulder length with bangs. In the appropriate follow-your-nose fashion, I found two promising storefronts and, incompletely concealed behind a copy of *Popular Mechanics*, posted myself midway between them. Time seemed to drag to a standstill and my amateur attempts at deception weren't fooling the newsstand operator. "Signorina is perhaps waiting for a friend?" he inquired slyly. With relief, I noticed a young boy who looked a bit like Stevo and followed him at a cautious distance— until he disappeared around a corner. Foiled again.

Reclaiming my car, I drove into an alley on a hill sloping down to Mission. Whenever anyone walked by on the sidewalk, I ducked low behind my steering wheel for cover. Hoping for quick rescue, I prayed hard that Stevo lived nearby and, ending my torment, would soon materialize at the foot of the alley.

And he did!

Just like that, one year older, looking fabulous, he came striding down the street. Snatching off my wig, I jumped out of the car and whispered, "Stevo!" Then more loudly, "Stevo!"

He paused, froze in place, and then, thinking fast, looked around to see whether or not anyone in his family was behind him. Jumping into my car, he ordered me to "Hurry!" After a few bumps and emergency wiggles, my old car lurched in relief onto the street.

Tracking down Stevo was hard on my self-image—I felt like a creep. My surprise appearance seemed to both delight and dismay Stevo, and I wasn't entirely sure he wanted to be discovered. The reasons why became apparent later.

AS SOON AS I COULD, I rented an apartment, one large studio room in the Cow Hollow section of San Francisco, an upscale area six blocks from the Bay.

The building came with high security. With all he had to protect at home, I didn't want Stevo to worry about the neighborhood crime rate. I didn't want to repeat the year of five moves and contend with unannounced visits from Tutsi. To reach my apartment required negotiating two flights of courtyard stairs—one inside, one outside—and three doors, two of which had double locks.

My studio grew into a jungle. In the fashion of the day, plants hung everywhere from the ceiling and crowded in pots on the floor. To celebrate the Mediterranean sky and the color of the nearby Bay, I purchased a pale blue cotton sofa that had been discounted at Sloane's Warehouse. I could stand there, snug and safe at the back window wall, the city sounds muffled by surrounding buildings, and see the tops of the lemon trees in perpetual fruit, growing lush from the yard below.

A new identity was required. The grandeur of our Wagnerian passion had segued into a light romantic comedy of sorts, something like one I had seen years before in Manhattan. At the end of the play, hundreds of crayon-color balloons sailed gaily from the stage into the audience, and floated to the ceiling. Ever sappy and optimistic, I think I was still expecting the equivalent of helium-filled balloons to unexpectedly pop into my life and punctuate an upbeat ending.

Entering into the spirit of my role as paramour, I gradually invested in the wardrobe of seduction—sheer negligees, lots of lace, bought on sale, of course. Stevo never commented on what I wore to the door, and maybe he didn't notice.

As I recall, the play with the gay balloons was made into a movie. But I don't think he saw it. The story went something like this: the heroine wasn't supposed to leave her apartment on any Wednesday, the day her lover was scheduled to visit. But, for us, Stevo and Djuhli, each day of the week was potentially Wednesday.

He gave me little notice. A day or two before coming, he would warn me by one ring of the phone, followed by a hang-up.

My reward for the detective work of finding him proved limited. No more singing together or leisurely days criss-crossing the city in the car. He never took me out. Of course there was considerable comfort in knowing we wouldn't be interrupted. But I was eager to deny my demotion from wife II to mistress. I felt I had been gratuitously dumped somewhere near the back burner, orphaned behind the meat and potatoes. Now I was creme brulée, the optional dessert.

The San Francisco Stevo kept a low profile; he was exceedingly cautious, parking several blocks away for each visit, checking the rear-view mirror to make sure he wasn't followed. It was disconcerting to be told I was required to keep his name completely clear of gossip. He particularly asked me not to mention him to the Gypsies; so, for years, I didn't. There were times I would have welcomed the chance to unload my frustrations into Katy's sympathetic ear. The possibility of complaining directly to him, I am astonished to recall, never even crossed my mind.

This was the time of Stevo's life when everything depended on a blameless reputation. Stevo had six sons to marry off. No Machvano will knowingly give a daughter to a man who isn't "all for family." His primary responsibility as a Machvano, getting each child married and preferably to Machvaia, entailed at a minimum a bride, a bride price and the cost of a wedding.

He didn't want any of his boys to repeat his experience as a bitter indentured groom. He wanted to make good choices, "girls that are smart, pretty, healthy and from good families." Considering his feeling of fatherly obligation, I can imagine what hell it was, sitting in that little "Palm Reading" storefront room, facing so many discontented bachelor sons, all stuck in a state of arrested development. I know that several of them were considered old enough by Machvaia standards to be elected head of their own beginning families.

Over the years, our roles had reversed. Now I gave him the Gypsy news. He, on the other hand, seldom attended Machvaia gatherings. He was saving every cent and said he couldn't afford the expense of social obligations, the suitable clothes, the requisite public generosity. Perhaps, with me on his weekly agenda, he hadn't the interest or the time.

We slowly became estranged because of our associates. He lived among Gypsies I didn't know, the Kalderasha. He didn't complain. But I knew his life wasn't easy. He and Tutsi had negotiated a truce: she told fortunes and he didn't spend their money. The truth was, Tutsi was winning. Perhaps she had already won. Perhaps the battle had always been a matter of luck, good luck like Lola's, or bad luck like that of Stevo's family. You would think no one would consciously choose the latter. But Tutsi always did, in Seattle and San Francisco, perhaps out of spite, perhaps to avoid disappointment.

"Gypsies are born to be poor," she'd spit out, taking a pin to his bubble. "Don't say that," he'd beg, heading for the door and the tavern. "You'll make it happen."

MEAGER AND PRECIOUS, our time together was a Sousa afternoon of tubas, snare drums, silvery clanging cymbals: a victory parade that never failed to wipe the slate clean of defeat.

But my sense of loss when he left, after being so close, pro-pelled me out the door. Grabbing my bag, I would hurry the two blocks to Union Street, where the row of Victorian houses had been transformed into boutiques, high-end restaurants, singles bars and discos. Mingling my leftover sense of celebration with the vacationing tourists, I would stare into the store windows at my familiar reflection, imagining how it would be if Stevo were actu-ally there beside me, his dark head a few inches above mine, his mustache merry and sly at the corners. I always half expected to turn and see him.

I saved up the best of my new experiences to tell him. I wanted to share the élan with which the street juggler balanced and spun his flaming torches. I wanted him to see how, with an ordinary mirror, the velvet-robed magician at The Enchanted Crystal would catch spears of light in the air and broadcast a sea of rainbows through his store. I wanted to share everything, big and little, some things immediately, like the surprise midnight appearance of our old Seattle tavern friend JoJo on my television screen, hale and hearty, promoting Rainier Beer.

I always planned to tell Stevo what he had missed. But when he arrived at my door, the terrible brevity of our meetings and the absolute significance of his presence usually made me forget.

Stevo came over once or twice a week. Collapsing into a chair that heated and vibrated—a gift from a fellow teacher, a cheap black plastic monstrosity, divinely relaxing and truly ugly—he held off any conversation until, as he said, "my head slows down." The transition might take three minutes, it might even take twenty.

"Wait!" he'd say, as if I hadn't waited quite enough. Sometimes he would pace, turn off the music and ask me, of all people, what it was that Tutsi wanted. But he usually arrived in fine humor, clowning at the door, making me laugh, my curly-haired satyr twin-kling after his Djuhli-nymph.

BEST OF ALL, I still had my mission: the Gypsies. My village had gone from just a few Seattle households to a population of at least three thousand.

I began to study my kinship charts, the ones Lola had given me. At the top were lists of the original pioneers, founders of the current Machvaia population. By tracing the descendants, I was following the lines through which kinship is found and various propensities can be determined: kinds of luck, degrees of prestige, reputation stories. So that I could add to them and tell who I was meeting and addressing in my "village," I carried copies in my suitcase and my handbag wherever I went.

Zhurka, Lola's uncle, was first; he came to America late in the nineteenth century. Liking what he saw, he went back to Serbia to sell his property, get his family and tell his friends. The estimable Zurka Adamovich, Lola's uncle, who she described as "smart, dark and quiet," became father of the illustrious Adams lineage in America. After that, over a period of several decades, eight more Serbian Gypsy families arrived. Two kept their original surnames (Uwanovich and Todorovich), two shortened Adamovich to Adams and one, the Williams, immediately adopted the name of the official on Ellis Island who had difficulty spelling Pavlovich; and one family headed by father Elia (sounds like ay-lee'-yah) became the Lees.

In America, three small Kalderash families—Merino, the San Diego Marx and the Los Angeles Stevens—married into the Machvaia group and have, in five generations, become assimilated to the Machvaia way. After a century in America, everyone of Machvaia kind is related to almost everyone else.

When they meet, Machvaia seldom resort to surnames. They will say so-and-so is the child of so-and-so, the grandchild of so-and-so, using first names and sometimes locations. Of course, some of the people have two or three first names (Katy had three) and it helps to know them all. For this reason, whenever I wanted to find out how someone was doing at the hospital, I had to call the immediate family and ask what name the patient was using. I was increasingly dependent on my kinship charts.

IN THE MACHVAIA WORLD, bloodline is destiny. Before he was six, one of Bibi's great-grandchildren taught himself to read by watching Sesame Street on his television. When we went to a restaurant, he read the menu aloud. Great grandmother Bibi beamed; she had never learned to read. The lad's exceptional skill was traced through his father, his father's mother, and back to his great-grandfather, a man reputed to be good at business and "smart."

But deeds, strong thoughts, emotions, everything has the possibility of power, and even a given bloodline inheritance is subject to amelioration. Curses, for example, can have an effect. Good wishes nearly always do. The generous good will that helps achieve the "perfect" party raises the level of luck of all those assembled. The goal of all Machvaia activities is to improve and raise experience in the "upward" and more spiritual direction. Sharing and contagion is the Machvaia way. To avoid contacting bad luck and make sure they rub shoulders with their good luck, the Machvaia have a strong proclivity for ranking. Bad luck people are usually avoided. Low on the Machvaia status rung are those who take the greatest risks, no matter the profit, generally Gypsies of other, unknown kinds. Also not to be trusted, likely to be desperate, are the impoverished Machvaia; better to avoid them altogether. The more compassionate and powerful, however, sometimes give them money.

Households with capable women and secure territories—territories known only to Roma and, possibly, the local American police—rank high; they often receive the descriptor of "rich." These tend to have smaller families, in part because a territory must be shared and a large number of needy kinsmen can dissipate any profit. The owners of lucrative territories are the ones who can sponsor the more sumptuous parties and ritual occasions, the kind that builds up name and reputation. Good and wonderful times full of "unforgettable moments" promote individual and communal good luck. Attributes and abilities like these, when combined with a reputation for ethical behavior, give a number of families high rank; they became a beacon and a challenge for the others to emulate. Everyone wanted to be near them, to share the benefit of their good luck.

In the seventies, every household had a shrine, although the Machvaia had no term for religion, no priests and no church. Instead, Katy's creed was wound into the warp and woof of ordinary days, at the service of purity, gossip and reputation, the judgment of *kris* (court). It was this more than anything else, the pervasiveness of the sacred in every element of life, that separated the Machvaia from the outsider and that defined the Machvaia person.

RITUAL AND BELIEF was my focus, and I went to every Machvaia party event I could. Of course, as luck would have it, I ran into Tutsi.

On a warm Christmas day that didn't need a wrap, we met at a party in a hall on the Avenues. Not knowing what to expect, I escaped into a room behind the bandstand and several women followed to find out who I was. As people began to dance, on the grounds that bad feelings can destroy the chance for communal gladness, Miller suggested that I leave. So I did.

I think I had lost some sympathy for Tutsi, however. Finding her there seemed less significant to me than the sight of two of her daughters, ages four and eight. The other little girls at the party wore pretty, form-fitting American dresses with puff sleeves, and Tutsi's were swathed in the traditional wrap-around skirt and top, likely hand-made, and ridiculously over-sized. In retrospect, I can see what a ridiculous emphasis I put on appearance and what lack of empathy I had for the family's impoverished situation. But, at that moment, my subversive link to Tutsi and humiliated fashion sense caused me pain.

I, TOO, WAS MANAGING on very little money. Without the advantage of friends and colleagues, finding a permanent teaching job in California had proved unlikely, and obtaining a research grant without an academic affiliation even more so. To avoid missing three-day Gypsy rituals and the enjoyment of the people's celebrations, whenever I could I preferred to work part-time.

I became wizardly at inventing job histories and got the impression that some of my employers found my intensely personal manner—the legacy of my quality time with Gypsies—unnerving. When money was scarce, my American girlfriend Sherrie and I hit the 5-to-7 happy hour at trendy bars and filled up on free food samples. When I wasn't working, I survived on whatever savings I had managed and the money I got from my unemployment check.

Lucky for me, the ambiance of peace and love from the Sixties, though a little strained, continued on. I had traded in my Volkswagon and bought one of the cars Stevo had for sale, a durable old Volvo. The doors didn't lock and I often parked it on the street, but nothing—magazines, clothes, suitcases—was ever stolen from it. When it needed repairs, I went to The Organic Mechanic in Mill Valley, a pony-tailed throwback to the previous decade and a mechanical genius who created his own replacement parts. His garage ceiling, like my apartment, was lush and green with plants, and he charitably charged only what the traffic would bear. "How much do you have?" he'd ask with a nobleman's air, settling on what one could give.

In truth, I was living hand-to-mouth like a Gypsy. I worked as a hotel "camera girl," several times as a salesman, a receptionist and a desk clerk, repeating the first job I held at age sixteen, when I worked for my father at the hotel he managed.

On rare occasions, I had the opportunity to give a public lecture on the topic I knew best, the Machvaia. I had the most financial success marketing silk-screened prints and hand-pulled etchings. I split the money with the artists, fifty-fifty, like Gypsies do with their working buddies. Although still a bit shy and never entirely sure of my reception, I learned to cold-call offices in the downtown area of San Francisco.

Pitting improvisational theater against the routine of corporate business, I would pull an etching out of my flat zippered case with a flourish. By this diversionary tactic, I found I could stop typewriters, telephones, even conversations.

I might even start the game of "time out for a little pleasure" that Lola never hesitated to recommend. I was kidded a lot: "You want me to come up and see your etchings? That's a switch!"

Selling etchings without a license, like selling cars or fortunes, could have resulted in my arrest. There were a few traumatic episodes when a building security guard asked for my credentials and my destination, and quickly marched me out the door. But I was usually lucky at selling. When I wasn't, I tried to break the bad luck by enjoying a leisurely lunch at the Pink Poodle Restaurant or the Sheraton-Palace Garden Court.

The times my luck went on extended hold and I grew desperate, I took my cue from Lola. I found a poor and art-deprived client and magnanimously gave away an etching. Giving makes luck. It was largely the coda of luck that fueled my efforts. Tuned into what Stevo had described as the "extra-sympathetic wavelength," I let my intuition tell me where to go and what to do. The days I felt lucky and in sync with the universe, a bounty of gifts careened my way. That's how I got to know the city and its secrets. If my customers had no available cash or the backup of a personal check, I gave them the faith of unlimited credit.

Then, in the late seventies, a series of bomb scares increased building security and I was viewed with more suspicion. Two of my more popular artists moved to Europe. My job no longer provided much in the way of surprises. Clearly, an era was ending.

AT FIRST, WHEN STEVO complained that marriage is the biggest risk a Gypsy takes, I wondered if he could be serious. I had assumed that getting jailed for fortune telling was the biggest risk. But then I recalled that jail hadn't seemed to faze his wife.

When we all lived in Seattle, Tutsi had been arrested for disturbing the peace, and I borrowed money from my sister to bail her out. Although her eyes popped with surprise when she saw me, she didn't seem especially grateful. Her back stiff with annoyance, rocking from one three-inch heel to the other as we signed her release, she looked betrayed when Stevo suggested she thank me.

I worried that Stevo and Tutsi might never find the money for brides and weddings. The boys couldn't have been much financial help; with so many Kalderasha nearby on Mission Street, the used car business had proved unusually competitive. Stevo's job was primarily to please Tutsi, and Tutsi's job was to bring in the money. I shouldn't have been surprised that she managed so well. All it took to transform her from financial failure into a high roller was sufficient motivation.

But the money from fortunes didn't come in as fast as they'd hoped. Confirming the belief that the unmarried tend to run amuck, one of Stevo's sons became notorious for bad behavior. I began again to hear about his exploits.

Stevo's family lived in the Mission, San Francisco's Latin Quarter, and it was there that the problem child Mikey had the naïve audacity to challenge a Latino gang. During the altercation that followed, Mikey's companion was shot in the leg. Because he was older, the Roma court blamed Mikey and, consequently, father Stevo. To clear their name, Stevo was required to settle the damages by paying a fine of several thousand dollars to the injured boy's family. The event was critically discussed by the local gossip network. The people agreed, as usual, that good luck doesn't approve of taking unnecessary risks, and that escape, not challenge, is the preferred Gypsy policy.

Then bachelor Mikey was arrested walking out of a store with a stereo speaker, in plain view. "Is he on drugs?" I asked in dismay.

Stevo admitted he was, but he didn't know what kind. "I kicked him out. I'm afraid he will involve the others." He was dressing, one arm in his shirt, getting more and more upset as he paced across the full seven yards of my cream-colored carpet. "But he doesn't go far. And he doesn't go for good."

Mikey, I remembered, was the son Stevo brought to my basement apartment the critical afternoon that I was at the University and he was leaving hopeful notes of running away on the table, on the bedspread, inside my refrigerator. Vexed by warring emotions, I realized that Mikey was the son we would have taken with us had we run away.

The next I heard, Stevo had driven Mikey to see Leo, praying that his good uncle on his bad side (his father's) could promote an improvement by offering advice and presenting a sterling example. But that didn't work either. Stevo said he had done all that he could do. He kicked Mikey out again.

"Look," I offered in encouragement, trying to cheer him up. "You're lucky. All your children are alive and healthy. And you do have a really big family." But, as the weeks passed, the heavy tread of his feet on my stairs sounded increasingly somber.

AS STEVO'S LIFE WENT out of control, so did mine. Whatever I did, whenever I left the apartment, I obsessed over Stevo, counting the minutes without him, wondering what he was doing and if he might be calling me on the phone.

Psychology had been my undergraduate major. In my Learning Theory classes, we had learned that nothing creates a greater, more lasting response—remember the rat frantically jumping up to push a particular lever?—than the irregular delivery of rewards. First, the rat is rewarded on a regular basis. Then the rat is rewarded only occasionally. First, a strong response is built; then rewards are meted out in an unpredictable fashion. Precisely what was happening to me, I thought. Intermittent conditioning. Stevo was my reward, and he was becoming increasingly intermittent. Desperate for his company, unable to call him, forbidden to share with him the substance of my days, I had no control over the levers of my life and had become a textbook case of conditioned rat running amuck.

Stevo stopped asking for my fidelity. When he left town for an extended period, he would turn away from the door and harshly shock me out of any abiding sense of security: "I can't be here. You do what you must."

The first time he said this, I had no idea what he meant. Then I remembered that the duties of the Machvano husband are comprehensive. He must supervise and protect his wife from the dangers of the outside world. He is responsible for taking care of her urgent sexual needs. Presuming mine would be unmet for an unspecified period, Stevo was gallantly giving me carte blanche to be with other men.

I wanted to reassure him, but that would negate his generosity. I tried instead to sound like the faithless social butterfly he had in mind. This led to a masquerade of sorts. One time, I didn't hear from him for four months, two of which, as I recall, I spent with Lola's relatives in Los Angeles collecting quantities of field notes. When I had returned and he finally called, a bit timorously, I knew he was indirectly asking if I was still available? Hiding all my rage and greedy longing, I staged an identity switch: "Stevo, darling," I sang gaily. "How have you been? What fun to hear from you!"

What we did was skim the happiness off the top and deny the pain of separation beneath it. I wanted nothing so much as to be available whenever he called. Together, we transformed a most unlikely thirteen years into the affair of the century. When things came apart at home and he had difficulty negotiating the time to see me, I reminded myself that in so many ways I was his only success.

"You don't have much of my life," he admitted once, as he tried to relax after a harrowing day. "Only a sample. But, believe me, you get the best part."

STORIES OF REPUTATION last for only two or three generations. I doubted that many of the younger Machvaia have heard about the man who ran the San Francisco Gypsy community in the 1940s, a Rom famous as "the man who went crazy for love."

Miller Uwanovich was known as the most beautiful of all Machvaia men. According to beliefs that still prevail, beauty deserves reward. But Miller's reward proved somewhat mixed. While Bibi, his wife, was telling fortunes in the Fox Theater lobby, Miller fell in love with an usherette, a pretty platinum blonde, and went crazy. Those are the facts of the matter. But, over several decades of gossip, Miller's history expanded into a major Hollywood feature.

The first time I heard this story, I was sitting in Lola's comfortable sunlit kitchen. In her version, the blonde usherette didn't just look like Jean Harlow, she *was* Jean Harlow. Lola's bracelets reflected the red and purple lights off the outdoor wind chime as she explained, her voice slowing to match the moment's drama:

"He went crazy for love. When Harlow died, which she did very young, Miller went crazy. Love too much and that's what happens." As evidence, Lola recited a list of those she had known who went crazy for love, most of whom died tragically.

Was she trying to warn me, I wondered?

Pouring us more coffee, she noticed the trail of my thoughts and how Miller's story had depressed me. Wanting to put it right, she patted my cheek briskly and coaxed, "You mustn't feel sorry. Miller got exactly what his heart wanted at the moment. You know that is even better than a long, day-to-day kind of life."

Twelve years later, seated at another dinette table, I heard Miller's story again. This later version was told me by the woman who should know, Bibi, Miller's Machvanka widow, now in her late eighties and renowned far and wide as Barvali Babé (sounds like Bah-bay), the Queen of San Francisco. (I call her Bibi, Auntie, a term of respect.)

With as little emotion as if she were totting up a grocery list, Bibi described how she had fallen to her knees and begged the usherette to give her husband back because he already had four little children—this part I could well imagine. "I told her how they needed their father."

Perhaps the coup de grâce for the usherette was the news that Miller had never worked a day in his life, that the car and the money he flashed around belonged to his wife, details he most likely failed to mention.

But love, gained or lost, can easily become a loose cannon. When the usherette charitably returned Miller to his family, he lost his luck. Depreciating into damaged goods, he went crazy.

"Really crazy?" I asked, feeling an immediate emotional connection with the man who went crazy for love. "Yes," Bibi stated positively, her neatly waved head nodding the force of a crisp, angry agreement. After several years of confinement, he died in the "the crazy house," she said.

Bibi married again, but only, she says, at her mother's insistence. Her second marriage was unhappy. Miller, Bibi confesses, had been the one she wanted. To keep him hers forever, she has built an imposing granite tomb in the Machvaia section of a Sacramento cemetery where, when the time comes, she will be buried next to Miller.

Machvaia are always bad-mouthing each other as "crazy." Anything or anyone unusual (including me, I realized), easily fall into that infamous category. Remembering that in the Forties, the grief-stricken and eccentric were often and routinely institutionalized, I questioned Bibi further. How did she know he was really insane? How could she tell his problems weren't temporary?

Imperious Bibi went on the offensive, steering the conversation to the time when she and Miller had been an effective team. At her husband's insistence, she took lessons in the proper dinner settings and employment of silver and crystal tableware. "We had maids, a big house. We entertained the District Attorney, the Mayor, the Chief of Police."

During that happy time, Bibi had prudently started her collection of expensive jewelry, a collection that had glamorized California social events for decades, raising their ante, and helped make

Bibi the most famous of all the Machvanki living. As was often typical during our interviews, she never really answered my question.

Gossip, on the other hand, attributed Miller's tragedy to excess: too much of the high life, too much money, too much time spent with Americans and not enough with Gypsies. But that struck me as poor rationale as well. Given that good luck so often involves parties and the happiness of good times, when do such benefits lead to disaster? Bibi's unsatisfactory answer? "It depends."

But I persisted. "Did he have too much time on his hands?"

Gentleman-of-leisure is the Machvaia male ideal, and Bibi indicated that too much free time was out of the question. An imperious frown cross-hatched between the lens of Bibi's wire rim glasses and, in a last-ditch effort to break through my wall of incomprehension, she returned from the bedroom with a massive studio portrait in a lead crystal frame. The profile, forehead, nose, lips were strikingly like Rudolph Valentino's, and I knew then that Lola had not exaggerated. Miller was, indeed, beautiful. A matinee idol.

Beauty implies the luck of great expectations and, as the natural result, great envy. The Machvaia like to believe they are all the same, a simple people, ordinary, *prosto*—a word prominent in the ancient eulogy on behalf of the Dead One. But Miller, an only son, was anything but ordinary. While still in his teens, he was already light years ahead of his time. When most of the men were still wearing the sloppy old-fashioned Serbian pants their women had sewed by hand, he didn't mind prancing into camp in his polo hat, polished riding boots, tailor-made tight-fitting pants, an elegant silver-capped riding crop at his side. After describing his elegant entry, Lola hastened to explain that as the new daughter-in-law, she had, of course, been anxious to make a fine impression on Bahto's family. Nevertheless, she couldn't help clustering around Miller's horse with the other young girls in order to see the rider better.

I know, from talking with her daughters, that Big Bibi was once a quite naïve and simple girl. It was marrying Miller that inspired her style—smart chic—and, as Lola tells it, "like the American movie star, Joan Crawford." It was probably Miller's defection that had turned her into the only Machvaia woman "boss," tough and undisputed, capable of running a city and keeping all the other fortune tellers out. Her reign ended in the late 1960s when she tried to extend her influence to Los Angeles and got sent to jail for bribery. Jail invariably shoots down status and respect, and it took Bibi several years to build herself back up.

It wasn't politic, but I had to ask Bibi how she had wound up married to the exotic Miller. She said her father, the parent she obviously preferred to her mother, had made the necessary arrangements. He gave her to Miller's family because, as her father put it, he was a fool for beauty.

Of course. So, I thought, am I.

LOLA EXPLAINED GOING CRAZY for love as a relatively recent development. "Before coming to America," Lola had said, pausing to raise her arms and secure the saucy curls of her ringlet fall, "We didn't know what love meant. So we didn't miss it."

Initially, before the people got the hang of it, the onset of what they called "the American disease," which involved personal choice, proved disastrous. In Lola's younger days, there were suicides, murders, even bizarre supernatural punishments. But to those who live in the feeling mode—and feeling is the genius of the Machvaia—going crazy for love was an intriguing prospect, one that was destined in some way, I expect, to become immensely popular.

ON THE LAST DAY of a three-day wedding, the bride returns home to bid farewell to her family, surely a melancholy few hours when the people were traveling and a dearly beloved daughter might never be seen again. Signaling her change of status and the sexual consummation of the night before, she wears her hair braided, studded with gold coins and bound by the head scarf of the married woman.

To show she is willing and knows what a woman should do, she waits on the assembled guests. Relatives and friends remark on her appearance and critically assess her deportment. Eyes mist. Wailing love songs rise and fall. Those who had no say regarding whom they married suck on the ice in their drinks and grow tearily pensive. As the ardor of lost loves smolders in the shadows, they sigh and remember the person they had desired and wanted—called *kamav* in Romani—but whom they never got to be with or marry.

In keeping with the orthodoxy of decision by elders, none of Lola's daughters married for love, although Keka had the good luck to fall into a spin, nearly fainting, at the first glimpse of her prospective husband Duiyo, the look-alike, it was said, for David Niven. Bandji had wanted a Machvano who was drafted into the Army, but Father Bahto refused to give her to a man with so little control over his future. To the mature Machvanki of my generation, tragedy is not love unrequited. Tragedy would be to have never found the one your eyes wanted, your heart yearned for, someone to remember.

Of course, today's young people don't tolerate this. When they find what they want, they figure out some way to get it. They run away to America for a time until they get the craziness out of their system, or until their parents accept and formalize their shame. Young girls were once, as Lola described them, "pretty stupid." But now, perhaps owing to movies, television and an increased association with outsiders, they are more American, more worldly and independent. Now, brides insist, sooner not later, on having their own living quarters and place of business. Several decades of run-aways and broken marriages and vendettas over child custody has altered public opinion and custom, increasing the tolerance for "going crazy for love." The extended family still provides advice, money and other kinds of back up. But the success of the individual family unit takes center stage.

But in the Sixties and Seventies, the arranged Gypsy marriages I saw hardly seemed idyllic, although perhaps not any better or worse than many American marriages. While visiting Lola in Seattle, I overheard emergency calls from nearly all her daughters, phoning to complain about intolerable living conditions. The calls that upset her most were from Baby Daughter in New York. Zoni called for years about imminent nervous breakdowns. "He doesn't do anything. Doesn't sell cars. He takes my money and leaves me alone."

One time, Zoni sounded really serious and Lola said, "She's going to do it." Then she stopped, appalled. "Oh, God. They'll stay with me. Zoni and all those children. The little boy cries all the time."

Lola called her back, hollering: "You leave the boys. You bring the baby and get your girl back from your mother-in-law." Her heels clicked with excitement on the kitchen tiles as she jumped from one foot to the other. "You won't come. I know you won't. You remember last time? Miller [Zoni's brother, named after his famous uncle Miller Uwanovich] sent you money for the plane and you didn't come." Lola laughed, and pointed to the receiver. "She's laughing. You see? She knows I'm right." Hanging up, she continued: "She needs that girl to help with the new baby. But she says she hasn't enough money to bring them all."

"Why would she go back to a husband that beats her?" I wondered.

"She has to. He'll get sick and die without her. Oh, this life is miserable. If there's really a God, why does he let these bad things happen?"

Once, seeing Lola's hurt reaction to the call from New York, her hand wrapping defensively around her mouth, I suggested that Zoni deal with the husband who hit her by taking lessons in karate. The word "karate" changed her mood, and Lola's throaty giggle turned into a roar. This was her reply: "She won't do that. She could do that. But she won't. All my family are dummies. I got rid of one of them though. That man (Bahto)."

BIBI BECAME IRRITATED when I repeatedly asked about first husband Miller; she informed me we were finished with that topic.

Pulling at the sweater that had slipped off her shoulders and, knowing my affection for Lola, she got her revenge by vehemently denying that *she* had ever been a fool for love like her sister-in-law, the bad example. "Lola," she said, "lost all good sense. She went crazy for love."

This was certainly news to me. All those years I had known Lola, nearly a decade, she had never mentioned an episode of foolishness and *dihlimos* (craziness) similar to mine.

"It was Lola's fault," confided Bibi, gruffly. "She was much older than Maneia's husband, Pepe. Maybe forty. Besides, she already had all those children, and he was only starting out with two or three."

They met when Lola was partners with Maneia, telling fortunes and sharing the profits. Pepe was "in and out" several times a day. Lola secretly gave him money, clothes and jewelry, or so Bibi told me.

He became known, like Lola, for the extravagance of his good times. When the people got wind of their shame, they convened a Roma court. As the story went, the defendant Pepe insisted he was innocent: "I didn't take anything. I didn't do anything." With a pang of despair, I realized that the inconstant Pepe had betrayed Lola, that she had wanted him and he didn't stick up for her. Pepe, then, was the missing piece of the puzzle, one motive for Bahto's angry beatings, the spur to Lola's drinking—the reason, perhaps, that Bahto agreed to divorce in an era that didn't believe in divorce.

Pepe. The name triggered the memory of a long ago evening with sheets of rain falling from a leaden Seattle sky. Earlier that day, Lola had called to say one of her daughters had just called her from Los Angeles with the news that a Machvano named Pepe had died that day in a phone booth. "All alone. He was by himself."

Something in her voice made me hurry and finish what I was doing and drive over to see her. After hanging my wet coat over a chair in the kitchen, Lola sat near me on the sofa, our knees barely touching. Gently, she offered me a bit of news that my heart was eager to deny: "When somebody really loves somebody, it always means crying. Pepe *Mulo* [Dead Man]." It was, as she always put it, the understatement of a "little sad moment."

Learning about Lola's *dihlimos* over Pepe encouraged me to dig out my Seattle field notes. I was pleased and gratified to find that turncoat Pepe played no role in Lola's final chapter.

I HAD BEEN TALKING about a trip down the coast to California to meet more Machvaia, and Lola was trying to delay my departure with the enticement of her life story. She called me early, before I had had breakfast, giving orders in her usual inimitable fashion.

I was to drop everything, finish the Gypsy book I was writing "you know, about the old style, what you call the customs" and "before it is too late," sell it quickly to the movies. Lola, of course, planned to play the leading role.

Then, while collecting our breakfast plates from the kitchen table to make room for my tape recorder, she reconsidered and allowed she wouldn't have to have the *starring* role. "I don't have to play myself. Maybe the studio likes Bette Davis for me. She has a lot of practice." Pausing, Lola decided to be fair-minded and, pursing her lips, allowed that if Bette insisted, she wouldn't object.

At one time, Lola was "the first woman in the world," that's how she put it. Now she was unwell and "not as good as I was. A little house near a grocery would provide relief," as she put it, from being always on the go. Now I'd like to be settled forever. Let everybody know where I am. Keep the same telephone number. Get a license and a sign. Not be bothered by the police or complaints from the neighbors. If it's my house, I own it. I don't have to move. If it's mine, I got rights.

"Nobody knows about Gypsies. So this is the story of the world. Nobody ever had so much happiness and so much suffering. I've been all by myself, all the way through. Going to the clubs to forget my troubles and not thinking about buying houses. America is good. America will understand my story. You tell them I could have bought a house before with all that money I made and spent like water. Well, none of it is left. Explain how I'd like to see a little of it back. That's what you should do before I get too old, tell the people what I need and where to send the money."

I turned on the tape recorder. The urgent tone of her voice told me she was ready to begin.

"I was the favorite. I was the youngest girl. My parents cared for me very much. We didn't have cars. I don't remember that anybody had cars. It was mostly walking. Yes, I remember lots of walking. Me and all the children. And my mother. Father drove the wagon from a chair in the front, like a Wells Fargo stagecoach. You could say *'Dik Roma po drom!'* Look at the Gypsies on the road!

"We knew how to do it. The horses, one on each side of the pole, pulled the wagon. We had a canvas top and a canvas door in the back. If we got to ride, I remember we had to sit and be very quiet because there was so much inside, the clothes, bags, pillows, baskets. And sometimes, all my sisters and brothers.

"Mother was gifted by God to tell fortunes. She told them in Serbian, Italiano, Polish, Greek, Spanish. Father was good, good-hearted. The people liked them because they didn't make trouble. My parents were good with their neighbors. They loved each other. They always liked parties.

"Father worked hard. He bought horses at auctions and sold them for a little more. He took them to another town and tied them to the biggest tree. We were on the road all day long until evening.

"I was little and pretty. So Mother sent me to the houses to get food and water. The farm people were also good, good-hearted. They felt sorry. We stopped where American people had something to spare.

"That's the time Americans and Gypsies, everyone, had soft hearts. Ask and you got it, whatever was cooking, what anyone was wearing. Now it's like nobody cares. People don't cook, they go to restaurants, they show off, buy too many clothes." She giggled, remembering all the "rags" that were hanging in her closet. "People got modern."

Then, one night "in St. Joe," Lola's father got up to take care of the horses and died, "a heart attack or something. Maybe it was lightning."

That left Lola's mother with a wagon-full of children and no help except her brother Zurka, the original Machvano pioneer in America and the one who had encouraged all the rest. According to Lola, "My mother had lots of offers [to marry again]. But all the men were already married."

When Lola was maybe fifteen, her mother gave her to a Machvaia family that she had known in Serbia. The bridegroom Bahto was at least ten years older than Lola. He was the oldest and smartest son in the family, and his father's favorite. "I didn't really want to marry him [Bahto] in the first place. But he wanted me. I was pretty and fun and I still am. The family was beautiful. I liked my sisters-in-law a lot. I loved Old Seka, his mother."

For six months of the year, Lola's in-laws split into two groups. Bahto's brothers, Pero, Blažo and Prahli, their parents and the children, stayed in Colorado through the winter with the wagons and horses, while Bahto and the daughters-in-law, including Lola, traveled by train, telling fortunes, through the south.

But, even regrouped in summer, life was pretty hard. Nevertheless, Lola said, there were compensations. For one, "almost everything was trade or free. You just put the horse in the field and let him eat." For another, "If someone got sick, we put him in bed and gave him a little brandy. No one had colds. Isn't that strange? The children ran loose. They were never any trouble. Not like now.

"Wherever we were, as long as we got along with the people who lived there, we stayed. What's the good of moving for no reason? But sometimes people wanted us away. The money stopped coming. There wasn't enough to eat. We had to move.

"Now I'll tell you about the tents, striped or plain, with fringe and scallops. Bright colors and big as this room. The tent and the rug that was all flowers, the Wilton went on the running board—when we got a car, that is.

"Ahhh! The summer tent was different. We call that a *pelogo*. My favorite. I made it myself. Silk chiffon, pleated sides, no floor, no door. One side fastened to the car and the other was stretched out with poles. The *pelogo* is for letting in the breeze and keeping out the bugs. You can see my bed is like a *pelogo*," she said of her white, Midsummer Night's Dream four-poster, with lace canopy, chiffon drapes and paper flowers.

In their youth, Lola and Bahto went to Hawaii with several other families. At first, Lola and her sister-in-law ran a prosperous storefront and did a lot of shopping. But Bahto was always full of entrepreneurial ideas. He created a traveling show of Hawaiian and Gypsy dancers, a show that proved immensely popular and went from island to island.

"He was all-right looking and he was a man ahead of his time. He wanted to live like Americans, inside. He found a big store and we moved in. But I couldn't sleep. I cleaned it again, more soap. I washed the air with incense to clear out the ghosts. I put tapestries around so it didn't look plain, tapestries with The God, the old man with white hair. And maybe Jesus. But not the one that looks like open-heart surgery. I put up tapestries with kings. Some ladies. Dancers. Children. Deer. Lambs like we have at *slava*. Trees. All colors.

"Then I got used to wallpaper and modern things. I looked at the houses in magazines for ideas. I was all the time sewing, fixing, decorating—like today. Everybody liked the house. Everybody came. They were always welcome. I showed the Gypsies how to stay in one place, keep that place up. They see how to do it. That's the way you learn."

The years in Sacramento, Lola said, were the good years. Her girls were growing up. The family had a big store on "J" street. In the back yard, on a wood platform, Bahto installed a big tent. When home, Bahto was usually in the tent.

"It was starting his business that made the big trouble, going to work at nine in the morning. He was the first Gypsy to own a business, a used-car agency. He was like your family, with a business like your brother. He paid for the license, the taxes, the Social Security, which is why I get it now. Work all day, and leave me and the family alone like strangers. I raised my children by myself, I paid for everything. After he finished work, he went to the clubs and to women's apartments, which I wouldn't mind if he didn't come home mad, fighting at four o'clock in the morning and waking us up, hitting me, hitting the children when they tried to stop him.

"He never explained to me about his business. Just kept it to himself. He was all alone; his brothers weren't much for business. He didn't read or write and had to trust Americans to keep the books. That's how he lost the money. Anyway, that's how he said he lost his money.

"He made all the children go to school, even when they didn't want to. That's why they all read and write. But I think they skipped school pretty often.

"Mostly he was jealous because he knew I didn't like him too much. We argued. We argued over the children, we argued about money. When he was drunk, he lost his mind.

"One day, I couldn't stand it anymore. I divorced him, which I knew I shouldn't do because Gypsies don't believe in divorce. I thought to myself, well, I can't do anything good with this man, can I! So I got a divorce because I was legally married: the American way, married. For the taxes, he said, we had to be married.

"The lawyer promised me one hundred thousand dollars. That was half the business. But he [Bahto] got a better lawyer and it was like the money disappeared. They said he lost it, spent it, hid it, something. I don't know. Maybe he bought my lawyer off. He had everything in his name and it looked like all he had left was fifteen thousand. He said I could have that. I said, 'No. You keep it.'"

I watched Lola pace it out, her life story flushed with the effort of recall, pausing for emphasis at the turns—horse and car, car and tent, child and adult—on the floral figured carpet. She obviously preferred favorable press, a good luck story appropriate to the high status of a lucky person, rather than a down-and-out recounting. At the same time, possessing a keen sense of drama, she knew that the only way to write "the story of the world" in all its glory, a story that would automatically translate into the Movie of the Week, required reckoning with the dark side. She tried. The effort alternately knocked her out, put her on the sofa, exhausted and with fingers shielding her eyes from the trauma of memory.

For me, the urgency of the unspoken remained. I could only imagine the desperation that drove her to divorce when, at that time, no one had ever broken the laws of the Machvaia in this fashion. Seeking recourse through an American institution is taboo. For a woman to go to America for justice would have been considered particularly unlucky. Even Katy was astounded: "Did Dei, did Mother Lola do that? Are you sure?"

Lola's divorce may have been too fantastic an event for the Gypsies to comprehend. Or, more likely, the scandal got buried under a bunker of denial and the erasure of time. The fact is, Lola's suit for divorce and the associated shame have disappeared from collective memory.

Before the divorce, Lola repeatedly tried to leave her husband. Once she got as far as the train station, but Bahto's brothers coaxed her back by threatening to keep her children. (At the time, offspring were considered the property of the husband, the patri-line.) Lola said she returned for the sake of her children. "The mother is always for the children."

During this period, Lola began drinking excessively. Understand that it is practically impossible to drink too much from the Machvaia point of view. Drink is associated with happy parties and happy times, and possesses the agreeable qualities of good luck. In fact, excess has a certain cachet among older Gypsies, indicating a sensitive and feeling nature. When the people were traveling *po drom*, drinking was limited by the urgency of daily survival and was, of necessity, episodic. But, Machvaia are no longer nomadic and the man-of-leisure Machvano can be sorely tempted. For many, alcohol has become a health problem; several I know have died young from it.

Lola's "crime" was not her divorce or the amount of her drinking. From the standpoint of reputation, her crime was that she would drink at the local bar with the American outsiders, at the wrong place, with the wrong group. Lola met her lawyer, the one with the promises of a large settlement, in that bar. Some of the people who knew her remember this, particularly her in-laws. She would stay out all night and, to avoid another beating, retire to a motel across the street where she could keep an eye on the storefront. Her children would see her there the next day, sitting in the window, reluctant to come home.

Why did she drink in such an unconventional fashion? According to Katy, her mother was trying to offset marital discord with the remedy of good times. Drink was Lola's escape, if not her salvation.

There were clues that, after the divorce, Lola's life hadn't been all summer tents and parties. The people usually avoid, if not fear, the police. But I noticed that the Seattle police force had a special place in Lola's heart. Passing a pair of patrolmen on the street, her hands usually flew to tighten her hair clips and adjust her belt. As she did when saying good night to the waiters at the Greek Village, her shoes might tap out a few coquettish dance steps.

She admitted that, moving from city to city, she had lived in "dumps," and been required by circumstance to call for protection. Her report of missing jewelry or masked prowlers still brought the men in blue—handsome, clean-shaven and concerned, as she described them the following day—to her door where jokes and cake encouraged them to visit any time for "company and safety."

"I called them and they came," she would giggle.

I BEGAN TO REALIZE that Lola was, in reality, tragically lonely. As she talked, the bid for a house of her own "to be settled forever" became superseded by a desire for company, to find a home with a man who cherished her. In the end, lack of a close male companion was her greatest sorrow.

But the appropriate man was truly hard, if not impossible. Lola was a woman of substantial reputation. Marrying a Rom of another kind would lower her respect, as well as the respect of all her descendants. Marrying an American would wipe it out entirely. In terms of marriage, Lola had no luck. In terms of romance, I like to believe she was a little luckier.

"I got a lot to say that I don't want to think about—too much punishment and misery. There were men who wanted me, Gypsies and Americans both. But I remembered my mother. How each time she married, my brothers spoiled it. My brothers were big, they were jealous and the husbands couldn't stand it.

"So, after all, she was alone. Like me. I didn't marry again because I didn't want to give my children another father.

"After the divorce, I lived everywhere. No rest, always on the go. Pretty Bobbie was home with me as well as Miller, Diane and Zoni. One by one, when they were at the age, they married. Zoni was last. Baby Daughter Zoni. Me and Zoni were visiting Boyd in Louisiana and I had to get back to my business in California. I was gone a few days and then I couldn't find Boyd, Zoni, Erusha, Bandji, any of my children. Six months I was traveling around and asking everywhere. In those days, people got lost too easy.

"Then I was by myself and very sad, in misery because I had hard times. Then Katy called me to help get the bride price for her oldest son. So I moved here. But the daughter-in-law we got keeps running away. So the money we made wasn't lucky.

"That's why I'd like to have a place of my own. So I could be settled forever. Before I die, I want to enjoy my life, which I didn't do too much lately. I'm not too old, maybe fifty," Lola said, though she was closer to seventy. "I want to get married again. I want to make a home because I never had any. I'd like a nice decent honest man to come to me and make a home. I've been by myself too long. It's time to find a little happiness. I used to have lots of company, but not the special one I wanted.

"Shit! I'm full of prunes! What am I saying? It wouldn't work."

"I SHOULD HAVE MARRIED the Greek man. The Greek man was the one I wanted. He was good-looking, rich. He had a restaurant."

Stunned by this unexpected information, my coffee cup froze in mid-air and I kept it there, afraid to move and disturb the confessional flow.

"I went back south. I called him and he said, 'Where are you? I miss you.' He swore on his children's heads he would marry me if I came back. But Miller and Zoni were still home and I thought about how they wouldn't want that."

The pause lasted so long that my cup involuntarily returned to the saucer. The tear on my cheek went unnoticed. "Why do mothers care so much about the children," Lola asked, slumping into her chair.

"I never saw his like. Nobody else. That's why I never married. I could call him now. We could drive to see him in Sacramento. I know where he is. How old? He's maybe fifteen years older than me."

In despair, her arms wrapped around the softness of her printed bosom and she shivered. "He's too old. Maybe he's dead."

THE NEXT DAY, her mood had changed. She called to say that "Americans don't care about the old days. You should write about today. You can tell them no one camps any more. The young people don't even know how to do it. Katy's girl, Sophie, tried it and she didn't know what to do next. So she was miserable when the people in the next tent told her they were Gypsies. And they weren't. But Sophie was ashamed to say anything.

"I can't do that myself any more. Now I like a hot bath with my arthritis. The heating pad. The television. You can write that."

WHENEVER I COULD, Thanksgiving, Christmas and sometimes in the summer, I flew north to Seattle. Lola often had a prophetic dream or two to tell me. One was a dream of Diane, her dead daughter, as *Shei Bari* (Big Girl). In the dream, Diane wore a familiar checkered dress, and her hair was looped up in braids and ribbons. She looked exactly, Lola said, as she had before her marriage. "She was making cookies, probably chocolate chip."

The dream told Lola that Diane's time capsule had gone into reverse. She was returned from wifehood and her family of marriage, "the family that killed her. They didn't get the doctor until it was too late." The dream absolved twenty years of guilt and self-recrimination; "I knew I shouldn't give her there." Relieved, Lola declared, "Now she's my little girl forever."

We were sitting at the table in her kitchen, drinking strong percolated coffee and eating wedges of soft French bread fresh from the oven. When Lola got up to put out a bowl of warm salted nuts, I was alarmed to see that the usual arpeggio of her steps had become more deliberate. A bright red rose pinned over one ear fell loose and bobbed saucily in salute. On impulse, noting the direction of my gaze, she took more roses from her vase and gave me several, "one for you, one for each of your sisters."

As we reviewed the dream about Diane, she watched me with that compelling Gypsy intensity and directness. Then, with a trace of sadness—the glimpsed good-bye—she sighed. "I tried and tried to see her in my dreams. She finally showed up. That means I'll be seeing her soon."

What a silly self-concerned snip I was. I put that remark and its implication immediately out of my mind. I suppose I didn't want to pay attention.

After that, Lola made one more trip south to the Bay Area and stayed several months in Katy's two-story Oakland house. I would have liked her to stay with me, but my apartment was too difficult for her to reach, being fifteen feet across a concrete court, a long flight up a narrow stairway and involving several keys and locks.

Katy and King gave Lola their baby-blue master bedroom, which was next to the upstairs bathroom. At the window fronting the street, Lola sat for hours, people-watching. She was an instant hit with King's children, in part because until she ran out of money, she liked to order the delivery of giant between-meal pizza snacks. Pinkie played all her records for Lola, and Lola enjoyed the coming-and-going commotion.

"It's nice here," she called me to say. "Not too quiet."

Torn between going back to Seattle and moving south to be with us, Lola admitted she would miss Sabrina, Miller's daughter, now twelve years old. To encourage the move, I said I would deliver her weekly groceries and Katy promised to look in on her daily. The three of us drove around Katy's neighborhood. That's what we were doing, apartment hunting, on the day Lola began choking and gasping for air.

I drove fast to the nearest hospital. Because she had left her medical card back in Seattle, we had no option but to sign her in on Katy's. In the Alta Bates Emergency Care Unit, we were questioned now and then by the busy nurses as they ran to help:

"Do you know this woman? She can't remember her name. Her card says forty-eight, but she's obviously older."

Stalling, speaking slowly and thinking fast, Katy feigned ignorance. She said Lola was a neighbor from down the block. She said the rumor was that the woman, whose name she didn't know, tended to become viciously uncooperative and forgetful, whenever she had a heart attack. As payment for our lie that we were unrelated to their patient, the nurses banished us to the lobby.

The wait seemed endless. When Lola's voice finally pierced the wall, Katy and I were considerably cheered by its loud and irritated timbre. "You want a life story and I'm dying! What happened to Florence Nightingale? She probably died from bad treatment in this bed."

That ended the questions. By then, the hospital had so much invested in treatment and tests that payment of any kind was welcomed. When we finally sneaked into her room, we found Lola sitting up, pumped rosy and festively full of oxygen.

Admitting, "I didn't feel this good for years," she joked about the tubes, the bottles, the staff's professional demeanor and how, when asked, she couldn't remember Katy's California name. She made fun of my driving: "You went *sooo* fast. I didn't know you had it in you."

Lola became so capriciously funny that the head nurse, who had seemed starchily unbending, couldn't manage a straight face.

LOLA'S IDEAS ABOUT LIVING and dying were clearly defined and tersely stated. She said that all you have in this life is "to get dressed up, live comfortable and have a good time. You should do that and quit. Without the least trace of self-pity, she added that "people shouldn't be sick for a long time like me. I want to get well and enjoy my life. Or I want to get rid of it."

Did she arrange to get rid of it? A year after that hospital visit, back in her Seattle apartment with the Christmas lights, the day came when Lola didn't answer the phone.

Boyd and Miller immediately flew up from Los Angeles and, together, the brothers found her, fully clothed and wearing her favorite jewelry, lying in state on her summer-tented *pelogo* bed. When she heard about the jewelry, Katy had her suspicions. "What do you think? Maybe *Dei* took sleeping pills? Like Marilyn Monroe?"

Lola died on Halloween, the time that ghosts and goblins are said to be about. But I didn't worry about her timing. I knew that, after the death of Diane, Lola had never been afraid of The Dead. She was confident that the spirit of her Big Girl daughter would provide whatever advocacy she needed with the Spirits on the Other Side.

At Lola's funeral, when the funeral director called to those assembled, "Friends first; then family," Katy insisted on pushing me out into the aisle.

As she pointed out, everyone else was family—nearly all the Machvaia seem, in some way, to be kinsmen. That's how I found myself walking alone up to the coffin. My solitary march felt somehow wrong and grotesque.

Keenly aware that Lola regarded nearly everyone in America—she hadn't the least idea of the sizable number involved—as her friend, I had to ask myself, where were all the others? How about the customers she adored, the busy grocer who took the time to read labels and fine-print cooking directions to her, the taxi driver who drove her places whenever he had a little free time?

Of course, none of the Americans she knew would know she was dead: who would tell them? I had the mad urge to run out onto the street and shout the shocking news: "Say good-bye to Lola, the American Machvanka!"

For Gypsies, the first year after death is a year *po drom*. So I wasn't entirely surprised that the banner stretching above the coffin at the capella wake read "Welcome Lola to Paris France!"

Why not, I thought, for that's where she wanted to go! Then, remembering how she never liked to wait, something funny happened to my eyes. Through a woozy veil of tears, I saw Lola leap nimbly over the coffin edge, wave a cheery good-bye and rush toward the door on her magic Springolater sandals. But she wasn't gone for good. I carry her, always, in my heart.

I studied her so hard and cared for her so much that, like those long-hand notes I scribbled in my car after dropping her off, she has been written into bones of my being.

At the graveside, while the people offered farewell flowers and money or poured a little good time wine on the coffin lid, I could hear Lola's youngest daughter Zoni at some distance, her voice high and strong, singing Lola's favorite wartime song, "There'll Be Bluebirds over the White Cliffs of Dover."

Custom forbids singing and dancing during mourning, but sometimes singing is the only thing to do. Why shouldn't music follow Lola to The Other Side as it had followed her everywhere else: on the car radio as we drove around the city; the radios in her apartments and Sacramento storefronts; the recordings in bars, department stores and elevators; the live music we enjoyed in night clubs; all the way back to the minor-key guitars the men strummed in the campsites of her youth.

LOLA PAID ATTENTION to the dead. Early on, in Seattle, she called with the news that Pero, Bahto's brother, had died.

163

"How could that happen?" she demanded, outraged. She was of the opinion that Pero was too young to die: "He was never sick. Besides, he's younger than him [Bahto]." I had to remind her that she hadn't seen him for a number of years, and that her brother-in-law was then in his late seventies.

Son Miller wasn't planning to attend Pero's funeral in Sacramento or the burial, or, as it turned out, the first two death commemorations. Lola was uneasy about going by herself because "it doesn't look right."

She was also afraid to fly. "I don't understand how the plane gets up," she'd say. But the offense of missing the last good-bye to Pero and the "last chance look" had troubled her.

So, I drove her to the Sea-Tac airport and ushered her into an airport bar for a quickie and she boarded the plane a bit smashed, grabbing the other passengers' arms for comfort. She called me several times later that day from Sacramento. "Just look what is happening! Miller doesn't care. Nobody cares anymore. It's like a nobody chicken that crosses the road and gets hit flat by a car, and it's over."

Lola's last send-off, in 1976, the *pomana* that followed the year of preliminary offerings, had no resemblance whatsoever to that of "a nobody chicken's." The ballroom at the Holiday Inn on Union Square was large, bright as daylight, and decorated in brass and gold. Modern chandeliers, fifteen feet across, ran a festive sky of continuous light across the ceiling. Hundreds of little candles stuck into round loaves of bread glittered the length of the U-shaped table. Everybody came: Gypsies from San Francisco, Oakland, Palo Alto, the Stockton-Sacramento bunch, plus the relatives from Los Angeles. Lola would have approvingly described it as a "turn-out."

We were seated on the sidelines just outside the kitchen, Lola's girls with me on the end next to Zoni. With sweet relief, we sighed and agreed that the evening had come off better than expected. We noted how well it was going. We admired our guests who looked like angels, the men scrubbed and polished in their best suits, the women gleaming in silken prints and fur-trimmed sleeves.

Wanting everything to be perfect, we had spent the afternoon industriously washing and polishing fruit. A luscious variety, including the exotic and out-of-season kinds, were displayed in great colorful heaps running down the table's center. At each guest's place, there were eleven different kinds of dishes, including salads and desserts. To get to the banquet, the guests rode an escalator from the first to the second floor and the direction—up!—was construed as auspicious by those attending. No one got lost: Miller had posted a sign in the lobby, *Feast for the Romanian Queen 7 PM.*

Stevo didn't come. He wanted to, but he couldn't afford to repeat the fiasco in Seattle when we both ate at the same memorial table, and he became a partial (maybe, maybe-not) outcast. He did what he could; he sent two of his older sons instead.

THROUGHOUT THE YEAR of traveling, the Dead One's clothes are believed to require renewal. The relatives must offer handsome and appropriate gifts, and it was Big Bibi, Lola's sister-in-law, who accepted the new "suit," the blouse, jacket, skirt and scarf on the Queen's behalf.

Bibi chose the material, while Miller and Boyd paid to have the suit made. After the ritual cleansing with incense, Bibi went behind a screen and changed into the suit, immaculate and new, pumpkin silk chiffon laced with golden threads. Above the diamonds at her throat, her eyes sparkled like diamonds.

The sight of Old Bibi, full of energy and years, exalted the people. She validated their lives by presenting the example of many life experiences, many descendants, an aptitude for survival as well as the power of wealth.

The eulogy began "Sun, Moon, Listen!" shouted in Romani so the sun and moon might hear through the floors and roof of the building, and pay attention.

The burning of incense sanctified and dedicated the food to the dead, offering it for the consumption of those in this world and the next. But Queen Lola's *pomana* wasn't like some commemorations of the lower-class kind, where the people snatch and run, swallowing a few nervous bites and then filling their take-home boxes as fast as they can with the leftovers, the papayas, melons, candy, roasts, floral arrangements.

Instead, the people lingered at the table in a stately manner, refilling and raising their glasses to address The Dead One. Occasionally, someone called out "Fly up!" in Romani. Or "What we eat here, may Lola eat in Heaven!"

Lola's last *pomana*, appropriately enough, was a happy time: a tribute to a long, good-living life and the final release of her family's mourning. There were no tears and no long faces.

After everyone else had left, Lola's oldest son, the invariably gracious Boyd, moved us into the adjoining room and led us in the singing. We sang "I Left My Heart in San Francisco," slowly at first—we hadn't sung for one year—and then faster and louder, until we were shouting it out with joy and celebration. When we finally paused to catch our breath, Katy, Zoni, and I linked hands and murmured the ancient prayer for a Dead One you have loved:

Open the gate.
Open the road.
Go into the luck.
Go into the sky.
Go into the sun,
not to be cold.
Let the sun touch and warm her.

LATER, I REALIZED THE REASON for such a glamorous turnout. The people heard that the BBC was filming a documentary about American Gypsies and they came, some of them at least, to be featured in the movie.

The original plan had been to record the Saint's celebration of a Kalderasha family. But those Gypsies had reneged or vanished, and, arriving in the Bay Area with his small band of men and equipment, the film director had found himself without the expected subject matter.

The students of American Gypsies are few, and, knowing of my connection to the Machvaia, Anne Sutherland, a fellow anthropologist, asked for my help. When I mentioned that Lola's last death ritual was going to be held only thirty minutes away, the director, David, by now suitably impressed with the mercurial character of his subject, was desperate enough, despite a limited budget, to offer Miller several thousand dollars for the privilege of filming the event. He couldn't help pointing out, however, that in England being immortalized by the BBC does not normally involve a fee.

At that time, bribery—it worked in Serbia and still works, on occasion—was second nature to the people and I didn't want Miller to think I had a vested interest in the outcome. "Miller," I said. "I don't care what you do, because you have to do what's best and right for you. Understand that David is not paying me anything. I only called to see if I might give him your telephone number. The death commemoration has never been photographed, that I know. It's an important decision. I thought you might be interested because of your mother. We both know the affinity she had for Hollywood and how she always longed to be in movies."

In the ensuing silence, I had a momentary vision of Lola framed in the doorway for her grand theatrical entrance, the Gypsy Bette Davis dressed as her favorite movie role, *Jezebel*, tossing her bangs and saucy curls, shrugging bare and fleshy powdered shoulders as she critically assessed the diners who had gathered to attend her one-year commemoration. "Who came?" she demanded. "Who showed they had a heart?"

Negotiations by phone—Miller in San Francisco (Miller had moved to San Francisco immediately after his mother died), David in Oakland, Boyd in Los Angeles—proceeded for several weeks on end. Miller insisted on reviewing every detail. Director David, enduringly patient, always listened and agreed.

At the last minute, however, the offer was declined. Miller said he worried about the camera crew. By then he had a certain regard for David, but the crew was still an unknown quantity. I suspected he was equally concerned about upsetting the implacable host of the Dead.

Not until I saw the brilliance of the room did I feel a keen stab of regret. One of David's chief worries had been that a room without floodlights would provide inadequate illumination for the filming process. But the glowing high-noon Hyatt chandeliers penetrated every corner. How appropriate, I thought, how like the forthrightness of the woman we honored, what suitable wattage for the dazzling invisible Queen.

But the rule is to follow the luck of intuition and no one, not even a Gypsy, can say what a roomful of Gypsies might do or how they might react. Despite the allure of being filmed—even with the presumed cooperation of The Dead Ones—there was no way anyone could have predicted the evening's outcome. The people might have left as soon as the BBC arrived with their cameras. In truth, that might be exactly what they got all dressed up to do.

Miller claimed the main reason for his refusal to allow Lola's memorial to be filmed was the serious respect in which he held his elderly aunt, Bibi. But I wasn't persuaded. Movies were part of Bibi's luck. At the beginning of what she called her "big money luck," Bibi would give readings in the afternoons in the sumptuous Fox Theater lobby. She says they gave her a spot in a gold lamé tent next to the main staircase.

Bibi was a tough old, nothing-more-to-lose woman, who always assured me she was afraid of nothing, and I never had reason to doubt her. I found it difficult to imagine she would have objected to being in a filmed documentary, particularly the one-year *pomana* which is the welcoming end of all mourning and offers a final celebration to The Dead One.

DIRECTOR DAVID WAS STILL desperate for footage. Finally, I gave him Katy's number. Somehow he managed to persuade her that news of her famous chicken *paprikash* had reached the British Isles and the English were anxiously waiting for the recipe.

The BBC crew, three unobtrusive men and their director, arrived at Katy's house about noon. They waited without complaint until Katy finished fussing with her hair, took a deep why-not breath and allowed she was ready.

During the filming, husband King proved to be an incorrigible ham, continually creating a diversion, stepping boldly up to the stove to provide a sing-song counterpoint as Katy cut and sliced, rephrasing her cooking instructions. As he later explained to me, he had felt obliged to grab the only opportunity he was ever likely to get for a screen test. I was amused by the way he kept the better side of his profile toward the camera, and impressed that he managed to avoid looking directly into the lens.

It seemed like second nature to my Gypsy friends to mimic, project, act out and share feelings. In the face of a problem situation, they are quick to assume the right mindset and intuit their way through the plot.

At ritual events, I watched them perform with regal grace and distinction. Given the motive and opportunity, I've seen them act like psychics, salesmen, "no hablo English" foreigners, bank managers, booking agents, doctors, whatever the moment seemed to call for. Maybe it's this highly developed theatrical sense that allows them to identify so handily with celebrities and find a rapport with the actors, musicians and dancers they see onscreen.

This fascination with Hollywood apparently began early in the past century. By the Forties, I am told that movies had tempted young Katy and her younger sister Boba to run away, disgrace their parents and their ancestors and damage their lineage reputation.

Katy candidly assures me that that's what people with ambition did back then. They "ran away to Hollywood and got discovered."

When they were traveling *po drom*, Lola had told me that there had been a special star for each individual: "That's my star," she said once, pointing rather vaguely at the night sky. "Unless it moved."

More recently, the tendency has been to assign everyone to a star of the cinema. Lola, of course, was described as the look-alike for the gutsy, flirtatious Bette Davis. The younger Bibi was known as the Gypsy Joan Crawford with "Joan Crawford hats, fur stoles, suits with football shoulders." Lola so admired her sister-in-law's American look, lifestyle and political clout that she named *two* of her daughters after her.

Tomboy Katy got her name from Katharine Hepburn. The family showed me an oil painting of the younger Pretty Bobbie, pointing out her remarkable resemblance to Yvonne de Carlo. Zoni modeled herself after a young, well-scrubbed Elizabeth Taylor, no makeup except lip gloss. And Stevo Polo wanted me to take notice of his remarkable resemblance to Clark Gable:

"That's what people have told me," he said modestly. Of course, I thought, chagrined, the devilish grin, the sly wink, the swooping, enfolding kisses. He thinks he's playing Gable.

THE MACHVAIA NEEDN'T HAVE worried about being caught on camera and identified as "Gypsies, Tramps, and Thieves," as the popular song went. The documentary, *Face Values*, a film sponsored by Prince Charles that ran in England as a television series, was apparently never released on this side of the Atlantic. Shortly after we finished the final scene, I was hired by Twentieth Century Fox as technical consultant on a movie that was to be "about Gypsies," more or less.

My contract with Fox saved me from full-time social work and a repetitive, deadly filing job. Before I left the city, I piled all the happy plants hanging from my apartment ceiling into a cab, ferried them to the office and, with abundant good wishes, left them on the desks of my fellow caseworkers.

Unlike the BBC documentary, the Twentieth Century Fox movie, eventually titled *Alex and the Gypsy*, involved union-scale actors, dozens of technicians, sound stages, locations, a book and a script. I championed the favorable portrayal of Gypsies, protesting, for example, when, as proof of the marital consummation, the desperate virgin heroine stains a bed sheet with catsup and throws it out the window. The people, I insisted, haven't checked for this kind of evidence for more than fifty years.

What the scriptwriter had in mind was a sexy Gypsy woman. But we were quickly, hotly into his own psychological motivation: "sexy," to him, implied a woman who was helpless, weak and victimized, if not worse.

"That won't do," I countered. "The bride price amount is predicated on practical matters, health more than anything else. The Machvanka must be strong and clever at survival. No family could afford to invest their savings and pin their hopes on a woman who is weak and helpless. The Machvano is her protector in terms of concrete dangers, jail and such. Healthy and smart is alluringly sexy to the Machvano who has better things to do with his life than bail a stupid wife out of jail, or earn the household money himself." I could have saved my breath.

For the wedding, wardrobe had in mind torn and ragged costumes. But pitiful and poor hadn't been my experience. I recommended the scene reflect the people's abiding concern with an elaborate and carefully orchestrated public appearance. As examples of what I had in mind, I borrowed some of Zoni's gowns, and one from Fatima's daughter, to show the wardrobe designer. Ironically, the latter, a Grand Colonial ball gown with panniers, was probably copied from another movie. I assured the disbelieving studio that many Gypsies live in houses and enjoy a comfortable lifestyle. I could tell that the idea of bourgeois Gypsies didn't excite them.

But while we were filming an outdoor scene on Sunset Boulevard, a ragged family, hair uncombed, the children barefoot in the mild winter air, circled aimlessly around the lights. One of the technicians came over to ask me if they were Gypsies. I had invited Srécha, Stevo's aunt who lived nearby, to the shoot, and I could see in her eyes that the answer was yes.

"What kind of Gypsies were they?" I asked her later. Embarrassed, she turned away, changing the subject. "Who knows? Thank God, we don't know them."

Given the people's enthusiasm for *Dynasty*, *Dallas*, Julio Iglesias and Hollywood in general, I thought it would surely be to my credit to be involved in making a movie. I rather hoped I might project a glitsy, glamorous show-biz image. But defending the people I loved, fabricating a story that would appeal to outsiders, satisfying so many points of view, had exhausted me emotionally and left me confused and depressed. I fiercely resolved never to be caught in the middle again.

MY HANDSOME SON FLEW to Los Angeles during the filming. Recently graduated cum laude with a double major, unemployed and sporting a Gable/Stevo mustache, he was in his budding actor phase and wanted to play a bit part as a Gypsy. Knowing a lot about Gypsies, he was convinced he could do that quite well. But the studio was casting short men as Gypsies and told him that, because of his height, he would have to be a Greek. The role of a Greek didn't interest him whatsoever, and he left.

To gain a sense of her role, Genevieve Bujold, the actress playing the Gypsy female lead, asked to meet some Gypsies. *Bujoh*, the word for money bag in the Machvaia dialect, is pronounced much like the French *Bujold*.

The coincidence connoted fortunate outcomes to my friends, and she was offered many good thoughts and Gypsy blessings. Zoni hoped the actress might correct some of the Gypsies' bad press by acknowledging Machvaia as "the best" class of Gypsy and acting Machvanka in the movie.

In preparation for the scene in which she runs away from her wedding, Genevieve requested I take her to a real Gypsy wedding. I wasn't comfortable sponsoring her on my own, however. In fact, I doubted that I could. I called the aristocratic Fatima, Lola's daughter-in-law, for back-up. But she sounded lukewarm to the idea and said she didn't think she would be going, adding she doubted Genevieve would be welcome. So I tried Lola's second daughter, Keka, whose attitude toward protocol was more relaxed. She invited me over to make a plan.

Keka's house, a tiny, cheery oasis of tropical plants and noisy songbirds, sat behind a wall of commercial billboards just a few blocks off a highway; it was easy to find. I knew Keka's husband, who was sweeping the sidewalk, was Stevo's blood relative and lineage mate. He greeted me warmly.

Keka, ample and beaming in a silken caftan, met me at the door. We sank onto twin sofas in the living room, drank coffee and talked about the former boss of Los Angeles, Big George. When I explained I was a writer—I had long ago given up calling myself an anthropologist—they said I should have met him, "the greatest man who ever lived."

George protected his people's territorial rights. He sponsored years of good luck and good living, settling disputes with the local police, and keeping the peace between Gypsies. "Then we had a big house," her arm circled majestically around her postage stamp room, "and no worries. Now George," Keka complained, "is dead and Hollywood is up for grabs."

When their fair-skinned, black-eyed daughter served us chocolate-mint milkshakes, I paid them a heartfelt compliment: "Where will you find a match for such a beauty?" Indeed, they didn't. A few years later this youngest child, their favorite, the girl they called Luluya, ran away to the American lifestyle and never came back.

As the afternoon slipped pleasantly away, Keka and her husband, much better informed than I regarding Hollywood and movies, seemed eager to hear everything about the film and were particularly interested in the male lead. We made a deal. If I agreed to introduce them to Jack Lemmon, Keka and Duiyo would sponsor the actress Genevieve briefly at the wedding.

Most days on the set, I had little to do but watch. Never having had the opportunity to speak with Lemmon, I had little confidence in the proposed arrangement. But it worked out much better than I had hoped or expected. Early on the appointed morning, Jack Lemmon was a joy, the soul of hospitality, graciously shaking the couple's hands in both of his, nodding his approval and holding their gaze with his in the appropriate Machvano fashion.

After a few minutes of convivial rapport, however, I had to hustle them out before the crew arrived. By the producer's order, no one who was actually a Gypsy was allowed on the set!

WE ARRIVED AT THE WEDDING in Genevieve's giant dressing room/mobile home. The Gypsy children ran to announce us. None of the adults, however, seemed particularly impressed.

Genevieve proved a quick study, adopting the low-pitched voice, the arrogant disdain of a Machvanka. When a Rom asked her to dance, she surprised me and gained public credit by modestly refusing. But after the wedding scene had been filmed, the studio sent word that she was to have nothing more to do with Gypsies. The reason given was that Gypsies—were they referring to jokey Keka and the elegant Fatima who had showed up at the wedding after all?—might upset the actress and hex the picture. It didn't matter. Genevieve, it seemed, had no further interest in visiting Gypsies.

When the film was released, the Machvanki admitted they were disappointed to find more lies, which I took to mean the standard Gypsy treatment. But the chief fault, they said, was the questionable subject matter.

The people live in terms of a fervently moral ideal and movies are public events the world can see. This movie was about running away from the Gypsy way of life, which, as no one knows with more poignancy than I, is forbidden. Because it failed to meet the recommended standard of excellence, several of the women I was sitting with, compassionately explained to me as if speaking to the feeble-minded, that the movie should have paid more attention to "right living Machvaia families."

The day my contract with the studio was terminated, I found I no longer existed. Once effusively cordial, my co-workers now looked right through me. The sudden attitude change was hurtful and disconcerting.

The Hollywood episode pointed out what I had begun to suspect. Outsider Americans had become more incomprehensible to me than Gypsies.

I WAS LIVING IN LOS ANGELES with Boba, one of Lola's middle daughters, when I first met Zoni. We had a house full of guests and Zoni, who had just flown in from New York, went from woman to woman, beginning with the eldest. She greeted them by name and gave them the news from the East Coast, most of which related to runaways, an incendiary topic.

While I waited impatiently for my turn, the conversation began to annoy me. For what was I, if not a runaway? Leaving my family in Seattle, I had run away to Gypsies.

Retiring to the far end of the kitchen, I bent in aggravation over Boba's old gas range, industriously stirring a restaurant-size pot of stew. Essence of chili peppers stung my eyes until they watered. Reaching blindly for a tissue, I sneezed and sneezed. When my vision finally cleared, I was stunned to find the women nodding their agreement and smiling at me with approval. A Hapsburg-nosed brunette, draped in pearls that hung past her waist, lifted her coffee cup in congratulations. Blinking in disbelief, I wondered what they might be saying.

Eventually, from what I could hear of disconnected snatches, I realized my value had appreciated considerably, offering them a victory of sorts. The evidence was incontestable. Here I was, voluntary daughter-in-law, Djuhli as Machvanka, cooking and wearing the apron, serving and listening without an argument, consummate proof of the superiority and persuasiveness of the Gypsy way of life.

"Mother and she are close friends," Boba said, to soften this impression and to rescue me from servanthood, glancing my way in dismay. Immediately, Zoni crossed the room and pried my fingers off the spoon. She told me to sit where I would be comfortable, and she would serve me.

Because I had made her mother happy, she owed me everything, she said, pulling a chair alongside mine. She even tried to give me fifty dollars which, embarrassed, I refused. "For years, you took her places," Zoni explained. "Whenever you could. She loves you. So I will too."

My reply was awkward and stilted. It was moments like these, when my words were not so ready or so fine, that I learned how liberating it is to sense what is in your heart and say it, putting words to the music of life without hesitation.

A FEW YEARS LATER, Zoni left her husband in New York and moved to San Francisco. We instantly became best friends. As warm and generous as her mother, and a great success at parties, Zoni knew precisely when to sing, when to dance and when to tell a story.

She was unbeatable at telling fortunes, in part because she listened with a sincere and rapt attention, followed by the gift of compassionate advice. Everyone, Gypsy and not Gypsy, wanted to be near her and share the benefit.

Zoni of the Good Luck, all eyes and curves, was the most beautiful of all the sisters. Her hair, thick and black, was piled high at the crown. Her lashes were unbelievable. I felt I could trust her completely. Among the more hard-pressed Gypsies I have known, the best intentions are occasionally overridden by necessity and unbidden crises. But Zoni was lucky, so lucky that she never acceded to, or seemed to know, hard times.

We found we had more than her mother in common. For one thing, we liked to move. To avoid sitting with the married women and listening to the same news over and over with embellished details, Zoni and I built up our credit for good service.

Joining the younger women in the kitchen, we took pleasure in the cutting and slicing, the communal songs and jokes, the bracing runs from room to room. Sometimes, when our tasks were done, we changed from high heels to flats and hiked around the neighborhood. Zoni is the only Machvanka I ever knew who liked to walk.

Zoni, Katy and I went together to all the Gypsy events. Zoni and I, the two San Francisco bachelorettes, went out on the town now and then.

We usually caught a cab to North Beach, first to a jazz club, on to a disco and then to a late dinner. Almost invariably, someone would appear like Aladdin's genie with the offer to pay the check, a middle-aged businessman, usually, anxious to ask me who Zoni was.

"You say she's an Argentine heiress? Let me show you two the city."

Zoni is the only one of Lola's children to address me as *Peio* (Sister). She was her mother's favorite, Katy's favorite, Miller's favorite. And she became mine.

"THE WEDDING WITH DOGS," Zoni called it. The dogs had seemed a bad omen at the time, disgruntled ghosts can materialize as dogs, according to Gypsy belief. In fact, many of the people said that because of the dogs the marriage couldn't last. They were right. It didn't.

Katy and I were shopping one 1978 afternoon in the East Bay, searching for fabric to make into dresses for the upcoming wedding. I had a particular shade of fabric in mind. The moment I saw the bolt of peach satin, I was captivated by an alternate vision of myself in a slinky bias gown, as stylish, cool and carefree as Holly Golightly pretended to be.

As it turned out, the Gypsy style of the time dictated the final nature of the garment. The bodice, edged with ecru lace, wrapped to the side and tied. Katy's dress was also wraparound, navy chiffon with a white bead trim.

The dressmaker, a Cuban woman with a genius for constructing full-circle skirts from whatever width of material we gave her, had only Machvanki clients and claimed she had so many she couldn't take more. Nevertheless, I was grudgingly accepted as Katy's half-sister. Katy enjoyed relating scandalous stories about just what kind of "half" I was—step, in-law, adopted—which, like so many tales she told, contained about as much truth as fiction.

We made three long trips to the dressmaker's before the dresses were finished. While the woman checked our measurements and heel heights in the bedroom, her husband in the living room, accompanied by the irritating yips of his terrier, would mumble discontentedly at what he took to be intrusion.

Zoni wouldn't say what she was wearing. She dropped tantalizing clues, however. The morning the three of us left for the Las Vegas wedding, we carefully laid out our dresses in their opaque garment bags in the trunk, with Katy's on top. Not until we arrived and had pulled them out and hung the contents in full view on the shower rod did we see Zoni's, a brilliant red organza—short, tiered and daring, a flapper dress from the American Twenties.

Wherever the three of us went, Zoni got all the attention. Rumors about the divorced Machvanka from New York—tall, attractive and good for business—were circulating throughout the West Coast community. The women would cluster around Zoni, pointing out a male relative, a brother, an unmarried uncle for her to consider.

Tired of providing financial support for unattached male relatives, they would remind Zoni of the benefits of marriage and "someone to keep you company." They encouraged her to take a second look and assured her that "a home is what he needs to settle him down." They often asked me why Zoni had left her other family and speculated that she might return. I always told them what I hoped was true: "Ridiculous. Never."

But then, within a year of her arrival in San Francisco, Zoni's former husband called and the three older children went back east to join him. Zoni was reluctant, but she let them go.

"This is America," she said, as she gave them the option of choice. "I hope they know what they want."

After that, the Machvanki no longer asked me about Zoni's availability. Nodding in agreement, they spoke from experience. Believing that "the mother is always for the children," they said Zoni would be obliged to return to her husband.

But Zoni in fire-engine flapper red, confused them. Red is not the color of sorrow. Red is happiness, health, the heat of passion and weddings. Instead of crying, Zoni was laughing. Instead of sitting wide-eyed, abused and forlorn, Zoni was dancing. Hair bobbed and unbound, Zoni danced like a dervish. She danced herself pink and disarmed her detractors.

Armed with the news of the children's defection, the women had been anxious to share their own difficult times. They were harboring and polishing stories about their stupid husbands, defiant daughters and impossible in-laws, and now they looked dismayed. They longed to suspect Zoni of something awful: a visiting lover, a plot to run away. They proposed that she might be having a little "breakdown." But Zoni's good nature proved too appealing. Public opinion acquiesced to her charm. Zoni was declared a "truly lovable" woman, the kind you can't stay mad at.

Zoni was lucky in so many ways. But her best luck, in my opinion, was the magical way she breezed through life, protected by good will.

THE GLAMOROUS THREE-DAY wedding in Las Vegas involved several notable and wealthy families. Many of those invited had rented suites, putting the women in one room, the men in the other. Where I stayed, there were mattresses all over the floor, makeup cases piled on the dressers and insufficient soap in the bathroom. Some brought sitters to watch the children and, in just a few hours, their children ran the Room Service tab up to an astronomical amount. The casino motel was a Disneyworld of entertainment, a self-contained city with stores and restaurants with oversized, eye-popping carnival themes.

Several hundred Gypsies, mostly Machvaia, were gambling and borrowing money from each other. The slot machines, the gaming tables, the music, the bars presented a series of room to room delays.

Taking it all in, good tempered Pinkie, Katy's stepdaughter, lifted her Armani sunglasses off her pretty nose and exclaimed: "Wowee! It's like dying and going to heaven!"

The room reserved for the wedding was at the far end of the casino's main building. There Zoni, Katy and I—visions in red, blue and peach, confident of the effect we were creating and the notice we were getting—danced in the center of the floor.

Katy hadn't seen Zoni for more than twenty years, and she insisted on buying all the drinks. New people, from Kansas City and Florida, had arrived. Anticipation grew when we heard who was coming from Los Angeles. Hollywood John, the Machvano Pavarotti famous for the unstrained quality of his tenor range, was said to be singing by late evening.

Excited guests streamed through the wedding room and out beyond to other enticing venues. When it came time for the ritual of putting on the veil, most of the guests were busy elsewhere. When it was time to offer the bride's gift, half of the men were missing from the table. Relatives left at home were called and urged to come, hurry, that this was undoubtedly the wedding of the century.

Although there was talk of extending the party another two days, by late afternoon of the first day we found ourselves forcibly evicted.

The Hotel was at fault, certainly. But hot-blooded Widow Donna was the instigator. Having remarried only months after her husband's untimely death—Ned was no more than forty—and long before his last death commemoration, she had given Ned's boat and car to Jack, according to gossip. Then, when she should have been in inconspicuous mourning and too wrecked by loss to express feeling for a glad event, Donna showed up at the Las Vegas wedding, large as life, with flaming lipstick, nail-polished toes and pink with love.

She arrived on the arm of Happy Jack, her new husband. (Jack was one of Stevo's older uncles.) Tanned, robust, rumored to be fresh from the prison exercise yard, Jack had either forgotten custom or forsaken its example. Normally, the public demeanor of couples is constrained to indicate respect for Machvaia rules. Instead, Donna and Jack brazenly smooched and cuddled.

"Like a scene from *Days of Our Lives*," I heard someone say.

Under ordinary circumstances the couple's lack of inhibition might only have revealed a regrettable lack of breeding and provided a windfall of gossip that could be eagerly phoned out of state. But Ned's vengeful sisters were just waiting for an opening.

They attacked when Donna went to the bathroom, scratching like wild cats and yanking at her curls. Before we could intervene, hair from Donna's wiglet, and from her head, was strewn across the bathroom tiles and out the door onto the carpeting.

The management called the police, who quickly arrived with giant dogs. The word passed around that we were required to be out of the building immediately, fifteen minutes at the most. We sent scouts to reconnoiter the restaurants, down to the lobbies, back up to the rooms. But hardly anyone was able to round up their family that quickly.

Not all the children, many of whom had found a slot machine away from the traffic and started to win. Not all the disbelieving cousins who hadn't heard the screaming, being involved in a hot game of roulette.

As the only Djuhli in the outlaw party, I tried to remain the calm temperate eye of the storm. But panic, I discovered, is contagious. I don't remember packing my suitcase or collecting my things. What sticks in my memory are the dogs, the menace of dogs as the lobby elevator doors slid open, harnessed and ready, held in check by armed men who refused to look at us directly or to answer any of my questions.

I had never been thrown out of a public place in my life. On the way back home, still dressed in peach satin, a little heady with champagne and disbelief, I wished loudly for some manner of punishing revenge on the hotel and everyone connected with it. The family tried to calm me.

Pinkie asked who I thought was to blame—the police, the fire department or the management? King was driving. He saw both sides of the situation in his usual conciliatory fashion. He said to remember the motel's investment, all that expensive equipment, the fragility of the windows and mirrors, the reputation of Gypsies—largely undeserved, of course—for violence.

Katy, an old hand at eviction, sublimely pointed out that no one other than Donna (who may have deserved it) had been injured. But Zoni knew what to do. She began singing an ancient Machvaia lament about loneliness, loss, separation from family and dying in jail, which spoke to the moment, our fugitive position; a song so absurdly tragic and overwrought that it mellowed me out, and we collapsed, giggling and face down, on the plastic-covered bed pillows.

WHEN ZONI WAS SMALL, Lola would station her double-luck child, all ruffles, batting eyelashes and full of smiles, in the storefront window to entice the customers in. That's where Zoni says she had her first inkling of a revolutionary future, her first baby—thought of escape. She began to realize that the ladies who arrived with the money were better off than the hard-pressed lady in the back. Zoni developed, as her mother had before her, her "own mind." She wanted to adopt America, to come and go as she pleased, to choose her own man, to be her own boss. The Machvaia call these behaviors "going American," "going crazy," "running away."

She attracted good fortune. Once, when she, Katy, and I were on holiday in Tahoe, she began winning on the billboard-size vertical roulette. A crowd excitedly circled around her as she hit three correct numbers in sequence, and she looked so full of money luck that the club rushed to shut the table down. "Can they do that, *Peio* [Sister]?" Zoni asked me in dismay. "Is it against the rules for both of us to concentrate on one number together?"

According to Lola, there was a valid reason for Zoni's exceptional luck. "Zoni," she said, "was born with a double veil wrapping her up." I supposed Lola was referring to the caul. Whatever it was, Lola ought to know, because she delivered all her children without medication and "easy as kittens." Easy births apparently ran in her family. Years before, Lola's older sister had delayed pedestrian traffic on New York's Lexington Avenue when, squatting down on the curb, she casually gave birth to a healthy infant. The news, Lola added, traveled through the community like "gangbusters," causing considerable mirth.

Zoni, the last of her children, was never far from Lola's thoughts. While she waited for a late evening client, Lola would call her New York daughter, adding minutes and dollars to an already formidable phone bill. Sometimes Lola handed me the telephone and ordered, "Talk!"

By the time I met her in person, Sister Zoni even favored a career change. Instead of telling fortunes, she would be a supper club chanteuse and sing in spotlights. She sang very well and, as she pointed out, already had the evening gowns appropriate for spotlight entertainment. Machvaia taboos, however, proscribe working for an American employer, a rule applying to females in particular. In addition, singing, like dancing, belongs exclusively to the people, the God and the Saints. Although the stigma associated with entertaining non-Gypsy Outsiders caused her some trepidation, Zoni rented a house in the Sunset District and was planning to buy a white baby grand piano for her wide-arching Moorish front window and to begin taking lessons.

After her teenage children returned to New York to live with their father, Zoni enrolled her youngest two, Michael and John, ages six and nine, in a nearby private school. With her boys gone all day, she had the opportunity to investigate matters normally forbidden. She learned about places and pleasures her people actively disdain: art museums and galleries, antique and garden stores, road shows. We saw the musical, *The Wiz*, together.

She discovered the wonders of the natural world, flowers, bugs, trees and birds, something the old timers took for granted and the younger generations have no use for. Non-Gypsy men friends invariably perplexed her: "Explain them to me, *Peio*," she'd say.

They liked to walk with her along the nearby beach; at first, walking barefoot through the sand struck her as an infantile waste of time. She told me about a geologist from Israel who she was dating and, afterwards, talked for weeks about geologic ages and the tides. With new experiences came new issues. She was especially curious about topics relating to telling fortunes, religion, extrasensory perception and psychology. "Gestalt, that's about how the answers suddenly fit together when I'm giving a reading?"

She had no one but me with whom to share the excitement of the changes in her life; I had no one but her with whom I could rhapsodize and anguish over Stevo.

For her "babies," as she called them, Michael and John, she wanted American careers. But first they must have time to be young children. I never saw her caution them to stay quiet, be serious, to be men, in keeping with custom and the realities of Gypsy life. Instead, she bought them kites and we took them to the Marina Green where the wind sweeps steadily off the Bay and the weekend sky blazes with flapping wings of color. Laughing, she pushed the boys out of my Volvo. "Go play!" she commanded, slamming the door shut behind them.

After the awkwardness of a few self-conscious minutes, the idea caught on. While we sat in the front seat and talked, the boys, hair in wild disarray, took turns playing out the kite line, jumping, shouting and running all the way.

We discussed living together and sharing the complexities of our Gypsy/American double lives. But how could I entertain Stevo in secret? And what about Miller, her brother, who was responsible to the people for her actions and who, given his political ambitions, couldn't afford the scandal of a runaway chanteuse?

We questioned whether or not being so beloved was worth the cost. Sharing the subversiveness of women, we researched the possibilities and solutions to our quandries. And did nothing about them.

Driving was crucial to Zoni's plans for independence. Duda, Miller's wife, already knew how to drive and offered to teach her. But Duda had several business places to run and too little free time. Zoni bought a car with an automatic shift and spent an incredible amount, thousands of dollars, on driving instruction. When I heard how much, I offered to teach her myself. But we had only gone a block from her house when the car veered sharply toward the center line, and we nearly missed the turn.

"Turn, Zoni!" I screamed. "Wait, Zoni!"

Something was wrong. We blamed the headache medication, not knowing about the tumor.

On the X-ray, the tumor looked rather like a small and insignificant potato.

WE FOUND ZONI'S BURIAL DRESS in the first few minutes of our search at a new boutique on Union Square, an elegant gown of white chiffon with silvery beads. A silver spangled sweater was added for warmth. Sister Katy discovered a matching evening bag under a dozen others less appealing. With housecleaning determination, Boba's grown daughter went through all the drawers near the dressing room and pulled out two chiffon scarves, one to tie back Zoni's hair, and a spare. Pointing out to the astonished sales clerk that "we're buying a lot," Duda and Pretty Bobbie tried to get the price down. They cajoled and underbid; my part was to appear intractable. The shoes were next, then the lingerie, the stockings. Duda, of course, knew all the sizes. She and Zoni had been partners, sharing earnings, business strategies, meal preparation and child care.

And then out onto Market Street and across the trolley tracks, half running and short of breath, six bright silky, slightly overweight butterflies—me, Duda, niece Ava, three of Zoni's sisters—slapping along in our backless pumps and generous yards of skirt. As the sun shot its impersonal blessings from the cloudless sky, our purchases were rapidly concluded. There wasn't time for anyone's shoes to pinch. Harmony builds community and welcomes contact with the sacred, and that day, I can't remember a single difference of opinion or complaint.

"Zoni is making shopping easy," we agreed. Katy summed up the reason: "She was that kind of person." And we piled back into my car.

Carefully, conscious of my chattering load, I pulled into traffic. In accessing the freeway, as we passed beneath the arching cement cloverleaf, I was reminded of the clovers that grew to lanky grass in Zoni's hospital window. Instead of flowers, I had brought Zoni clovers packed in a little square cardboard box, seedlings to nurture and transplant into her garden, the miniature promise of a future and much better time. "Here, Zoni. There's bound to be a four-leaf in here somewhere." But I had been tragically mistaken.

"Romnia," I began tactfully. "Zoni always looks beautiful in white. But, as you know, emerald green is her favorite color. What we buy her next, the little things like her comb, her mirror, let's look for green. Green will please her." No one disagreed. It was that kind of day.

Miller, a short man bursting with command, met us at the mortuary door, eager to show us what the husbands and brothers had accomplished. Obviously proud to have remembered, he tangoed a few steps across the carpet circled with coffins. Pleased with his choice, we tenderly ran our hands over the length of the cool green lacquer surface and agreed this must be the "box" Zoni had in mind, the one she must really want—for the Dead One leaves by degrees and Zoni Dead was still a palpable presence. We shared the stack of Kleenex Ava found in her purse. We agreed we were crying out of pity for ourselves and the loneliness of the days to come.

NOON, THE NEXT DAY at the mortuary. Zoni Dead is lying in her box. We are tucking her in and talking to her. Although she doesn't answer, we know she can hear. We check the incense and the candle to see if they are burning. We wonder, are the lights too warm? Duda pours a fresh glass of water and takes away the breakfast roll. For Zoni's lunch, she leaves a ham sandwich and a freshly opened soda on the table. Ava cleans the ashtrays. I sweep up the autumn leaves that shift and drift and hesitate, before skidding through the open door.

We ask if she is comfortable? We wonder what is wrong? It is not like Zoni to look sad. Even with the pain in her brain, her lips had smiled at us and she had told us stories. Even sick and dying, she had been the Zoni we loved and an undeniable pleasure.

Katy and I huddle over the box to study Zoni's expression. Before she went to the hospital, the three of us, together, had taken offensive action. Twice, we had sallied bravely to the healing remedy of Tahoe where we drank, laughed, gambled and had fun. Now, trying to cheer her up, we remind Zoni of those better times.

"Zoni, you jumped up from the front row to reach Humperdinck's hand and he gave you his handkerchief, remember?"

"Zoni, remember the gambling and the time you won three thousand?"

"Zoni, remember how we danced at the weddings and parties, and the people stood around and clapped?"

"You are coming back, little sister," Katy said. "You don't look happy to go. You'll be back, an American this time. We'll see you someplace. Or someone who looks like you. We'll hear all your gold bracelets tinkling, and you'll be wearing a new green dress. Or," Katy continued, mischievously peering over her harlequin glasses, "red, white and blue if you like that better."

That's when I realized Zoni had shared her plans for a chanteuse future with her sister Katy. Or maybe Katy had guessed.

Now, Zoni was packed and ready for the next leg of her journey, and it must be admitted she still looked depressed. We began by folding her best dress, a flowered sequin, under her feet. We tucked in the green and black that was her favorite. We didn't forget a house dress for everyday, some shoes, her familiar woolen cape for the cold, a comb and cosmetics.

While we were packing, we spoke so she could hear us. We reassured her that some of her more valuable jewelry would be added later, tied into the Chinese dragon jewelry case embroidered with sequins.

When she arrives on the Other Side, these familiar, beautiful and useful objects would remind her of us, and that we love her. While we packed, we spoke to her and about her:

"What was the name of that song Zoni liked?"

"Remember two birthdays ago at the Hyatt Regency when Zoni just got off the plane in San Francisco?"

"Remember the wedding with dogs?"

THE OTHERS BEGAN TO ARRIVE. They came in families, separating into groups of men with men, women with women. Sabrina, Duda's oldest daughter, passed around the dipper of cold drinking water said to ease the thirst of tears; only a Big Girl, unmarried and pubescent, can do this. When the moment felt right, when they were ready, the people approached the box to settle accounts, to ask Zoni's blessing and forgiveness. To ensure she has whatever might be necessary on the Other Side, the people placed the fresh paper money of good wishes on her chest.

"Here, Zoni, a little money for bus fare."

"Zoni, here's five dollars. You might have to bribe the *gendari* (police)."

That night, Duda and I removed and counted the money together, returning it to the box in the morning.

By afternoon, the funeral director was nervously shutting doors, moving the chairs back into rows, clearing his throat. He was obviously distressed by the army of men on the patio, so many teenagers in the parking area, Zoni's room full of women, and the way we stayed and stayed—until he locked the doors.

Then there were the forms to fill out. He asked us if Zoni was married, divorced or separated. Miller, Zoni's take-charge brother, couldn't have been more agreeable. He answered, "Divorced, I guess. Or separated. Or never legally married. Whatever works out best on your papers."

WHEN ZONI'S OTHER FAMILY arrived from New York, a hush fell on the gathering. John and Michael were last, the youngest covering his eyes in terror. There was an anguished commotion at the box when the older children caught sight their mother. Gusha, the mother-in-law, announced she was required to sit down before she fainted. Sailor, the discarded husband, immediately turned to the first row and solicited Valium, demonstrating his need by pathetically clutching his back. Some of the more tender ran toward the two offering comfort. But not me.

Zoni had blamed Gusha for Sailor's drug habit and the terrible example this set for their children. In the hospital, she had refused to see Sailor or his mother. "Never, sick or well," she said. Of course, her sisters and brothers and I respected her wishes.

She was, nevertheless, required to deal with the pleas of her older children who, while Zoni spent her days in New York giving readings, had been raised by Gusha in suburban Yonkers. The teenagers begged Zoni to forgive and forget; in terms of future luck, the forgiveness of the dying is a critical matter. But, to Zoni, forgiveness implied a return to New York and the defeat of life with Sailor, a possibility she refused to sanction.

To defend Zoni, one of us always remained at her side. As long as Zoni was conscious, we held Gusha off. Old Gusha camped in the hallway and hollered at everyone who passed and to anyone who would listen, that Zoni's running away to the West, the divorce, headaches, the tumor, the operations, the catastrophes she was experiencing were all our fault.

LEANING AGAINST ME, little John whispered that the lady in the box didn't look much like his mother. We agreed that perhaps she was not. With a fresh pang of grief I discovered something of Zoni in his small sober up-thrust face. With another pang, I realized that the dreams she had for him—public school, an American childhood, an American career—were now lost forever. But maybe not, if I obeyed my heart and followed the impulse to snatch him up and race with him through the crowd and kidnap him for America!

Seeing the women's eyes upon us, I remembered these are the kind of crises that Gypsies live for. I tried to rise to the dramatic potential of the tragedy, to create an Unforgettable Moment.

A kidnapping would certainly have done it, would have given the moment meaning and direction, set it apart from what Lola called "the day-to-day side of life." I had a sudden, passionate impulse to clasp John to my chest, to waltz him up and down the aisles and between the people, screaming "No!" so he would never forget where and when the fabric of his childhood was torn by his mother's aberrant departure. The possibility of singing crossed my mind—a poignant, heart—wrenching and melancholy ballad, composed on the spot.

I knew my responsibilities. I longed to invent a farewell commensurate with our loss. But I am not nearly as emotionally expressive and musically accomplished as the Gypsies. All I could manage was a feeble, "My dear boy. Always remember the kites."

The events of that afternoon became history. Sailor baited Miller, and I was surprised at Miller's calm. Usually prone to argument, now that everyone was losing theirs, Miller kept his temper. But when Sailor switched his tactics and cursed Duda's father, Duda changed into a Fury, and I had to hold her back from assaulting him. Several of the others ran to fill in the gap between them and, from the benches under the grape arbor, the soft hands of the elders waved their worried, fluttering fingers of reproach.

Angered by the disapproval she sensed, Gusha screamed, "You take care of her then. *You* bury her." Calling her family to the car, they left, spitting gravel behind them.

Like naughty girls conspiring to play a prank, all the sisters ran to tell Zoni. But sister-in-law Fatima placed a restraining hand on my arm. Fishing a loose Lucky Strike out of her jacket pocket, she promised, "They'll be back."

AN HOUR LATER, they had returned and Gusha confronted the elders. Zoni, she claimed, "made thirty thousand in that fine office on York Avenue I bought her." And then, like a thief in the night, "She stole it."

Gusha wanted her money back. She pointed out that as an old, sick widow, she was now responsible for Zoni's five growing children. She needed whatever help she could get, help with the capital expense of getting four boys married, help finding another bride for Sailor—Duda snickered, "As if anyone would have him!"—help making ends meet without the support of Zoni's upper East Side income.

In truth, Zoni couldn't take it with her. So perhaps it was justice. But I was wounded by the sight of all the personal items from Zoni's four handbags heaped for public display on the peeling picnic table near the parking area—all her bankbooks, notebooks, address books, letters, rings, charge cards, her tiny treasures. Some of the rings had missing stones. Gusha picked one up and looked suspiciously at Miller.

Sailor, puzzled, asked about a famous diamond set in platinum that the East Coast Zoni was never seen without. I told him I had no memory of such a ring and described the one that West Coast Zoni always wore, a black onyx oval with a big diamond center. The current estimate of Zoni's handbag valuables was a negligible several thousand dollars. Everyone was busy speculating. Where had all the money gone? I mentioned ten or so thousand for driving schools and private schools for the children. But expenses of such kind made no sense to those assembled, so no one paid any attention.

We retreated inside, to Zoni's side again. And what followed, although entirely in keeping with official Roma rules, struck me as criminally insensitive. In fact, Katy, noticing my concern, kindly turned my chair away from the scene and recommended I speed my mind away to someplace else. I didn't want to watch, but I couldn't help it. Zoni's green lacquer box was pillaged, her good-bye wardrobe and all the good luck gifts unpacked. Assuming the rights of the nearest relative, Gusha carelessly pulled everything out and took Zoni's measure, starting at her head, cutting the ribbon when it reached her feet, and looping it into her pocket. Because her family had paid Zoni's bride price, the measuring ribbon—a kind of magical protection that hypnotizes *gendari* (police) and ensures the success of escapes—would be Gusha's prize. Without the solace of kind words or sweet thoughts of remembrance—and without folding them!—Gusha carelessly stuffed Zoni's traveling wardrobe back inside her box.

That, to me, was the final insult. I couldn't believe there was nothing we could do to rectify this horrid situation, to make Zoni's good-luck life end on a more consistent note. I looked to my Gypsy sisters for solace. They were pretending not to notice or to care.

Then Duda made us smile. She reminded us how fastidious Zoni had been. "You know she wouldn't be caught dead in wrinkles." Duda ran a forefinger across her throat: the matter was out of our hands.

Zoni was on her way to becoming *Muli*, an ancestor with the power to judge, reward and penalize the living. But how could we wish Grandmother Gusha harm? She was now, by some unbearably grotesque twist of fate, the primary caretaker of beloved Zoni's children.

THE LAST EVENING that Zoni lay in the open coffin in the chapel, she lost her stern expression. We were gratified to discover a dimpling tilt to the corners of her mouth.

That night, only Zoni's western family was faithfully in attendance. Young girls put paper plates of meat on our laps and beer and bread in our hands. At the box, beside the flower arrangements drooping from a late September heat wave, the gentleman of the family—brother Boyd—spoke to sister Zoni.

He told her how she had pleased him. He spoke decorously and with the sincerity and style for which he was known. He said everything he needed to say to his sister. He spoke for us all, and we listened.

The unseen hand of a good-bye breeze lifted the lace veil draped above Zoni's lifeless head and then dropped it. No one bothered any longer with the procession of dead leaves that scooted through the open door, whispering emissaries from the Other Side, racing to collide and pile around the box.

Fatima and I went out for a breath of cool night air. When we returned, Duda was standing, arms raised melodramatically, excitedly relating the story of the two brain operations, and how, before the last one, our beloved Zoni was wheeled down the corridor on a gurney, singing in her bravura soprano, *She'll Be Comin around the Mountain when She Comes.*

The sisters and I couldn't believe Zoni was really dead. To us, despite the tragedy of her last chapter, the months in the hospital, the standoff with Gusha and all that trouble she had with her husband and children, she was still our lucky, laughing Zoni. How could bad luck sneak up on and outflank our double-luck sister? It certainly can't be good luck to die before you're forty.

Gusha got her revenge by flying Zoni back to the East Coast. But, before she left, she assured us she knew what Zoni liked better than we did. When she got to New York, we heard she ordered another box, more conservative in color, and another dress.

My Machvaia family and I missed the funeral service, the rituals at the burial, the opulence of the three death tables and all the big and little offerings. At six weeks I bought some candy Zoni liked, had it wrapped as a gift and gave the box away to an astonished stranger. But we had no word about who took the fresh traveling clothes at any of the commemorations—or how they looked. Sometimes I see an American look-alike, a passing resemblance, and Katy says that's a good sign. But we had no final endings. My sister Zoni seldom visits me in dreams.

Several years later, I looked up John in Yonkers. Now a likely lad of seventeen, his close resemblance to his mother—the same big eyes and long lashes, the sweetly generous mouth—stopped my heart. He told me East Coast Zoni is buried somewhere in New Jersey. But what became of Zoni West?

MY DESPONDENCY, WHAT I think of as The Great Depression, started with Zoni's coma. It lasted for what seemed like centuries. I couldn't party, I couldn't work and I had to sell my car.

For endless days that slid into nameless months, climbing out of my bed required a vast effort of will. I had traveled to the far corners of my psyche and lost my compass heading back. Flat on my back, tracing the fine cracks in my studio ceiling, I anxiously waited for the other shoe to drop. Robbed of the hubris that had backed my sales approach, I gave up selling etchings. Instead, I sold my belongings, piece by piece, and went on General Assistance.

Only the rituals associated with the sick and the dead seemed essential; only they could get me dressed and out the door. Duda called and invited me to a summer picnic in Golden Gate Park, assuring me that everyone I knew would be there. Hours later, I found myself, sock in hand, staring dumbly out the window. Was it more than grief for Zoni?

Dismayed by my sniffles, red swollen eyelids and complaints that my etching sales had dropped to zero, Stevo offered me a little emergency cash and the usual bonus of Gypsy advice.

"Well, she's safe now. You should look at it that way. Nobody can make her do anything. The kids can't bug her to go back to Gusha and Sailor. She doesn't have to worry about hurting the people she loves to get what she wants." He sank despondently into the toucan print pillow on my bed. Passionately sincere, he mumbled, "I wish I could be so lucky."

What a way to cheer me up! His rags-and-patches attitude infuriated me. All those years of cherishing and waiting, and he remained unsalvaged. The critical mass of my loss suddenly smashed into the only available target, and I shocked us both by attacking him ferociously.

"You can't do anything right! You will be remembered for nothing! The only fame you will ever have is as The Djuhli's lover!"

BEFORE I REACHED THE BOTTOM of the well, for a change I tried some of America's celebrations. I went to the San Francisco Symphony, and found I couldn't stay, couldn't sit through it. I couldn't comprehend what I was doing there or the lack of response by the audience. Why, I puzzled, weren't we all shouting along with the trumpets' ennobling cadenzas and swaying in time with the bass? How absurd to sit like a regiment of dummies, eyes staring straight ahead, row upon row. The music called, and I longed for participation. I missed the joy of the Gypsies dancing.

My mourning lasted longer than expected. Duda called me to the happy events, the picnics, weddings, Saint-days, and parties: "Come! Everyone will be there." But I didn't feel up to going. Racked with foreboding, my life was not good time. Since I was still adept at sleeping, I began to collect and study my dreams: colorless dreams of underwater shipwrecks, endless trudges through deep-sinking gray sand; a series of Ondine dreams, cataclysmic with longing. In the fairy tale of the same name, Ondine is a sea nymph who falls in love with a mortal. For years I had lived a mythic dream of desire for the "other." Now, in despair, I obsessed on the dreams of the night.

From my knocked-out and prone position, there was every opportunity to study the double sliding closet doors that ran next to my bed and along the entire end wall of my studio. As the doors opened, one behind the other, the contents could be viewed by halves. On one side I had hung clothes for work and knocking around, comfortable clothes of wool and cotton. On the other were costumes for carnival moments, all of them billowy, sumptuous, fanciful.

Looking up from the depths of my ennui, it occurred to me I had become overly invested in the latter. I had given the Gypsies too many of my hopes and memories, all the excitement and glamour of Christmas, Easter, Saint-days. I could see the red silk ball gown and velvet jacket from the previous New Year's gala in Las Vegas; the magnolia-white sheer Stevo adored; Lola's black organza with pinpoint gold stars that she had positively assured me was full of good luck; the dress with the matching apron that put me on the map, socially speaking, in Sacramento, the time we were too few in number and had to cook for days; the print of green and orchid crepe I had anticipated wearing to an upcoming Gypsy wedding; the sumptuous suit hemmed in fur, floor length like the others, an extravagance bought with the Hollywood money that proved unsuitable for dancing; the low-cut peach satin from the notorious wedding with dogs. There they were, statement after statement of enchantment, story after story, visually apparent, so achingly near at hand.

Crammed into the same side, underscoring the message, was the wardrobe of filmy pastel negligees in which I greeted the man who could never hang around long enough to change a light bulb or balance the weight of my despair.

Once, to step into that other reality, I had only to change my clothes, my hair, my mindset. But my game of pretend had turned into *Prikadja*, a hydra-headed demon with a million angry and demanding mouths. Enmeshed in this situation I was trying to fathom, I found myself wanting too much, wanting what I could not have.

I tried to sort it out, to reorder my affections and loyalties. Why was it, I wondered, that the company of Americans felt bloodless, even inane, while the tolerance of the Machvaia seemed so amazingly rich with support and welcome? How had my passion for Stevo become confused with my passion for Gypsies? To what degree were they in cahoots or, possibly, one and the same? By continually rephrasing the questions, I hoped to discover an answer.

Being familiar with hard times, Katy could hear my desolation through the phone line. She offered me the standard Machvaia remedy: "Forget it, whatever it is. Come over and we'll go to the clubs."

UNAWARE THAT MY SELF-ASSESSMENT was at least a decade out of date, I told my neighborhood therapist that I thought I might be having an identity crisis. He was usually silent. When he finally spoke, he reminded me of what I seemed to comprehend only intellectually, like something I had read (but for which I'd forgotten the page reference). He pointed out that I was not born Machvanka and could never really become one. Oh, no?

But the fact had become painfully clear. Although I had tried and had been given every chance, there was no way I could truly live the Machvaia lifestyle. Once, in a more heroic time, the intrigue of expectation had been quite enough, and I could pack blind hope into the car and head out to the challenge.

Those first years with Stevo, anything and everything had seemed possible. *My Gypsy* won the Seafair Hydroplane race in

Seattle. A man landed on the moon. *Mr. Tambourine Man* played his song for me. My world had revolved around the University, a hippie-dippie world promoting peace and communal sharing—so much like the Machvaia. In that world, with Stevo's arms around me, I had no reason to doubt that we were in keeping with the times and our own deepest nature. That was then, when everything was a match. Now, what I had once taken for granted seemed illusory and simplistic, and most certainly out of date.

I had to admit that certain acting bit parts over the years were light-years beyond my dramatic range: the time Leo refused to forego his fishing trip, and Srécha thrust her bare fist through the kitchen window, returning from the ER with a forearm lined with stitches. I remembered the disasters involved when Erusha's daughters ran away. To find and bribe the girls to come back cost Erusha a lifetime of savings, her business license, her office and her home. She said it was worth it, even though she lost thirty pounds, and, it must be said, neither girl seemed especially grateful.

Falling in step with this kind of drama was as alien to me as flying through space to the moon was for Lola. Even when my agony was real, I was never able to compete with the over-the-top Tutsi: breaking my front teeth, screaming threats of suicide, smashing restaurant windows, putting my children's lives at risk, inviting jail time by yelling at the police.

The truth is I don't enjoy suffering. Not really. I can't imagine trashing my furniture, my antique Meissen soup plates, my work, my friends, my health—as well as every prospect for the future.

If I were playing the Gypsy in the Third Act of *Carmen*, the music could have risen in crescendo, the minor notes sliding down the warning scale. But, like Lola, I don't look for trouble. Before succumbing to the bullfighter's red tassels and swagger, I would have suggested the remedy of a healing Zen meditation retreat to my former lover. If that didn't work, maybe a Europass to his home town girl, Michaela? I would have been a considerate ex-lover and waited until he recovered his spiritual center. Or would I? I could never stay away from Stevo.

EVERY DAY, IN SILENT, one-way conversations, I was always telling Stevo what I was doing and feeling. Then, at night, I turned the time back to an earlier period and went to visit Stevo in my dreams.

Before falling asleep, I imagined—was it imagination?—soaring over the city and down to his storefront. The store was dark, except for the streetlights, the passing cars, the neon PSYCHIC letters flashing through the drapes against an interior wall. There, on the sofa beneath the pulsing colors, one sturdy arm circling his silk dark curls on a pillow, Stevo slept.

Making myself narrow as a ruler and as weightless as one of the shadows, I snuggled there beside him. The heady scent of him unfolded in my nostrils and mouth. Turning, looping his free arm around me, he held me. I could stay, moored in that safe harbor, as long as I concentrated fiercely.

Sometimes I awoke from dreams of him with the peaceful certainty that we had been together. But how that might be, I couldn't say. My traveling was witchcraft, and I knew it. At first, evoking him this way was as inadvertent as a craving. But, over the years of trying to drum him up into a viable presence, my need for contact had built into deliberately conjured spells.

Mary Catherine Bateson has said that good fences may make good neighbors—but maybe not good anthropologists. I was pretty weak on current theory and no great shakes on the more recent publications. But I had journeyed far to know the other, the stranger, to break through every exotic and resistant barrier, to plumb the range of human possibility. Now, having transgressed some invisible guard rail, I had crossed into Limbo. Or was it the Land of the Dead?

THE GREAT DEPRESSION MOVED from bad to worse. My mind exploded into a conflict of interests, one part sane and rational; the other sneaky, crafty, overwhelming, a sudden diabolic impulse that could catch me unaware.

Terrified by powerfully seductive urges to fling myself into the sea, I had to stop running in the Presidio or riding my bike along the beach. I had sold my car when after a close call: one night while driving over the Bay Bridge, the steering wheel unaccountably nosed toward the railing, and only by a superhuman effort of will and desperate prayer could I hold it in the forward direction. Who or what was I battling? Had Tutsi's curses begun to work?

I had always enjoyed living near the wide blue stretch of San Francisco Bay and the Marina. I loved watching the wind fill the blossoming sails of the boats and playing with the waves, the damp feeling of fog against my face, the hoarse Tibetan sound of the fog horns.

How could what I love have become a threat? Why would the Angel of Death, *Marteah,* beckon me from the watery depths of spells and enchantment? My alternate consciousness was only a flicker, familiar and then not—a *déjà vu,* alluringly peaceful—a powerful, inexorable advocate for transition like the wheel of destiny spinning and turning.

Would the wanting and needing and not having destroy me? Was I hoping to avoid the uncertainty of Stevo's phone calls and cement myself to him forever by turning into a vengeful Unforgiving Ghost?

GHOSTS AND WITCHCRAFT brought poor Tutsi to mind. Long ago, when we were still a dysfunctional threesome, she had explained why their usual summer trip to Idaho had to be aborted. "We were driving up the mountain. We got as far as Snoqualmie. Some music played on the radio and Stevo pulled over to the side. He sat there, studying his knuckles. Then he couldn't stop crying. He couldn't drive on. So we came back."

Her voice sank into a confidential whisper and her eyes brightened with fear and respect. "What did you do to him?"

Lola had warned me that witchcraft can reverse and fall back upon the witch. That's how the ghost of me gave up on the ghost of him. During the day, I stopped initiating those lethal one-sided conversations. I quit scheduling his storefront on my nightly dream itinerary. Fighting flashbacks of the happy smell and feel of him, I suffered long days and longer nights without him. Cries of anguish and loneliness rose in my chest only to stay there, dumb as a bell without a clapper.

Sensing my desperation, Stevo appeared one evening to take me out, the first time in our years in San Francisco that he was willing to risk it. And I had no party clothes to wear except my floor-length Gypsy dresses.

He was disbelieving. "Don't you have a dress, American and short? You did. I remember a dress you wore when you worked at the Colony Club." Long ago in Seattle, so long it seemed like a previous lifetime, I had quit my weekend cocktail waitressing job and given that dress to my sister Nancy.

He came, his brows in a marching line because of Dzhio. Dzhio, a Kalderash Rom, had died suddenly, almost instantly, slumping forward off a barstool at The Silver Clouds. As Stevo said, "It was good that Dzhio was drunk at the time and didn't know what hit him." But how sad, he added, to think of Dzhio being alone—for none of his people or family had been present. I tried to find the chord of empathy for Dzhio's drunken demise. Instead my mind went back to something Lola said. She had been right; too many of the people died too young. Zoni had been thirty-seven. Dzhio was only fifty.

I asked if Dzhio drank too much. But whiskey is on the same preferred list as good times, good health, good luck. "As often as he could," Stevo said.

Dzhio's bad luck was my good. Wanting to share his sorrow over Dzhio, Stevo took me to The Silver Clouds. To be near the main event, we sat at the bar and drank good-bye to Dzhio. Then Zoni. Dzhio again. Then Zoni. But something was wrong. After my long-ago bout with hepatitis, one drink, possibly two, had become all I could manage. The music was too loud. The smoke bothered my sinuses. Apparently, Stevo didn't feel like singing. He never wiggled his mustache. Instead, he cried a bit for the friend he had lost and the nights at the bar they would never again spend together.

Later, at my apartment, I rubbed his shoulder blades and carefully trimmed the wiry edges of his mustache. We played mellow Getz-Gilberto music on my sound system, and I showed him snapshots from the latest Machvaia wedding. Toward morning, while he slept, I lay wide-eyed and desperate.

This was my long-sought opportunity to share my sense of impending doom, of losing control and even losing my life. This was the time, the right time, to tell him about the nightly trips no longer taken, the mystery out-of-body experiences, the panic attacks on the bridge, the sinister allure of the sea. Now was the time to solicit help.

But unfettered pleasure had been our story line. Being with the man who couldn't stay—for reasons beyond anyone's control or blame—was exciting to an extravagant degree. The tease of his arrival put a sharp edge on our moments together; pinpoints of desire were kept alive by the frequency of his escapes. Once, the space between us had been illusory, and there was nothing we couldn't share. Once, as I remembered, the mere fact of his presence put me in tune with the times, my own deepest nature, the creative forces of the cosmos, the teachings of the spirit-making me feel invincible. Now I stared all night at the fleshy wall of his back, unable to escape the trap of happy endings. All night I tried, and I couldn't tell him about Death's spectre.

He had always viewed me as privileged; how often he mentioned that I was lucky to go where I pleased, to do as I liked, to spend my time and money on myself. What could he do with more problems? What to expect from a man who would be gone the next day, back to another life? There had been times, when he was standing at the door and reluctant to leave again, he would turn to remind me that I was his only joy. Joy, I found, is a high-maintenance job: demanding, bitter and lonely.

THE MAGICAL MYSTERY TOUR was bottoming out. The options available to me in San Francisco were on the wane. My dreams and my therapist had failed me, as had the security of funding from the Unemployment Office. The man who could never stay provided increasingly brief and occasional comfort.

Lola was dead. Zoni too. And gone were the dance-filled disco days of *Boogie Fever, Freak Out* and *The Hustle.* Bomb scares and shootings in the Financial District had ruined the ability to cold-call for my etching business. Two states away were my parents, children, sisters and now Katy who, since King converted the bulk of their Oakland house into apartments, had moved back with her children. Looking for distraction, I began to review the field notes from my time with Lola.

Studying the history of Lola the Lucky, fearless Lola, the essence of that other earlier Gypsy life *po drom* and, as it has turned out, a Machvanka for the future, I realized that Lola was an original. I might study Gypsies forever, but I would never find another Lola. I became so lonely for my beloved friend that I added to my notes with a rich tapestry of recollections. I obeyed her request and began to write "the story of the world."

As I recalled, read and wrote about her, I began to occasionally have happy, marvelous dreams of Lola in turbans, feathers, flowers. Once she wore an exploding headdress of iridescent moons and sapphire stars. The dream put me in such an exuberant mood that I headed for the local House of Pancakes and ordered a serving of strawberry waffles. A generous carafe of coffee arrived promptly. But the dishwater taste was unfamiliar. The waffles came with a choice of sugary syrups that made the taste of unripe strawberries especially sour. Only Lola's company, I thought, would have made the waffles palatable.

I began to wonder how Lola did it, how had she shuttled with so little effort between eras and worlds? When young, she had traveled constantly, by horse and wagon and car and tent, eventually moving from farms and open country into the heart of the city, and, after the infamous divorce, city to city. When we met, she was still traveling on a daily basis, walking or taking the bus to the grocery store, to Katy's, to go shopping downtown to Woolworths, Frederick & Nelson or The Bon Marche. She moved equally well, agelessly in fact, between the generations. I might have called her Old Lola out of respect, but I had never really believed she would ever be old.

Remembering her enthusiasm for the unfamiliar, I wondered if adapting to the novel kept her young. When, a decade earlier, *Fiddler on the Roof* came to town, I had bought tickets for four: Lola, me, my daughter and one of my sisters. It was Lola's first musical comedy and she loved it. Although I assured her she looked quite resplendent in her favorite colors, cardinal red and gold, she noted with concern that the other women were wearing stockings and she wasn't. As we reached our seats, not the kind to let a minor setback get her down, she assumed her "time for enjoyment" expression and was immediately transported by what began to unfold on the stage. After that evening, however, I noticed that Lola never left her apartment without pantyhose or stockings.

Shape-shifting Lola, that's how I thought of her. Once I drove by a bus stop and noticed someone who looked a little like her. Later, I told her what I had seen—she was always interested in resemblances. Admitting that "it was me," she explained she had been on the way to her bank, in a plain black wool shift and pearly earrings.

"You didn't look like yourself," I said, a little irritated by her successful deception.

"It's better to look like where you are going," she sniffed imperiously.

Endlessly adaptable, even the transformation of her idol Bette Davis from siren to psychopath couldn't dismay her. When the movie *Whatever Happened to Baby Jane?* was released, Lola called me and two of her children over to see "something important."

At the time, she was living by herself in one of Miller's rental houses, and she high-stepped slowly down the stairs in a giant pink hair bow, baby doll dress, cotton anklets and a generous polka-dot of rouge on each cheek.

"Who am I?" she challenged, pausing on the landing, holding out the hem of her thigh-high skirt and assuming a girlish pose. Miller, eyes popping, was unable to speak. Katy hadn't seen the movie. She hazarded a guess, "Baby Snooks?" Exasperated at the failure of her staging, turning back up the stairs to get the warmth of her robe, Lola blew me a quick, conspiratorial farewell kiss and called over one puff-sleeved shoulder, "You can tell them who I am."

I RECALLED ONE SATURDAY night in Seattle when I had gone to Lola's. There, facing the pictures of Baby Daughter Zoni and the life-sized, wood-backed Art Naif Saint, I was served a bounty of refreshments and royally entertained. Lola turned the television dial to a program she described as "big with luck": her favorite, featuring Lawrence Welk.

She didn't exactly watch the show. Instead, she flitted through the room, rearranging the lace-draped tablecloth, stirring something in the kitchen, now and then settling on the edge of her wine-red sofa to point out a particularly engaging dance step or to pay attention to a voice that showed the truth of feeling. To give her pleasure and for the pleasure of her company, Lawrence Welk was something I endured. Welk's old-time ballads that climaxed in the oompah of a polka, and Welk's people with their ear-to-ear smiles—forced, I thought—their vapid comments, the men's conservative haircuts, all struck me as hopelessly stuffy.

I compared them unfavorably with the young people in my building, every one of whom, including my son, decried the artifi-

cial. They wore their hair in the shaggy rumpled manner of Bob
Dylan, and took heart in the whining social criticism of Dylan's
songs.

Now, thinking of that evening, recalling her enthusiasm, her
party dress appearance and the ceremonial way she had laid out
the table, I finally understood what had been going on. In Lola's
view, Welk was the American counterpart to the worth and stylish-
ness of Machvaia parties. Lawrence "Welch," as she called him,
was a man "full of luck." He appeared on screen in concert
with impeccably attired women and men, "his people," as Lola
described them. During his "time for enjoyment," people danced
and sang and basked in the reciprocal charisma of dazzling
white smiles and teeth. They "put a face on things," which is what
Gypsies do to demonstrate respect. "Americans," I would often
hear the Machvaia say, "don't have respect." But Lola didn't agree.
"No difference," she would say. "Americans and Gypsies. Just the
same."

What I had perceived as pretentious, Lola had found inspirational. Welk's was a world remote from the heartache of youth,
the damage of time, the burden of the everyday. Like a Gypsy *slava*,
Lawrence Welk provided an hour of faultless flowing moments, a
sample of life as it ought to be.

WHEN LOLA WAS EIGHT, her godparents Drago and Lubché
bought her a bright red American-style dress and coat to wear at
her baptism. It was the gift that set the compass for her life and
bound child Lola in the American direction.

As an adult, *Amerikanka Lola*, the American Machvanka, had
her own mind—that's what she said—and followed the American
directive. She had bypassed Gypsy law and instigated an American-
style divorce. In Seattle, with no husband/boss, she did pretty
much as she pleased. For one thing, she made friends with a
Djuhli—that was me!—and insisted on foisting me on the others.

Some of her efforts to communicate that we were a match, and essentially the same, were incredibly obvious. So why hadn't I paid more attention? Shortly after we met, she had hung a giant American flag, commercial size, in her living room. Understanding so little about Gypsy ladies and their decor, I must have thought (if I thought about it at all) that there was nothing particularly unusual about a Gypsy hanging an outdoor flag indoors. The size of it was remarkably outstanding, however. It completely covered one wall and lay in folds and rolls at the edge of the hardwood floor.

"Where did you get that?" I gasped.

"I got it, that's what counts," she retorted. The flag showed up several days after she announced to me, "We're going to be best friends."

How did I manage to miss the point? Instead, I simply recorded the captive flag event in my notes—typed, dated—and forgot about it.

Only in retrospect did I appreciate Lola's genius for adapting. Between the social groups I found so disparate, Americans and Gypsies, she had perceived the midpoint and was always re-establishing the necessary harmonic balance. Undaunted by cultural barriers, she refused to be categorized and conveniently filed away. When I asked her a question and she refused to answer, saying, "I'm American, not old-fashioned," she wasn't trying to undermine my studies. She was giving me the opportunity to extend them.

SHE IMMEDIATELY RECOGNIZED and embraced me as her luck. How do I know? Whatever felt unlucky to her, she rapidly discarded. Whatever I gave her, she kept: a five-foot Saint, an oil painting by my sister of a mother sewing for her daughter, two electric heating pads that she applied to her increasingly arthritic joints, a pair of dangling earrings I really liked, a quilted nylon raincoat that struck me as too conservative for the Sixties.

Lola also saw my value in her auspicious dreams. In one, I was painting her room pale, pale pink. The paint, she said, was "shiny and curly." Paint, pink, shiny and curly—each was a favorable omen.

In another, I was pulling hundreds of fish that were caught in my net into a boat. This, we all agreed, was good luck, a dream of beneficent bounty.

But not until I moved to California and was welcomed and sponsored by her pro-American children and their other relatives did I begin to appreciate to what an extraordinary degree Lola had returned the favor. The things she knew intuitively, I had to list and analyze, paying particular attention to belief.

Belief creates experience. A major theme of Machvaia belief is luck, *baX*, the wellspring of which is received through the blood-line. The inheritance of luck is fulfilled and sustained by following the rules of Romaniya, which advocate the avoidance of outsiders and calls for following the lead of your feelings. As outsiders possess their own outsider luck and blood is unforgiving, according to traditional thought, the two bloodlines ought never to mingle; that's the way, I was told, the God has made it.

How did I, a Social-Democrat who knew, scientifically and intellectually, that all *Homo Sapiens* are more or less born to a similar physiognomy and potential lean in the Machvaia direction? Of course, the differences between our cultures had been my focus. But I had become so engrossed in my research that I began to think, at least some part of me thought, along the politically correct Gypsy line. By obsessing over the caste-like separation of soaps, towels and "kinds of people," by finding rapport with Lola's family and attending to the lesson-plan of ritual, by meeting the challenge of Stevo's continual good-byes for reason of our disparate bloodlines and karma, my motherboard had unwittingly, over time, and in a manner that my intellect would never countenance, become rewired.

I detected this Gypsy side of myself in my dreams and realized it left me stranded on a tiny island of my own making, as emotionally isolated as Lola must have been at times. In terms of cultural belief, Lola and I were really hybrid splits, neither this nor that entirely—a direction, it would seem, that the entire world is currently taking. When she first visited my Eastlake apartment, even *Amerikanka Lola* hadn't been able to fight her gut-level reaction to refuse coffee brewed by an outsider—even though I announced the coffee was being served in brand new Wedgwood cups!

Initially, I was only aware of our differences. She had seemed so incredibly exotic, provoking my imagination into loops and spins, spiriting me away from the known. Yet, by listening with our hearts, by caring enough to make an effort, we became partners in the dance. How amazing that the two of us who were so incidentally selected could be transformed by the passing years into such deep and lasting significance. Looking back, I find that my casual, occasionally reluctant relationship with the Gypsy Lola, my mentor, had blossomed into my Holy Grail—the unexpected central theme of my life's adventure.

Rescuing me from my existential pit, Lola's ghost offered the gift of wisdom as well as the usual bits of well-meaning mischief. While reading my field notes, I remembered the many ways she showed me that life was short, too short, and the best plan of action was to "live like you are going out of style." I remembered how she taught me that the great adventures are those of the heart, and that loving is always a risk. And that not loving enough is riskier. That giving generously, with gladness and abandon, is something a person can count on; getting love back is serendipitous. That's when I realized I was failing my family, my heritage and myself, by neglecting to cherish those of my own kind. I knew I had to fight my way back to America. I had to learn to feel the same empathy for and close identity with American "outsiders" as I had for the Machvaia.

Maybe my depression had been a premonition. At any rate, how fortunate that I was feverishly looking for a new persona because that's when the Lord of Disaster struck in earnest.

HE PACES, SITS, STANDS and paces again. He takes out a filtered cigarette and forgets to light it. What he needs is emergency money, he tells me, and not an inconsequential amount.

"Thousands!" Every moment counts; he must settle this crisis as soon as he can. "Mikey did it. But I'm the one they blame."

Stevo wants me to ask my *father* for money! His own father, the man the people refer to as a look-alike for Cesar Romero, has already helped with "all he had," which was three thousand dollars.

To avoid my refusal, to allow me time to reconsider, Stevo warms my hands between his and switches topics. He asks the question I have been waiting weeks to ask him: "Where have you been?"

I had been to Seattle to visit my family over the holidays. But on the unlikely chance that the phone might ring and I would hear the sound of his smooth cello-like voice wishing me the standard good health and good luck—*Sastimasa tai BaXtasa*—I didn't leave for the airport until mid-morning Christmas Day. Now, with the holidays over, I was back in San Francisco. But, still upset by his negligence, I felt an urgent need to complain.

I slid my hands out from under his to pour more coffee. My father is the last person I can imagine ever asking for money. He says I have wasted my life on Gypsies. A careful man, a lawyer for a bank, he is appalled by fieldwork jobs that don't provide a salary and that entail expenses he deems frivolous. The summer before, when I used his phone for a news-laden call to California, he angrily stomped out of the house an hour early for his five-mile morning walk.

Stalling to avoid the crime of killing hope, I don't answer Stevo directly. Instead, I return the question: "Where were you at Christmas?"

The answer is, in Los Angeles, looking for his son. "Mikey stole a girl from Fat Fred." When I ask who this fellow Fat Fred is, he ignores my question.

"They ran away. They took all four of her children."
"*Four?*"

"Yes." Stevo answers in his firm-jawed, face-the-Armageddon mode. "I'd like to give them all back. Really. I nearly caught them when they telephoned for money. They called me from Gardena. That's where my father lives with his poodles. You know, the funny French-clip kind. I don't have his number. But I know where he lives and I drove there. Mikey and the girl were gone."

Stevo moves restlessly from the sofa, to the bench, to the black plastic chair. He wants me to know he has done everything he could to right the situation. He has returned three of the children. I don't ask him how.

The girl says the fourth is Mikey's and refuses to give the baby up. Fat Fred, the legal father-in-law, claims that she lies.

"*Hatchiares?*" You understand?

Overwhelmed, I forget about Christmas Past and his failure to phone. The thing is, while we sit here talking, the problem is compounding. Paternity claims involve incendiary matters like sexual potency and male authority. The reputations of Fred's family and the honor of the lineage are threatened. As the final settlement, a Romani court has officially recommended five thousand dollars, a king's ransom and twice what Stevo paid for his last daughter-in-law!

"Why so much?" I mutter, choking back my alarm. "Two or three thousand would seem more like it. I never heard of anyone getting such an unfavorable judgment!"

"Only Palo Alto Pete stood by me," he says stoically. "The court was stacked against me. Everyone else there was a relative of Fred. *Hatchiares?*"

I can guess why. Preoccupied with making ends meet, juggling the logistics of dealing with his oversized family and finding time for me, Stevo has neglected to build the critical friendships with the important men of his tribe whom he might have called upon for help.

"It's bad, very bad," he tells me. Fat Fred is Mexcaia (Roma from Mexico). He has brothers the size of Sumo wrestlers who have promised to destroy Stevo and his family. Mikey, his bride and somebody's child have fled and are moving fast. No one knows what they do for money. But, since she's not Machvanka, Stevo doubts that the young woman has been trained to tell fortunes *po drom*.

Stevo's terrified wife and children are hiding in a motel outside the county line. They spend their days watching television from tunnels in the bedclothes. Food is sent in; the washing sent out. One son, Paul (my favorite, the one with the lively eyes), was kidnapped, beaten and held for ransom. Luckily, he escaped.

"Call the police and get them arrested. You have to!"

"That won't help. Fred is the much better liar. You don't know those Gypsies. His family would destroy us. The women would accuse us of rape and thievery. They'll injure themselves, make cuts, file complaints and get us for dope-dealing, fraud, knife wounds, attack . . ."

Distraught, Stevo grasps at straws. "Do you think I could get Mikey arrested on fake drug charges? He might even have a little angel dust in his pocket, in which case the charges would be real."

He has the look of a man desperate for a suggestion. But I don't know what to suggest. I resent my low profile in these affairs, pulled in as legal consultant after the fact. What kind of rule is it that holds the boy's father responsible when the girl is already the mother of four? How can anyone suppose she has been stolen, considering the ingenuity required to collect and get away with all those children?

Stevo lives on a one-way street where emergency is the only direction. The girl lives on the same street; why didn't she have a plan? She could have left her husband, returned to her parents until the bride price money and relevant children had been returned—and then run away with Mikey. I can't help pointing out that smart Gypsies know the ways to get what they want and how to bend the law.

Bewildered, he rocks his head in his great sun-bronzed hands. Then he gets up to make a call. As he leans toward the phone, my mind races off in a contrary direction. I think how gorgeous he is and how the arrangement of his teeth and eyes and short straight nose still excite me.

In Giraudoux's *Tiger at the Gates*, Helen explains her attraction to Paris: "There are some things, and certain people, that stand out in bright colors for me." She has seen her lover Paris "vividly; in the clearest outline against the sky and the sun."

That is precisely the way I see Stevo, even now, even in the midst of this latest chaos.

FINALLY, HE UNDERSTANDS THAT I will not ask my father for the money. He is too proud to ask again. Instead, he pensively recalls, "I kept ordering him to leave. Mikey left. But he didn't go far. The girl lived only six blocks away."

Stevo seems so pathetically sad. I think he may be shrinking. Even his cigarette droops at a dejected angle. Although I have heard many historical accounts of his failures and know, in my heart of hearts, that he must be full of anger, I have never really seen him angry. Here, in my apartment, in order to please me, he always makes the effort to arrive in good humor. Here, we keep the stage set for good luck with an earnest good intention. Like the televised hour of Lawrence Welk, our programming is designed for auspicious moments. But, rather than the oompah of polkas, here we dream among the green of jungle plants and frolic to the bossa nova.

Seven years have passed since I first followed Stevo to San Francisco. But the lid is off our secret. Betrayed by the hours spent apart and the moments we didn't share, a vast gaping hole, bigger than my apartment, has just opened above our heads, exposing us to the outside elements, hot ungovernable winds, the wails of the lost and lonely. I am besieged by premonitions of a future, black and bleak without him.

The man sitting across from me, his curls rubbed into confusion, looks at me with enormous heart-stopping eyes that put me to mind of prehistoric carvings. They meet mine with unaccustomed anguish. We embrace again. But there is this irredeemable difference: I have failed to save Mikey, the impossible problem; and failed to save Mikey's father.

THE YEARS APART BEGAN with the paranoid phone calls that made me furious. "I can't tell you where I am," he'd say. Who did he think I might tell? Who did he think he was fooling? He always called collect from a telephone booth, and I could read the origin of his call on my monthly bill.

I don't even know how or if the Fat Fred problem was settled. Stevo was running, hiding out. The move from motel to motel was difficult and costly. He didn't come to rest for a year or two, maybe longer. The Machvaia State of California is divided into business territories and defended by families. As far as those Gypsies already established were concerned, Stevo's three-car family was an Evil Empire of men and boys notorious for stealing women, and not desirable as neighbors.

His last calls came from San Jose. "I don't want to give you up." But after waiting nearly a year without another phone call, I did the only thing possible. I went traveling. I went to look for my luck.

The worst that could happen had happened. I resolved to run away again, this time from the Gypsies. Sunken deeply in memory and fighting to forget, I floated from apartment to room to house, and from city to city. When the emptiness in my heart turned to despair, I fought the desire to resurface for my fix of Gypsy life, for community gossip. My long-time fear of losing track of the people, that at any moment my Gypsy *Brigadoon* might disappear forever, became irrelevant. The outsider—Americans became my study and focus. In the best Gypsy manner, I "put my mind" with theirs, determined to appreciate and understand them.

At the same time, I began to realize the magnitude of my loss. Eventually, I would relent a little and phone Katy in Seattle or San

Jose—she, too, was traveling—Duda in San Francisco, Fatima in Los Angeles to hear about the major rites of passage, who had died, who got married. But, I missed the smaller details. I missed the frisson of excitement at every social event, always aware that I wasn't supposed to be there, making my good luck entrance and not knowing what to expect.

I missed dressing in my Gypsy clothes and stepping into another dimension. American life seemed poignantly lacking in drama. For many, many years I hadn't needed to take a vacation. The company of the Machvaia had been entertainment enough.

Katy promised me I would come back to the people. "You and me, we left our families and went to California and now we are family for each other."

In my new American life, my intention was to avoid the topic of Gypsies entirely. But Gypsies were all I knew. I tended to blurt out involuntary statements like, "Gypsies would say each time you count your money, it becomes less." Or, "Old Lola believed there is no luck beyond the truth of feeling." I must have been tiresome company.

I went on a health kick, jogging daily, quitting smoking and eating meat, and taking up a multiple vitamin regimen. I bought a suitcase with wheels, stored a few of my favorite Gypsy clothes in the old leather one and gave away the rest.

Although, by the next year, the vast stretches of ocean and beach along the Bay had lost all menace, even yet, I hadn't the nerve to confront the Bay Bridge in my car and maybe for good reason. In 1989, part of the upper deck gave way during the Loma Prieta earthquake.

I had been given two magnificent gifts, the boon of community acceptance and love without moderation. Passion breeds generosity; opened up to the virtue of feeling, I needed to share. There was no end of opportunity. When I thanked a clerk for helping me at the store, I sent an arrow of gratitude speeding from my heart. I treated everyone, all the outsiders, with inordinate kindness, and, as Lola had promised, sometimes the bounty of kindness came back.

Then, after what seemed a millennium, but was only thirty minutes by car from where the Mexican Gypsy crisis began, the savage sharpness of my loss eased into a lingering sadness. I had been walking in Marin County, among tree trunks so massive they boxed out the hum of the highway. Wrapped in unaccustomed silence, I became conscious of something seen—yet not seen—many times before, the blinding light pouring into the shadowy forest, vertical gold columns floating with a luxuriant petit-point of particles and motes. Each breath, I realized, loaded my lungs with sweet fresh air and tree stuff. Each step kicked up a little more. I considered how dust from other galaxies, ancient glaciers, the dying and the dead had been bathing me every moment of my life, even the days and nights with Stevo.

Between the fanning arms of majestic branches, the sky suddenly blinked its blue eye at me, and waved. Maybe it's because those redwoods are so fantastically tall and old and have been growing there so long, since all the continents were joined as one and long before human memory, that I finally felt the bird of death release its hold on my heart and vanish.

Losing Stevo—the worst that could happen—had happened. The world didn't end. The sun rose and set. The stars came out. The seasons changed in their usual progression. On each birthday, I became exactly one year older. I cut my hair, dated other men, read books, wrote academic articles, worked on Lola's story, practiced rhythmic yoga breathing and stopped listening for his footsteps. Phones might ring, but the call was never from him. I was on the road and traveling. He didn't have my number.

In time, I found I couldn't really remember how The Great Depression felt. But I went to Seattle, New York, Hawaii, Seattle and back to San Francisco, to all those places without breaking a fine thread of connection.

How was the connection? Was it the thirteen years of our intoxicating roller-coaster ride, or the cotton candy of indigestible longing? He no longer stood at my door like blue-faced Krishna come to tease and tantalize his adoring milkmaid.

216

Eventually, in part because I was curious and in part because I couldn't help it, I looked him up at the location of his last phone call, a pay phone in the hall outside a tavern. A woman's voice answered. "You've called The Red Coach Inn," she said.

WHEN I FIRST ARRIVED at the Inn, Stevo didn't admit he was involved with someone, a former go-go dancer who apparently still had some electrifying moves. I never saw her, but she certainly had him in her pocket. When he explained, "We match, we look right together," the half-life of my expectations dimmed quickly out of sight.

"Matching" is one way good luck is created, and looking right together suggests foreordained intimacy. What was I doing with a man I didn't match? Numb, I went on automatic pilot and, without saying good-bye or finishing my beer, rushed out of the tavern and across the twilight street. He followed. Maybe he was worried I might hurl myself under the bus when it came, or start breach of promise proceedings by slashing his tires. "Are you all right?" he asked, sounding solicitous. I didn't give him the satisfaction of an answer.

FOUR MONTHS LATER, STEVO called to say his relationship with the dancer had ended. I didn't ask what had happened or what he meant; instead, I maxed out my credit cards and bought a second-hand Honda. The day after, I drove south, San Francisco to San Jose, to console him.

We usually met at The Red Coach Inn, a windowless tavern notorious as a singles hangout. He was never on time.

Week after week I waited with the lost boys at the bar, having the same conversations: "What's your name?"; "Where you from?" They never remembered me—like them, I was a shadow—

anymore than he seemed to remember the days when we had
risked everything, family, sanity, even our lives, for the stolen
moments together.

In the permanent dusk of the lounge, the man I had thought
I knew was both an enigma and familiar. The razor-sharp urgency
was gone, burned out of his brain by the eighty-proof effects of
DeWar's and Jim Beam. The evidence was there in the shock of
white that blazed from the sideburns at each of his temples.

At the Red Coach Inn, I watched the party boy, mustache wrin-
kling at the women, go from table to table, buying and accepting
drinks, joining his Gypsy good times to America's, proving his
incontestable worth and popularity in the smoke-filled room.

Here, he didn't have to deal with his family. Cued to be selec-
tive about incoming calls, the bartender would say "Let me see if
he is here," cover the mouthpiece and holler "Hey, Steve. Want to
talk to David?" Here he had no responsibilities, no unending problems, and no painful history of failure. He was Gypsy Steve, bon
vivant. The Red Coach Inn had discovered his talents.

Once, mustering my courage, I shouted across the clamor of
the second-rate band, "You're killing yourself." I had to shout it
twice before he understood. "That's what my last girlfriend said,"
he replied.

Sometimes we had lunch at a mall and went shopping (for
him, of course). He liked charcoal-gray Mafia shirts and black ties.
I think he enjoyed looking dangerous. He tried to impress me with
his thrift, as if he were spending the day with a Machvanka who was
bound to provide his income and support. We went to discount
stores; we went to The Men's Warehouse. I paid.

To please me, he usually suffered through several hours without drinking. Then, sometime after lunch, he would begin to
fidget, hopping distractedly from rack to rack, searching for his
size. "How does this look?" he'd ask, holding an item up to his
neck for the mirror's reflection, striving for the image of success,
trying to impress someone, him or me, I was never sure. By four or
five, we were back at home plate, The Red Coach, facing the militant array of lighted bottles against the wall and straining to hear

each other talk. Drink by drink, he became less pensive. For a time, the genial, flirty, funny Stevo was back, recast into the role of generous host.

"Bartender, give these good people another drink!"

Inevitably, the process went into reverse and he turned a bit nasty, often toward the bartender, a gentle well-intentioned soul. I never stayed to watch the silk-dark curls sink in the table's direction. At that point, ten or eleven, I was glad to go to my apartment in the city.

But maybe I misread him. Maybe the droop of his head and the drop in morale suggested surrender. Maybe he hoped I would take the initiative, pop him into the car, drive him to San Francisco and surprise him with another life plan in the morning. I might have restored him to health with therapeutic massage, organic vegetables, nourishing fruit smoothies, long walks in the Presidio and the sensuous reminder of the Joao Gilberto records. Maybe he really wanted to run away with me, but couldn't remember how it was done.

I TOOK HIS DRINKING PERSONALLY. How could he do that, I wondered, deliberately destroy his perfection, the body I had cherished, held, idealized, adored? Over the course of the marathon afternoon-to-evening drinking sessions, obliged to accommodate his growing vagueness and inattention, I grieved for every cut-off capillary, no matter how minute, and every dying brain cell. Our time in the red leatherette lounge held all the fascination of a wake.

I would sit morosely, with the band three feet away, the sound crashing into my head, the people laughing and dancing. While studying his square, capable hand on the glass, I wondered if he still pounded out fenders, and if the end result of "going crazy for love" was this noisy, plastic lunatic asylum.

Sometimes, toward the end of the month, his hand on the table would be bare—his diamond ring having gone into hock. But that never kept him away. Men liked to buy him drinks, slapping him on the back, punching his arm. Other times, waiting for him to arrive, pivoting away from the neon-lighted bottles, I found him already sitting alone at a table, defended by a double shot. Had he forgotten our appointment?

Once, just for a few brief moments, the old rush returned. An emergency phone call and the warning, "Hurry! Johnny's coming!" Someone in his family had been informed that I was in the lounge, and someone else had called to alert him.

Confused, remembering the hair-pulling fights in Seattle, I grabbed my shoulder bag and ran behind him to the car. The car engine died in the middle of the mall's parking lot, and he slumped unconscious over the wheel.

Johnny, son number two, arrived, braking, flashing headlights, shouting something I couldn't understand. Jumping out, I answered him back, screaming and crying, finally finding someone to blame. "Why do you let him drink this way? Can't you stop him?"

Climbing back into the car to cradle his lolling head from injury, I wondered what we thought we were doing. Wasn't the "other woman" role a bit dated? He lived with his divorced daughter, not his wife, and all his children were grown. This was precisely the time I had waited for, gambled on, tried not to think about; and I had lost.

The wiring in his brain might be fried to a vapor. But Stevo had found freedom in a bottle. The reality was that the head in my lap had escaped me, Tutsi, his problems, and the problems of this century. So what was I doing, losing my temper, vulnerable to physical attack, out in the cold without my jacket, and locked in a car with a drunken sleeper?

BECAUSE I HAD TO, because nothing could keep me away, I kept making the trip to San Jose, over the connecting maze of freeways, through endless business parks and treeless apartment blocks. The trip was never easy. I left the city under the pressure of the possibility that I might miss him, that he would forget our appointment, be required to leave town, or die suddenly of a heart attack like his mother had.

When I got to San Jose and saw him again, I immediately found comfort. Was it the actual fact of his bodily presence after all those years of separation? Or the stone-cut peace of knowing he was still alive? I would drive home, brimming with content, reaffirmed in knowing exactly where I stood and what he was like, which was drunk and out of the question.

I would swear never to make the trip again.

But, then, time would pass, and he would apotheosize in my brain into the man he used to be: my *Man of La Mancha*. My Impossible Dream. My habit. And I would have to drive back down there and get the cold shower treatment of seeing for myself.

When I tried to explain to my daughter what these predictable extremes were like, she pointed out the obvious; "He always drank. Didn't you notice?" was her response.

But he never sang songs to me now, as he had then. Inarticulate rage was the most passion he could muster. The years of hard disappointment had drained an endless ocean of tenderness to a trickle. Even our lovemaking in a nearby apartment, to which he had a borrowed key, brusquely bypassed intimacy.

Besides, some sober Greek tragedy part of me sighed with relief when I left, thrilled to escape with my life.

DURING THE 1989 EARTHQUAKE, I was working as the apartment manager in an Art Deco-style building from the Thirties. In fact, I was showing an apartment to a prospective tenant when the shaking began, and the lights went off.

They didn't come back on for three long days. Without electricity, a stove, the television, unnerved by the continuing aftershocks and my youthful tenants' unsteady rows of lighted candles, I felt obliged to keep a close watch on the building. For a good many days, the telephone lines were overloaded. When calls went through again, I had no number and no way to reach Stevo. But why should I try? What was the point of waiting again for his call, of keeping up this masquerade and avoiding public mention of Stevo? Why continue the secrecy and lies, of holding to the good-behavior letter of Romaniya law while ignoring its content?

Two weeks later he called. Without uttering a word, I hung up on him. He never called again.

RECENTLY, AT A CELEBRATION with the Gypsies, I saw him. I went with Katy and her new husband, Machvano Chally.

The children greeted us at the door, vying for our attention, jumping with excitement, chattering in perfect English. Years ago, the children's English had been a bit awkward, and often required restructuring with Romani jokes and phrases.

The women were in the kitchen. Katy and I, always glad to be together, discovered the knife drawer and began slicing vegetables for the salad. Pinkie, King's agreeable daughter, now a young matron, covered the pans of cabbage rolls with foil and lifted them into the warming oven. Preparing a feast is an enduring comfort; it always seems as if we have done this forever and that the kindly virtuous Dead, who did it before us, wreath us with approval and garland us with merit.

Now that he was an elderly Gypsy man, a *Phuro*, Stevo had begun to attend public events again. I must learn to tolerate the twitch of excitement I feel whenever I see him and not give in to confusion. Withdrawing to the far end of the room isn't always going to protect me. Indeed, after we ate, he walked by me unexpectedly and the alarm of heated blood raced to my womb as if in response to a summons.

Love, Lola had assured me, always means crying. But, startled, I giggled.

After the feast, we sat at tables on opposite sides of the room; he was near the bar, Katy and I near the kitchen. I smiled and nodded. But he squinted across the room, uncertain, and turned to look again. Does he need eyeglasses? Is he, like most of the people in this room, too vain to wear them?

He had the same vulnerable expression as *The Gypsy Kings* when they strode to the edge of the Old Fillmore stage, shyly polite young Gypsy men, stunned by the applause and the cheers, with little except their guitars for defense. He had done what he had to do; he saw to it that all his children married. He gave up honor to be with me and now he must live with disgrace. Technically, being a woman, I am not the party responsible. The people say he is the guilty one. I have no sympathy for this aspect of Gypsy life, for the Machvaia belief that men rule the chessboard of political life and women are the pawns—a belief that is presently undergoing modification. But I was never really subject to that authority, whereas he, king of a growing family dynasty, a Machvano of conscience and heart, can't seem to escape it.

What do I know of him really? Except that his life was hard and mean in ways I cannot comprehend and, in any case, would prefer not to experience. What I know are the physical facts, the approach of his foot on the stair, the valentine face at my door, the shape of his mouth and joy of his touch—the rest has vanished.

A MELANCHOLY BRIEFLY CHILLS my heart, and I sigh. Then, feeling the weight of obligation, I sigh again. Shouldn't sharing go both ways, a two-way street? These people have given me so much; the hospitality of a bed on the couch, a chair at the table, their best advice and heart-felt blessings, the fantasy of a musical comedy, song and dance. For years, while serving me coffee, they patiently answered my questions, searched their memories and tried to figure out what I was getting at. Once, long ago, Big Bibi even offered me her only son, an Americanized runaway, in marriage! So what did I give them back? What could I give them?

Duda comes in late. She and Miller had trouble finding the hall. We hug and I hand her colored snapshots taken at the latest

Gypsy wedding. Among them are some of my children and their friends. Duda rapidly checks them out, shuffling one on top of the other. She smiles and tells me, "They look like Gypsies."

Katy holds up a snapshot of my daughter in a platinum bob and agrees. "That's right. I remember her as a Big Girl, the same age as my Sophie. Now she's looking more and more Machvanka."

"It's in her," Katy says. "I can tell."

I look again to see if my Gypsy sisters are fooling; Katy has an antic sense of humor. But the pictures are passing around the table in a circle, and everyone thoughtfully agrees my family looks quite like a family of Gypsies.

I study each photograph. Yes, my son, possibly; he has a mustache like Stevo's and a little of Stevo's old twinkle. My son's friends? Doubtful. Their wives? The real question is my daughter's daughter, who is half Chinese—how could she possibly resemble a Gypsy? Of course, she is a beautiful dancer and already, although young and inexperienced, her small and perfect face shines with the dawn of fortunate outcomes. Could that be apparent to these women of fine-honed intuition?

Then I remember how often it took a stretch of imagination to understand Lola, a leap of faith to meet her mind. I studied her so hard that the period of time when Gypsies had "soft hearts," the traveling days when the people were good with each other and shared everything—the sun on my back, the creaking and lurching of the wagon, the tremolo of anticipation as we round the bend— became the bone and sinew of my being. Nothing is safe from the retrofit of imagination. The women at this table have learned to see themselves in me.

THE GYPSY BAND is taking a break. A slow-paced ballad from a tape recorder begins, Andy Williams singing *Charade*. Stevo approaches the dance floor. The designer suit he is wearing has been custom fitted and looks expensive; I wonder who bought it.

He leads his granddaughter, a chubby little girl of maybe eight, through a few short turns. I note the cavalier grace with which he shows her off, matching his steps to hers, carefully balancing her pirouette. His investment in family was always my rival and, at the same time, one of his many consistent attractions.

Everyone knows the story of Stevo and the Djuhli. Ours is an old love story now, an established chapter in the book of Machvaia history—as famous, for those old enough to remember, as the stories about Miller and the Movie Star.

Moving down the floor in deliberate half circles, they are only a few feet away. Recognizing the potential of the situation—musical, dramatic, stylistic—he has followed the luck of his feelings to my side of the room. With kinetic grace, he is turning. As the music swells, he is bending. With a nod of acknowledgment my way, he is doing what he does so well, creating the perfect and unforgettable moment. Song, story, dance and ritual signify the moments in life we share and remember, setting them apart from the mundane of human affairs, and tempering heartbreak with glory.

I can appreciate the gift. For since I became joined to Gypsies in some unconventional fashion, I have been collecting heroic moments. This one, however, seems especially poignant. In learning to understand the Machvaia people, Stevo and Lola were my main tutors. But the excellent Lola taught me the most—how to survive Stevo, how to live "like you are going out of style." Good luck Lola will always be my luck.

I smile to myself, and start talking to Katy.

AG 1-8-09
PL 3-12-09
TC 5-14-09
SI 2-13-09
QM 2-14-09
OS 16-09
WH 21-CO
ET 3-25-10

DISCARD

ET 3-25-10